OUR SUPREME COURT

A History with 14 Activities

RICHARD PANCHYK

CHICAGO REVIEW PRESS

Library of Congress Cataloging-in-Publication Data

Panchyk, Richard.
  Our Supreme Court : a history with 14 activities / Richard Panchyk., 1st ed.
      p.   cm.
  Includes bibliographical references and index.
  ISBN-13: 978-1-55652-607-7
  ISBN-10: 1-55652-607-5
  1. Constitutional law—United States—Juvenile literature.   2. United States Supreme Court—Juvenile literature.   3. United States Supreme Court—Interviews.   I. Title.
KF4550.Z9P36   2006
347.73926—dc22
                          2006009018

Cover and interior design

Monica Baziuk

Cover photos

Sandra Day O'Connor: Library of Congress, LC-USZ62-86846 ★ Thurgood Marshall: Library of Congress, LC-U9-1027B-11 ★ John Roberts: AFP/Getty Images ★ Justices John Roberts, Clarence Thomas, Steven Breyer, and Samuel Alito: AFP/Getty Images

Interior images

Courtesy of the Library of Congress: P.6: HABS PA, 51-PHILA, 6-128 ★ P.23: LC-USZ62-119056 ★ P.24: LC-USZ62-3462 DLC ★ P.31: LC-USZ62-13017 DLC ★ P.33: LC-USA7-73981-14 DLC ★ P.47: LC-USZ62-21718 ★ P.49: LC-USZ62-75578 ★ P.63: LC-USZ62-121473 ★ P.68: LC-USZ62-30519 ★ P.74: LC-USZ62-83877 ★ P.77: LC-MSS-78637-1 ★ P.80: LC-USZ62-65770 ★ P.91: LC-U9-10364-37 ★ P.92: LC-USZ62-12960 DLC ★ P.95: (top) rbpe 0220120b ★ P.97: LC-U9-10364-37 ★ P.98: LC-USZ62-5399 DLC ★ P.101: LC-DIG-ppprs-00354 DLC ★ P.110: LC-DIG-ppmsca-09733 ★ P.111 LC-USZ62-60141 ★ P.118: LC-USW3-016536-E ★ P.122: LC-USZ62-33516 ★ P.125: LC-USZ62-41653 ★ P.132: LC-USZ62-10218 ★ P.136: LC-DIG-ggbain-04272 ★ P.142: LC-USZ62-111068 ★ P.144: LC-USZ62-23414 ★ P.148: LC-USZ62-92326 ★ P.151: LC-USZ62-10218 ★ P.162: LC-USZ62-2188 ★ P.167: LC-USZ62-80283

P.76: Courtesy of Lillian Gobitas Klose

P.81: Courtesy of Jim McCollum

All other images, unless otherwise noted, courtesy of the author.

Published by Chicago Review Press, Incorporated
814 North Franklin Street
Chicago, Illinois 60610
ISBN 978-1-55652-607-7
Printed in the United States of America

5   4   3   2

For Caren

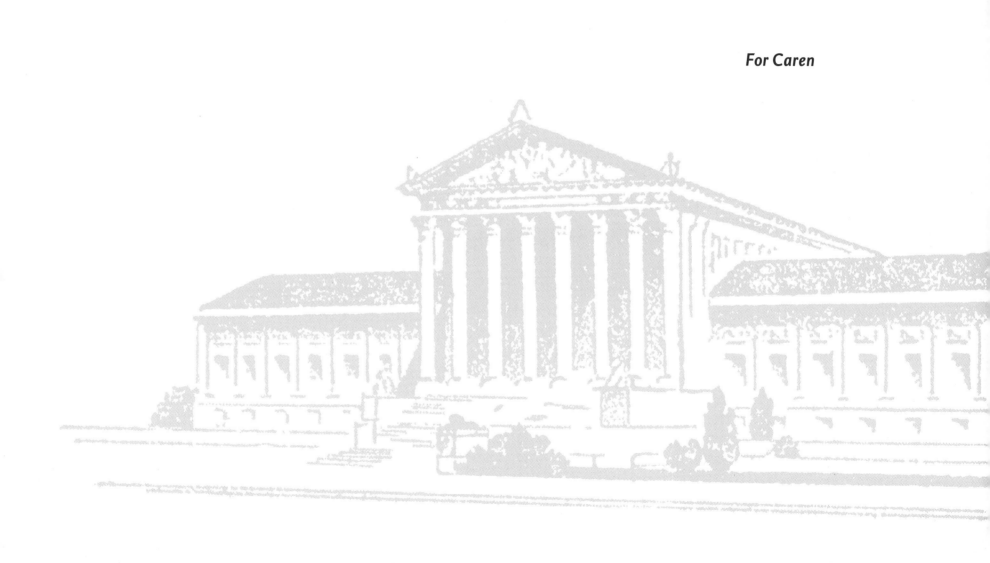

CONTENTS

FOREWORD

by Senator John Kerry

I'm glad you're reading about the Supreme Court!

Learning about our nation and its history is one of the most important things you can do.

Over 200 years ago George Washington, Benjamin Franklin, and the rest of our country's founders knew how important the Supreme Court would be. They were right about the journey our country would take to remain the best example of freedom and democracy all over the world.

The Constitution and Bill of Rights did so much good—protecting the freedom of speech and the freedom of religion—but the founders knew it would take a special group of people to defend these freedoms and help answer the great and difficult questions at the heart of our democracy. Someone would have to protect and interpret the Constitution and the laws of this land. That is why they created the Supreme Court.

Look at the history our Supreme Court has helped to define. The Supreme Court made our public schools open to every child, made sure women's rights to play sports were treated the same as men's, and made it clear that every American has a right to a lawyer, regardless of his or her ability to pay.

The Supreme Court is one of the most exciting parts of our democracy. Some of the greatest Americans have served on it.

As you read this book, and keep working hard to learn as much as you can, know that you can do anything—I'll bet even be a Supreme Court Justice one day.

John F. Kerry

A decorated Vietnam veteran, **John Kerry** was first elected to public office when Massachusetts voters chose him as Lieutenant Governor in 1982. He was then elected to the United States Senate in 1984, as Ronald Reagan began his second term as President. In 2002, he was reelected for a fourth term by the largest margin in Massachusetts history. During his time in the Senate, Kerry has voted on the confirmation of several Supreme Court Justices. In 2004, John Kerry was the Democratic candidate for President against the incumbent George W. Bush. He received more than 57 million votes, more than any other Democratic candidate in history.

Author's Note

I have tried to organize this book thematically, by major issue types. This is probably the best way to study the Supreme Court. Some cases touch upon several issues, and there I have tried to place them where they seem to fit best.

In writing this book, I have tried to mention as many relevant cases as possible. Still, I realize that there is no way to include every important case, every **precedent**, and every issue. In each chapter, I wanted to follow an issue chronologically through the years and go in-depth into some of the key cases about that issue.

The Supreme Court exists to protect *our* freedoms. I have tried to remember the humanity of the Court while writing this book. Sometimes in history books the personal and human side of things gets lost. To help kids gain a deeper understanding of the Supreme Court and its cases, I have conducted 35 interviews with participants in landmark cases and with political figures who have key insight into constitutional issues, the Supreme Court, and the justice system.

There are 11 interviews with people (or children of those people) who had the courage to take their fight to court. Most often, the case and the bigger issues are what are remembered. The people behind the cases are just as important. In these brief interviews, they explain how they felt and what they went through. They voice their opinions about the decisions, and about how their lives have changed because of them. I have tried to represent a variety of issues, and the cases I cover with these interviews date between 1940 and 1988.

The political and legal figures I interviewed include some of the most important lawyers, judges, and politicians since 1970. Some of these figures have argued important cases before the Supreme Court and have unique insight into those cases. By including these interviews I tried to give readers a broad view of not only the Supreme Court, but of the entire justice system. Supreme Court cases do not happen in a vacuum. For example, cases often revolve around laws made by Congress and signed by the President. Rulings by the Court have to be enforced by the Department of Justice and by United States Attorneys and District Attorneys.

When reading these interviews, remember that each person has their own particular insight based on their experience. Seth Waxman and Theodore Olson, for example, have each argued more than 40 cases before the Supreme Court. Edwin Meese III helped President Ronald Reagan select Supreme Court nominees. Kurt Vonnegut is a writer whose books have been banned. I encourage readers to find out more about these Americans to understand their backgrounds and experiences.

Remember that while some of their answers may be fact, other portions are opinion. Some people try to be very diplomatic, while others are opinionated. Some are brief, while others are quite thorough in their answers. These interviews are meant to supplement the main text. As you read the answers, see if you can tell what political party the person may belong to. I have tried to include equal representation among Republicans and Democrats, along with a few Independents.

Important terms are bolded upon their first appearance and are defined in the glossary at the end of the book. The first through fifteenth Amendments to the Constitution are included in the Resources, as is a listing of Web sites to further explore these important cases.

Acknowledgments

I want to extend a very special thanks to Senator John Kerry for taking the time to contribute the foreword to this book. I also want to extend deep appreciation to Professor Nadine Strossen for writing the introduction and to James A. Baker III for writing the afterword. Their belief in my mission was a source of strength to me while writing the book.

I was fortunate to interview many people whose opinions and stories greatly enrich this book. My most sincere thanks to these many illustrious figures: Floyd Abrams, John B. Anderson, James Baker, William Barr, Griffin B. Bell, David Boies, Benjamin Civiletti, Mario Cuomo, Walter Dellinger, Michael Dukakis, Charles Fried, Alberto Gonzalez, Rudolph Giuliani, Lawrence Lessig, Edwin Meese III, Walter Mondale, Robert Morgenthau, Ralph Nader, Theodore Olson, Robert Reich, William Ruckelshaus, Morley Safer, James Sensenbrenner Jr., Arlen Specter, Kenneth Starr, Dick Thornburgh, Kurt Vonnegut, and Seth Waxman.

Extra thanks to those who referred me to others I might talk to, especially Dick Thornburgh and Morley Safer. Also special thanks to those who answered extra questions and offered words of encouragement and support. Their participation has made this book something truly special and unique.

Special thanks to Linda Bernstein, Victoria Jean Benson, Gathie Barnette Edmonds, Steven Engel, Cathy Kuhlmeier Frey, Lillian Gobitas Klose, Dollree Mapp, Jim McCollum, Norma McCorvey, Tim Miller, Ellery Schempp, and John Tinker for discussing their landmark cases and sharing their ideas, insights, hopes, and fears with me.

Thanks also to all those who helped me set up interviews or gave me feedback: Elaine Adolfo, Amanda Bonzo, April Boyd, Jason Burkhart, Conrad Erb, Donald Farber, Anne Kienlen, Beth Kroger, Denise O'Neill, Theresa Pagliocca, Jacqueline Parke, Jane Safer, Terry Shawn, Amber Streit, Linda Vadasz, John Williams, and Wileen Wong. Thanks to anyone whom I forgot to mention or whose name I never caught along the way.

Of course, none of this would be possible without the efforts of Cynthia Sherry and Lisa Reardon at Chicago Review Press. Thanks to them for helping shape this book.

Special thanks also go to those who have supported me along my journey, especially to Caren, Matthew, and Elizabeth.

INTRODUCTION

by Nadine Strossen, President, American Civil Liberties Union

The U.S. Supreme Court is constantly at the center of public attention and debate since it has so much power as the ultimate interpreter of the U.S. Constitution. In 1803, the Court held that it has the power of "judicial review" to strike down any law or other government action that it considers to be inconsistent with the Constitution. This means that Supreme Court Justices can overturn decisions by elected officials, including the President and the Congress.

The Court's nine Justices are appointed by the President, with the Senate's **concurrence**, rather than elected. Moreover, along with other federal judges, they essentially have lifetime tenure, being subject to removal only through the extraordinary process of impeachment, for committing "high crimes and misdemeanors." No Supreme Court Justice has ever been removed from office through the impeachment process. In short, Justices are not directly accountable to the people in the United States, in contrast with our elected officials.

The Constitution deliberately shielded all federal judges, including Supreme Court Justices, from the political pressures that elected officials face. Their independence makes it easier for the Justices to enforce the Constitution neutrally, even on behalf of individuals and groups who lack political power, or who are unpopular. The Supreme Court eloquently explained the importance of this judicial independence in an important 1943 decision, in which it upheld the rights of public school students who were members of the Jehovah's Witnesses faith to refuse to salute the American flag, because that salute violated their religious beliefs. The Court declared:

The very purpose of a Bill of Rights was to withdraw certain subjects from the vicissitudes of political controversy, to place them beyond the reach of majorities and officials and to establish them as legal principles to be applied by the courts. One's right to life, liberty, and property, to free speech, a free press,

freedom of worship and assembly, and other funda-mental rights may not be submitted to vote; they depend on the outcome of no elections.

Throughout U.S. history, the Supreme Court has often lived up to its independent responsibilities by upholding fundamental freedoms and striking down government measures that violated these freedoms, even though the invalidated measures enjoyed wide-spread political and public support. A fairly recent ex-ample, which is especially important for young people, is the Supreme Court's decision in *Reno v. ACLU* (1997), which unanimously struck down the first federal law censoring the Internet. That law was designed to shield young people from material that might be considered "indecent" or "patently offen-sive," but the Court concluded that these vague terms could suppress much valuable online material.

Since young people do not have the right to vote, they lack political power, and therefore cannot nec-essarily depend on elected officials to protect their rights and welfare. Accordingly, the U.S. Supreme Court has issued many important rulings that have upheld minors' constitutional rights. In one of these key decisions, *Tinker v. Des Moines School District* (1969), the Court protected the rights of public school students to express ideas with which their school offi-cials disagreed. The Court declared that students do not "shed their constitutional rights to freedom of speech or expression at the schoolhouse gate."

While advocates of civil liberties and equal rights support the Court's relative independence, which enables it to enforce constitutional rights even when they are politically unpopular, critics denounce such rulings as unwarranted "judicial activism," or even "judicial tyranny." From their perspective, laws that have been duly enacted by elected representatives, who are accountable to the voters, should not be struck down by nine unelected Justices. This criti-cism is especially strong when the Court enforces rights that are not explicitly set forth in the Consti-tution. For example, in March 2005, the Court held that the death penalty cannot be imposed on anyone who was under 18 years old at the time of committing the crime in question. The Court concluded that any such death penalty would violate the Constitution's ban on "cruel and unusual punishments." Is this an appropriate interpretation of a provision that the Constitution's framers deliberately wrote with open-ended language? Or is this an inappropriate judicial decision of an issue that should instead be left to our elected representatives?

The debates about the meaning of the Constitu-tion, and the power of the Supreme Court to inter-pret it, go back to the founding of our country and will never be resolved, since they reflect enduring questions about how to strike the appropriate balance between government power and individual freedom. Therefore, no matter what the Court decides, it will always be criticized by some segments of the public. Nonetheless, public opinion surveys show that, in general, the Supreme Court is one of the most highly respected and trusted institutions in the whole coun-try. The Court is also widely respected around the world and has served as an inspiring model for courts in many other democracies that protect human rights.

Under our Constitution, all persons—including young persons such as the readers of this book—are equally entitled to certain basic rights, just by virtue of our common humanity. If those rights are not fully protected by other government officials, then the Supreme Court should provide the ultimate safety net for them. This essential mission is summarized by the words that are inscribed in the pediment atop the Supreme Court's imposing building in Washington, D.C.: "Equal Justice Under the Law."

Nadine Strossen has been president of the American Civil Liberties Union since 1991 and is a Professor of Law at New York Law School.

1

THE FOUNDING OF THE COURT

illiam Howard Taft was elected the 27th President of the United States in 1908. Though it was an accomplishment anyone should be proud of, Taft was not satisfied. He had greater aspirations. His true ambition, his lifelong dream, was to become a Justice of the Supreme Court. "Presidents come and go, but the Supreme Court goes on forever," he said.

Taft's dream finally came true in 1921, when he became the nation's 10th Chief Justice of the Supreme Court. He served nine years on the Court quite happily. One of Taft's biggest accomplishments, however, was not a legal one. He successfully lobbied Congress to get the Supreme Court its very own building. Though he did not live to see the Supreme Court Building completed in 1935, it was thanks to him that the Court got the majestic home it deserved. The huge new building, with its marble columns, looked like a structure out of ancient Greece. It was certainly a far cry from the Court's humble and uncertain beginnings during the country's infancy.

THE CONSTITUTION AND THE BIRTH OF THE COURT SYSTEM

The Supreme Court was created through the work of 55 distinguished delegates from the former colonies who assembled in 1787 to write the Constitution. The completed Article III of the Constitution said "The judicial Power of the United States shall be vested in one supreme Court and in such inferior Courts as the Congress may from time to time ordain and establish." While the Constitution established the Supreme Court, it did not say how the Court should be run or how much authority it possessed compared to the President or to Congress.

The drafters of the Constitution had been careful to create a system of "checks and balances" in the new country, where one branch of government could not rule without answering to another branch. Yet the Constitution devoted only a few brief sentences to the Supreme Court, compared to 13 paragraphs about the President's responsibilities and powers. One of the first items of business for the Senate was to put down on paper more details and specifics about the new judicial system.

The Judiciary Act of 1789 divided the country into 13 judicial districts that fell into three larger areas called circuits (Eastern, Middle, and Southern). One important section of the Act said that any case in a state's highest court where a treaty or law of the United States was ruled to be invalid could be **appealed** to the Supreme Court and "re-examined, and **reversed** or **affirmed**." The same was true for any case where the constitutionality of any state's law was in question.

The Judiciary Act also proclaimed what cases the Supreme Court would have **jurisdiction**, or authority, over. The Court would have exclusive authority to hear most civil cases where a state is a party, and it would have the right to hear appeals from the lower courts around the country.

The Supreme Court was to be located in the capital city of the United States. It was supposed to consist of a Chief Justice and five Associate Justices who would be appointed for life. During the drafting of the bill, there had been some argument as to the number of Justices that would be appropriate. Arguments were made for more than six Justices, but some felt that too many Justices would reduce responsibility and complicate things. After 1789, the number of Justices increased several times until 1869, when the number was finally fixed at nine (one Chief Justice and eight Associate Justices).

Upon passage of the Judiciary Act on September 24, 1789, President George Washington immediately set out to pick the appointees to the nation's first Supreme Court. He selected John Jay from New York as Chief Justice, and as Associate Justices he chose John Rutledge, from South Carolina; William Cushing, from Massachusetts; James Wilson, from Pennsylvania; John Blair, from Virginia; and Robert Harrison, from Maryland.

Only a few days after being confirmed as an Associate Justice, Robert Harrison received word that he had been chosen to serve as Chancellor of his home state of Maryland. The 44-year-old Harrison chose to serve his state and informed Washington. The President did not give up so easily and asked that Harrison rethink his decision. Harrison could not be swayed, and Washington replaced him with 48-year-old James Iredell of North Carolina, whose commission was dated February 10, 1790.

THE FIRST SESSIONS

When the United States was established, New York City was named as the nation's first capital, over rivals Boston and Philadelphia. The Supreme Court was supposed to hold its very first meeting in the middle of winter, on February 1, 1790, in the Merchants Exchange Building on Broad Street in downtown Manhattan. Except for the native New Yorker John Jay, the other Justices were coming from some distance. Because of transportation problems, they could not reach New York in time for the scheduled meeting, so it was pushed back a day.

Many local dignitaries were on hand for this landmark event. In the evening, a celebration was held at a local tavern in honor of the Court's first day of business.

The business of the Court in its first session was limited to administrative items, including how the official seal of the Supreme Court should look. The Court soon adjourned and did not reconvene until August, the appointed time for its next session. Once again, there were a few administrative matters to be attended to, and then the Court officially adjourned for lack of further business.

President George Washington was very supportive of the young Supreme Court. In fact, he wrote a letter to the Justices explaining how important it was for the judiciary to be independent. He asked them to keep him informed of their progress and any comments they might have.

RIDING CIRCUIT

Each Supreme Court Justice is assigned to cover cases arising in a specific court circuit or region of the country. During the early years of the Supreme Court, Justices were required to "ride circuit" twice a year, as dictated by the Judiciary Act of 1789. In the beginning, there were three circuits covering the United States: Eastern, Middle, and Southern. This meant they had to travel around the country to various courts, meet with judges, and hear cases there. These duties were exhausting and involved travel down country paths by horseback, around winding and rocky roads by stagecoach, and on great rivers by riverboat. They stopped at taverns and inns along the way.

After the Court adjourned in February 1790, the Justices began their first circuit assignments. Chief Justice Jay held the Eastern Circuit (covering New York, Connecticut, Massachusetts, and New Hampshire; Rhode Island only ratified the Constitution in May 1790 and so was not yet covered) in New York City on April 3, 1790, before moving on to other locations within the circuit. Justices Iredell and Rutledge traveled to the Southern Circuit (South Carolina and Georgia; North Carolina had also not yet ratified the

Chief Justice John Jay.

Constitution when the Judiciary Act was written and so was not covered), and Justices Blair and Wilson journeyed to the Middle Circuit (New Jersey, Pennsylvania, Delaware, Maryland, and Virginia).

Riding circuit gave them a chance to spread the ideals of the new nation's justice system to courts throughout the land. When John Jay gave instruction to the first grand jury in New York, he tried to instill a sense of duty and honor in them.

Nonetheless, riding circuit was an exhausting and dangerous affair. In fact, a stagecoach crash injured Chief Justice John Marshall while he was riding circuit in the 19th century and may in fact have led to his eventual death. Before Congress limited the duties to just once a year, Justices may have traveled up to 10,000 miles of rough terrain on many trips.

Only two years into their **terms**, the members of the Supreme Court were already exasperated with their circuit duties. They wrote a letter to Congress on November 7, 1792, asking for sympathy for their situation. They explained that they thought of the original system as temporary rather than permanent and that it would be revised as soon as possible. The Justices went on to say that they would have written sooner but did not want to interrupt Congress as it dealt with "affairs of great and pressing importance." They finally wrote:

That the task of holding twenty-seven circuit courts a year, in the different states from New Hampshire to Georgia, besides two sessions of the Supreme Court at Philadelphia, in the two most severe seasons of the year, is a task, which considering the extent of the United States, and the small number of judges, is too burdensome.

That to require of the judges to pass the greater part of their days on the roads and at inns, and at a distance from their families, is a requisition, which in their opinion should not be made unless in cases of necessity.

That some of the present judges do not enjoy health and strength of body sufficient to enable them to undergo the toilsome journeys through different climates and seasons, which they are called upon to undertake . . .

The Justices asked that the situation be addressed. In 1793, the Justices' circuit trips were reduced to once a year, and the practice of riding circuit was alto-

Stagecoaches in front of a tavern in the mid-19th century.

gether abolished during the 19th century. However, even today Justices are responsible for different circuits around the country. They can issue in-chambers opinions for the circuit that they represent. They can also issue a **stay** or an **injunction** on a case in their circuit.

Much of the Supreme Court's first year was spent getting organized and figuring out how to best run this new branch of government. The very early Supreme Court was not nearly as prominent as Congress and the President. Few citizens even knew anything about the Court in the beginning. When the Court was called back into session in August 1790, there were still no cases to be heard. In February 1791, the Court moved to City Hall in the nation's new capital, Philadelphia. John Rutledge resigned in March 1791, after only two years on the Court. President Washington asked Charles Pinckney to consider the position. Pinckney rejected the offer. Washington also asked Edward Rutledge if he would like to be considered as a nominee, but Rutledge also refused. Finally, Thomas Johnson, who had been the first Governor of Maryland, took the seat in August 1791. However, he resigned in 1793 due to failing health and was replaced by a Senator and Governor from New Jersey, William Paterson. The first actual case was not heard until 1792.

Meanwhile, President Washington was still trying to set the young nation on a proper course in the world. He composed a series of questions about international law and treaties with France that he intended to submit to the Justices of the Court for their learned opinion. Chief Justice John Jay and his associates respectfully declined, because they felt it was improper for them to give any official opinion on such matters as might arise later in a case before them. This was a landmark step for the Court, maintaining the importance of its separation from the executive branch of the government. This action also established a key rule. The federal courts, per Article III of the Constitution, would not give their opinions about important questions of the day unless those questions were brought to them in the form of actual legal disputes. The Court had in effect declared its neutrality and limited its own powers.

While on a mission in London, Chief Justice Jay was elected by the people of his home state of New York to serve as their Governor. When he returned to the United States, he could not refuse this honor, and resigned his position as Chief Justice. He was replaced by John Rutledge, who reigned only during the summer of 1795. The Senate refused to permanently appoint Rutledge to the position of Chief Justice because of his outspoken opposition to the treaty former Chief Justice John Jay had negotiated with Great Britain that year. Oliver Ellsworth, a Senator from Connecticut who had been one of the primary authors of the Judiciary Act of 1789, followed Rutledge as Chief Justice. John Blair also resigned in 1795. He was replaced by Samuel Chase of Maryland.

The number of cases heard by the Supreme Court was slowly rising during the early years. Between 1791 and 1798, the Court heard only a few cases each year. In 1800 the Justices heard 10 cases. In 1805 they heard 24 cases, in 1810 they heard 39 cases, and in 1814 they

Justice William Paterson.

The Supreme Court's chambers in Philadelphia.

heard 48 cases. As they ruled on more cases, word spread throughout the country of their authority. The Attorney General of the United States (who occupied a cabinet-level position in the executive branch of government) was called upon to argue cases before the Supreme Court on behalf of the government. The Solicitor General was also called upon to argue cases after that position was created in 1870.

INTERVIEW

Dick Thornburgh

Dick Thornburgh was Attorney General of the United States from 1988 to 1991 under Presidents Ronald Reagan and George Bush. He also served as Assistant Attorney General in the Criminal Division of the Justice Department under President Gerald Ford from 1975 to 1977 and as Pennsylvania's Governor from 1979 to 1987. President Reagan nominated Thornburgh as Attorney General in July 1988. As Attorney General, he argued two cases before the Supreme Court.

Q: What is the Attorney General's relationship with the Supreme Court, and how much contact is there between the Justice Department and the Supreme Court?

Thornburgh: Most of the contact between the Justice Department and the Supreme Court is carried out through the office of the Solicitor General, who is the third-ranking person in the Justice Department. The Solicitor General argues all cases on the government's side that appear before the Supreme Court. Occasionally, he will solicit the Attorney General himself to make the argument. But, normally, this duty is carried out by the Solicitor General's staff. They file all the **briefs** and make all the **oral arguments** before the Court.

Q: What was the nature of the two cases you argued before the Supreme Court?

Thornburgh: One had to do with propriety of drug testing in the transportation industry (*Skinner v. Railway Labor Executives' Assn.*, 1989). There was a dreadful crash on Amtrak. The drug testing program was designed to detect abusers. It was contested by the unions. The lower court ruled in favor of the unions, but in the Supreme Court we won a reversal. It opened up the right of employers to test their employees. The second case involved the admissibility of victim impact statements during a death sentence hearing in a murder (*Payne v. Tennessee*, 1991). The question was whether testimony could be received on whether the crime had an impact on the members of the community, including the victim's family [see page 126]. The Solicitor General asked me to argue these cases because he felt there were broad policy implications being addressed. I had also argued one case as an Assistant

Attorney General in the Ford administration, and I have since filed *amicus* briefs in two ADA [Americans with Disabilities Act] cases.

Q: *In many Supreme Court cases why are there* amicus *briefs filed by state Attorneys General?*

Thornburgh: In any case that has a broad implication for state government you shouldn't be surprised to find state Attorneys General involved.

Q: *Why then would you see only 20 state Attorneys General filing briefs rather than 40 or 45?*

Thornburgh: There are two sides to every case. You may even find cases where different state Attorneys General file on opposite sides of an issue.

Q: *What is one important case in recent history?*

Thornburgh: One case that was, in my view, wrongly decided was *Buckley v. Valeo* [1976] [see page 69]. It was the first of many largely unsuccessful attempts to govern political campaign spending. To me, it simply doesn't make sense that an individual can spend millions on his own election, but is limited to paltry amounts to help elect someone else. That doesn't sound like free speech to me.

Q: *What challenges does the Supreme Court face in the future?*

Thornburgh: Their challenges are unvarying. They interpret the Constitution, and they have to do so in a way that does not reflect their personal or political views but is as faithful as can be to the principles that gave rise to the Constitution. The issue *du jour* that may be center stage in a particular nomination process may never come up later. There are two features of the Court that are not focused on much. The first is that the Supreme Court is a purely reactive institution. They can't reach out like the other two branches, executive and legislative, and make laws in any areas they want. They can only decide "cases" and "controversies" that are brought before them. Second, the Court is purely a political institution. Not partisan, but political. It is a policy-making institution. It doesn't operate the way the lower courts do. As the saying goes, the Supreme Court is not final because it is infallible, it is infallible because it is final.

EARLY CASES

Many cases heard during the early years of the Supreme Court were concerned with property rights, breach of contract, fraudulent contracts, deeds and titles, taxes and duties, wills, insolvency, inheritances, and colonial laws. Because the country was still very young, there were many questions and disputes over land. As people explored and settled in the westernmost states and territories, there were conflicts over who was entitled to what land, which deed superceded which, and who had rights to the land in question. Some cases concerned surveys that were made many years before and the problems that arose with the language of these early surveys. (An example: ". . . beginning at a large black ash and a small buckeye marked thus on the side of a buffalo road leading from the lower blue licks a northeast course, and about seven miles north-east . . .") One problem was that landmarks such as trees and roads changed over time, as more and more settlers populated the areas that were once nothing but wilderness. Another problem was that early surveys and land grants sometimes overlapped each other.

Taxes and duties were also a common theme. This issue had been very important during colonial times; taxes were one of the main complaints of the colonists and were a major factor in the discontent that led to the American Revolution. The shipping business was in its heyday during the first half of the 19th century, and the duties charged on imported goods were sometimes an issue.

Another common thread among early cases was maritime concerns. The legality of salvaging ships, seizing ships, and other admiralty cases came up again and again during the early decades of the Court's existence.

As the years went by, the nature of cases heard by the Supreme Court continued to evolve to reflect the legal, social, and political concerns of the times. The

The U.S. Capitol Building in 1837. The Supreme Court moved to the Capitol Building in 1801 and remained there until it got its own building in 1935.

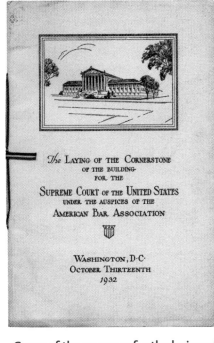

Cover of the program for the laying of the cornerstone of the Supreme Court Building, 1932.

The Supreme Court Building in the 1930s.

nation's view of the Court evolved as well over time. Some were undoubtedly perplexed by the complicated language used and the fine legal issues tackled by the Court. A satirical epic poem written in 1826 and published in Boston said the new Supreme Court term was "Full of strange oaths," calling it "a long dull term of dry and sober fun, the everlasting tournament of brains!"

How the Court Works

Selecting Cases

Every year, the U.S. Supreme Court receives requests to hear thousands of cases. All across the country, lawyers file official petitions for a **writ of *certiorari*** (*certiorari* is Latin for "to be ascertained") with the nation's highest Court. This petition must be filed within 90 days of the ruling from the United States Court of Appeals or the highest state appellate court. The request for *certiorari* is basically a carefully explained request or petition for the Court to hear the case. The petition contains all the pertinent information, including the legal issues, a summary of the facts of the case, and the lower court rulings attached as appendices. Normally, these petitions are filed through a paid lawyer or legal team. When the petitioner is poor and does not have enough money to pay the Court's filing fee, he or she can file *in forma pauperis* (Latin for "as a pauper").

The side that files the petition for *certiorari* is called the **petitioner, plaintiff,** or the **appellant.** They file their case against their opponents, known as the **re**?

spondent, defendant, or the **appellee.** The petitioner may change through the life of a case. For example, say that Jones sues Smith (*Jones v. Smith*). A lower court rules in favor of Jones, the original petitioner, and against Smith, the original respondent. Now Jones is happy, but Smith is determined to fight the ruling. If Smith decided to appeal the decision, he becomes the petitioner and Jones the respondent (*Smith v. Jones*).

Every term, the Supreme Court receives about 8,000 petitions; the Justices must sort through these requests and narrow it down to about 100 cases, just about 1 percent of the total. These cases reach the next level where the Supreme Court will hear oral arguments from lawyers. This is known as plenary review. A few dozen additional cases are ruled on without any formal oral arguments. The rulings that are issued every term take up about 5,000 pages when published.

Over the decades, the number of petitions the Court receives has more than tripled, in part due to the growth in population and size of the country. Thanks to Chief Justice Taft pushing the Certiorari Act (1925), the Court is now able to be selective about which cases it will hear (before then it had less choice in the matter). But just because the Court hears only a fraction of the cases for which they receive petitions, that doesn't mean that the Court has no impact on the rest of these cases. The impact is simple; by virtue of refusing to hear a certain case, the Court is in effect letting the lower court ruling stand. This is especially important in a death penalty case.

A case can be rejected for many reasons. If the legal points are not presented clearly, the Justices will not bother to hear the case. Sometimes it is simply a matter of selecting the most important issues. As the guidelines for filing a petition state: "The denial of a petition for a writ of *certiorari* signifies only that the Court has chosen not to accept the case for review and does not express the Court's views of the merits of the case."

Sometimes, the Court will notice a trend in a certain type of issue that seems to be showing up often in petitions, and will decide to set a precedent on the issue. Other times, the Court will combine several like cases into one, such as happened in *Miranda v. Arizona* (1966), where the *Miranda* case was combined with three other similar cases. The Court is likely to consider the importance to the public of the issue(s) being presented in the case.

The Court might be more likely to hear a case when several lower courts have confronted a common question in different cases and answer it differently. For instance, if some federal appeals courts held that executing convicted criminals who are minors is unconstitutional, but several others held that it is acceptable, the Supreme Court will likely take a case on that question to resolve the conflict.

The Justices have no choice but to narrow their case load, or they would have to work 24 hours a day, 365 days per year (and even then they would *still* not be able to cover all the petitions they receive). Rejected cases might be a matter of life and death, when death penalty appeals are concerned. When the Court refuses to stop an execution, the order from the bench might simply read: "The application for stay of execution of sentence of death presented to

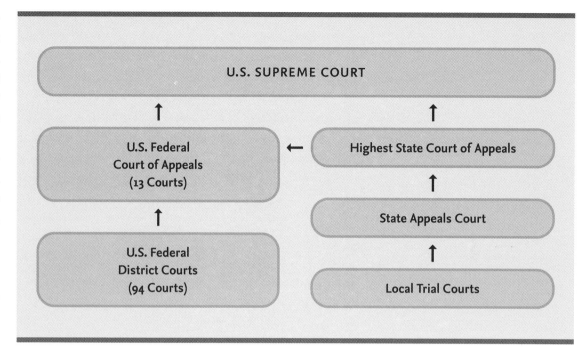

the Chief Justice and by him referred to the Court is denied. The petition for a writ of *certiorari* is denied."

How Presidents Select Justices

Ordinary people have enough trouble making decisions. You can just imagine how difficult it must be for a Supreme Court Justice to make a decision that will possibly affect millions of people. The Supreme Court can be a highly diverse body. There are many ways to approach each case, and few Supreme Court decisions are unanimous, where all agree.

Presidents usually prefer to select a Justice who is going to rule in a way that the President would favor

A case may get to the Supreme Court through a few different paths.

on certain key issues. A liberal President may want a liberal judge while a conservative President would prefer a conservative judge. When a position opens on the Court, the President may be bombarded with suggestions and advice. Between October and December of 1864, President Abraham Lincoln received more than 40 letters from prominent persons, each offering their own take on the vacancy for Chief Justice that resulted when Chief Justice Roger Taney died.

One letter Lincoln received in November 1864 was from a lawyer named B. White, who wrote about the characteristics he felt the new Chief Justice should have:

We should have a man of middle age, healthy and vigorous in mind and body—able and willing to labor day and night "to spend and be spent" for the honor of our profession [lawyers] and for the good of the common country; one familiar with the science of government, with the history of civilization, and at home in all the knowledge that civilization brings in its train; one, not only learned in the law and familiar with its practice but deeply imbibed with its philosophy; one, who is and always has been a lawyer, and never an office-seeking politician; one who desires to be only a Chief Justice, and will never seek to be President.

Presidents themselves rarely know enough or have the time to select a Justice without assistance. The President may call upon the Attorney General or close advisors to run the selection process. President Rea-

gan received help from his trusted friend and Attorney General Edwin Meese III. The selection is never instantaneous. There is a short list of several candidates, each of whose judicial records are usually explored. How did the judge vote on this or that issue? The President's selection committee may interview a judge who is being considered for nomination. Only after careful consideration is a nomination announced.

The nomination process then heads to the Senate Judiciary Committee, where a vote is held. With enough support, the candidate's nomination will proceed to the full Senate for a vote. Without enough support in the Judiciary Committee, the nomination is considered dead. Sometimes a nominee withdraws his or her name if it seems the nomination process will be especially difficult and the nomination will not be approved.

While Presidents are in office for only four or at most eight years, Justices may remain on the Court for 20 or 30 years, or sometimes longer. Justice John Marshall served 34 years, as did Justices Stephen Johnson Field and Hugo Lafayette Black, while Justice William Orville Douglas served 36 years. Several others have served more than 30 years, including the late Chief Justice William H. Rehnquist.

Justices continue to affect the country long after the Presidents who nominated them have left office. As time passes, Justices may shift their views. A conservative may shift more toward the center, while a liberal might become more conservative. A President can never guess all the different possible issues that might arise during a Justice's tenure in the Supreme

Court. The Constitution ensures that the President cannot remove a Justice if he or she does not approve of their decisions.

When one or more Justices are near retirement or are in poor health, the selection of their replacement(s) can become a hot political issue. During the fall of 2004, the presidential candidates (President George W. Bush and Senator John Kerry) were asked in a debate whether either of them would have a "litmus test" for selecting a new Supreme Court Justice. This referred to the nomination of a Justice based on his or her views on only one or two key subjects. The litmus test in that election was whether a Justice would be nominated based on his or her stance on the legalized abortion case, *Roe v. Wade* (1973). The politically correct answer for a candidate is that a Justice will be selected based on his or her qualifications and not on any one issue.

George Washington appointed the most Justices (10), but Franklin D. Roosevelt's eight appointees spent more time on the bench, an average of 17 years each compared to 8.3 years for Washington's appointees. Only four Presidents have appointed no Justices.

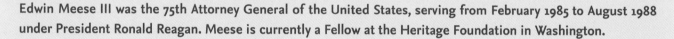

INTERVIEW | Edwin Meese III

Edwin Meese III was the 75th Attorney General of the United States, serving from February 1985 to August 1988 under President Ronald Reagan. Meese is currently a Fellow at the Heritage Foundation in Washington.

Q: In your opinion, what are some of today's more pressing constitutional issues?

Meese: One issue is "*What is the proper role of the judge in our federal system?*" For example, the founders had in mind that the judiciary would be what Alexander Hamilton called, "the least dangerous branch" to the principles of the Constitution. As he stated, the judiciary has neither the power to enforce the law nor to make the law, but only the judgment to apply the law. But some judges want to go beyond what the Constitution says, or what the laws passed by Congress provide, to substitute their own ideas of what the law ought to be, and therefore go beyond the role of the judge as an interpreter and usurp the legislative function.

Another issue at the current time is the relative powers of the Congress and the President in regard to the handling of the war against terrorism. To what extent does the President need the authorization of Congress to engage in military activities? This has been a controversy between the branches that has lasted from the early 19th century (when Thomas Jefferson was President) to the present. Closely related is the extent to which the federal courts have any involvement in the handling of the war, such as the treatment of prisoners and the manner in which enemy combatants are detained.

Q: What was President Reagan's view on judicial supremacy and the Supreme Court's role?

Meese: President Reagan felt strongly that the role of the judiciary was limited by the Constitution, and that was to interpret the law, not make the law. He said on September 26, 1986, at the installation of Chief Justice William H. Rehnquist and Associate Justice Antonin Scalia, "The founding fathers were clear on this issue. For them, the question involved in judicial restraint was not—as it is not—will we have liberal or conservative courts? They knew that the courts, like the Constitution itself, must not be liberal or conservative. The question was and is, will we have government by the people? And this is why the principle of judicial restraint has had an honored place in our tradition."

In other words, this is why he felt it was important that judges should not substitute their own ideas for what the Constitution and the laws enacted under it actually provide. For the courts to usurp the legislative function is a violation of the separation of powers and the allocation of authority in the Constitution itself.

Q: What was your role in assisting President Reagan with the selection process for Supreme Court justices?

Meese: All of the work was done by the Justice Department, by a small team under my direction. . . . We started with probably a list of about twenty [candidates], thoroughly researched all of them, and then brought them to the President, and he narrowed the list down and then made the final decision.

Arguing Before the Supreme Court

It is a special honor to argue before the Supreme Court. Not just any lawyer can be admitted before the Court. A lawyer must first fill out a detailed application to practice. Upon approval, the lawyer is issued an official certificate admitting him or her to the Bar of the Supreme Court. The Court receives 5,000 applications per year; since 1925, more than 200,000 lawyers have been admitted to the Supreme Court Bar.

Though accepted, most of these lawyers will never argue a case before the Court. This is due in part to the fact that thousands of petitions are submitted every year but only 100 or so cases are accepted. Among the present attorneys who have argued the most cases before the nation's highest court are Seth Waxman and Theodore Olson (both former Solicitors General of the United States), who have argued more than 40 cases each.

Those lawyers who do get to argue before the Supreme Court must follow many rules. As the highest court in the land, there are certain standards and rules to regulate the process of oral arguments. Though lawyers submit written briefs on their cases, the oral argument is the time to summarize their most pertinent points and try to sway the Justices to rule in their favor. Thirty-minute time limits for each side are strictly followed for the oral arguments. If you were a lawyer arguing before the Supreme Court, you would be expected to do several things, including dress in dark colors, speak clearly, use precise language, not read your argument from notes, stress only the most powerful arguments, never interrupt a Justice (they can interrupt you, though), always make eye contact with the Justice who is speaking to you, and when your time is up, stop talking immediately.

Court Facilities and Staff

There are many people who help make the Supreme Court run smoothly and efficiently. A staff of 400 people works inside the Supreme Court Building. Among the most important of these people are those holding several key positions that are appointed either by all the Justices or by the Chief Justice alone. These include the Administrative Assistant to the Chief Justice, Clerk of the Court, Librarian, Marshall, Reporter of Decisions, Director of Budget and Personnel, Counsel, Curator, Public Information Officer, and Director of Data Systems.

Each of these has a critical function. For example, the Librarian runs the Supreme Court Library, which is open to the Justices, members of Congress, and any member of the Bar of the Supreme Court. The library's collection consists of more than 500,000 books. Without assistance, the Justices would never be able to research legal precedents for their cases. In fact, each Justice has four law clerks to help with research on similar cases. Each Justice also has two secretaries (except the Chief Justice, who has three secretaries) for correspondence and a messenger.

Hearing a Case

After a petition has been reviewed and the Justices have decided to hear the case, oral arguments are scheduled. Lawyers for both sides file "briefs on the merits" that go over all the legal points of their arguments. The Justices carefully review these briefs. The

The Supreme Court room in the Capitol Building, early 20th century.

briefs are 50 pages or less in length, but are densely packed with references to other cases. Different groups and associations, such as the American Civil Liberties Union (ACLU), religious groups, and others may file special briefs called **amicus curiae** in support of either side's argument. These briefs may also be filed by the Attorneys General of different states, or other persons or groups who have something to contribute on the issues at stake. These *amicus* briefs are 30 pages or less in length.

The Court is generally in session from early October until late April. Up to four oral arguments are heard per day, three days per week, in two-week sessions. Between oral argument sessions, the Justices use their time to write decisions and review the many petitions they have received from around the country. The arguments are an opportunity for the Justices to ask questions from the attorneys representing both sides of the case. Sometimes more than one attorney will argue for one side or the other, but the time limit is still 30 minutes per side. Legal briefs serve to explain the numerous details of the legal arguments, but the oral portion allows the attorneys to summarize the pertinent legal points and try to sway Justices who might have doubts about certain issues.

The public is allowed to attend the oral arguments (go the Supreme Court Web site, www.supreme courtus.gov, for details), and when the Justices arrive in the courtroom, all present rise as the Marshall announces:

The Honorable, the Chief Justice and the Associate Justices of the Supreme Court of the United States.

Oyez! Oyez! Oyez! All persons having business before the Honorable, the Supreme Court of the United States, are admonished to draw near and give their attention, for the Court is now sitting. God save the United States and this Honorable Court!

Because of the limited time, Justices do interrupt attorneys whenever they wish. While the attorney may have practiced a set of key points to make, he or she must defer to the Justice and answer any and all questions before trying to get back on track with planned arguments.

How Do Justices Decide a Case?

There are many influences that help a Justice decide a case. Although Justices are supposed to put their personal views aside, people can't help but have their own opinions on controversial issues such as abortion, the death penalty, gun control, and government regulation of businesses. Conservative Republican Justices usually have different opinions than liberal Democratic Justices on many of these issues. But having personal views does not mean a Justice is not objective. Most cases have two viewpoints, and both viewpoints may have perfectly valid legal arguments on their side.

Legal precedent is also an important factor. Justices hear arguments and read briefs that cite precedents, or previous rulings, on similar cases, and use these to help guide them toward a decision. There are many thousands of cases that have been recorded all across the country to choose from, not only in the Supreme

Court, but in lower courts as well. The majority opinion and the **dissenting** opinion might cite legal precedents representing two opposing views on the same issue. Justices may cite sentences or entire paragraphs from previous decisions to support their arguments.

The values and circumstances of the times can also play a role in how Justices decide a case. The social climate of the mid-1800s was quite different from what it is today. The Court might look at a case where it has to sustain or overturn a very old ruling on a certain issue. The changing times may dictate that a change is needed in the way business is regulated, or the rights of criminals. A wartime ruling may be based on the immediate concerns of patriotism and a nation under threat of violence.

When they consider a case, the Justices hold a private conference behind closed doors to discuss the pertinent points of the arguments and to review legal precedents. Normally, the time between the oral arguments and the decision is several months. A case argued in October may be decided in March or May of the next year.

The Justices spend a great deal of time drafting their decisions, or opinions. They realize that the wording of their opinions is very important. They have to make a logical case for their decisions and explain their thinking carefully and clearly. Each opinion follows a Justice's thought process as he or she justifies the decision. Opinions are rarely only a few pages long—sometimes they are a few dozen pages long. They rely upon many case citations from prior decisions within their opinions, and all of these points must be carefully researched. A Justice will

BE A COURT STENOGRAPHER

IN TODAY'S Supreme Court, audio recordings are made of the oral arguments, but it was not always so simple. In times past, the arguments were taken down by a court reporter who could take shorthand notes at a rapid speed and then transcribe them later into normal English. Shorthand notes are made by either abbreviating or eliminating letters from the middle of the word. For example, "plaintiff" becomes "pltf."

Most courtrooms today still use court reporters. But today these experts attend special schools and type more than 225 words per minute using stenography machines. These machines have 22 letter keys, as well as a number bar. The consonants on the left side of the keyboard represent the initial sound of the word, and the consonants on the right side of the keyboard represent the last sounds of the word. The bottom bar has four vowels that are positioned so they can be keyed using the thumb. The resulting letters are printed on a strip of paper and have to be decoded later.

Try your hand at shorthand.

YOU'LL NEED

✔ Paper
✔ Pencil

What letter combinations (four letters or fewer) could you use to make the following words still recognizable?

Appeal	*Question*
Warrant	*Argument*
Opinion	*Constitution*
Decision	*Jurisdiction*
Contract	*Injunction*

Now try to type the following paragraph in abbreviated form. Try to reduce three-letter words by one letter, four-letter words by two letters, and larger words by at least three letters. Do not make any typed abbreviation longer than five letters. Make sure you shorthand a word the same way if it appears more than once. When you are done, put the paper aside. Come back to it a couple of hours later, and try to decipher what you wrote. How much can you decipher?

The defendant's rights were clearly violated in this case. The First Amendment states that Americans shall have freedom of speech. How can the defendant not be allowed to distribute pamphlets that do not incite violence, but only suggest what changes might make the future better for our great country?

SELECT YOUR SUPREME COURT

THE BEST WAY to understand how the Supreme Court works is to hold your own version of the Court. First, you have to select who will serve on the Court. Supreme Court Justices are first nominated by the President, and then have to be approved by a majority of the Senate. That means at least 51 of the 100 Senators have to vote in favor of appointing that Justice. Nomination hearings are held prior to a vote to discuss the reasons why the nominee would make a good (or poor) Justice.

Though the Senate more often than not approves Justices, there have been some who have failed to get enough votes. One more recent example was the conservative judge Robert Bork, who was nominated in 1987 by President Ronald Reagan and did not receive enough votes in the Senate. The next nominee, Douglas Ginsburg, withdrew his name from consideration after a controversy about his past. The President's third choice, Anthony Kennedy, was finally approved.

In this activity, your class will nominate and approve nine "Justices." These Justices will be used to rule on a few cases in this book.

YOU'LL NEED

✔ Index cards (twice as many cards as there are kids in the class)

✔ Pencils

One kid should volunteer to run the nomination proceedings. Every kid in the class gets two blank cards. To nominate a Justice, write down the person's name and the reason why you think he or she would make a good Justice for the Court case activities. Examples you could put down include:

She is very smart, He always listens to both sides of an argument, His father is a lawyer and so he might know a little about the law, She is very logical, He doesn't always follow the crowd and thinks for himself, or She is very patient and a good listener.

The kid in charge should collect the cards and organize them by name. Everyone in the class will receive an alphabetical list of all the students. The kid who has the cards should call out the name of a nominee and read each positive comment about the person, and so on until all nominees' names are called out. Then, each kid in the class will vote for his or her nine choices to serve on the Court by circling those names on the sheet. The nine kids with the most votes are selected. (Those kids not voted in get to play the parts of lawyers or clerks in one of the cases in upcoming chapters.) If for any reason you need to approve fewer Justices, go with six, the original number of Justices on the Supreme Court.

normally be selected to speak for the majority, whether the decision is 5–4 or 9–0. Other Justices who agree with the decision, but have slightly different interpretations of the issues, or want to make different points, might issue their own concurring opinion. In a concurring opinion, a Justice might agree in principle with the majority decision, but sound some of his or her own reservations or warnings about the decision. A concurring opinion may also allow a Justice to add strength to the majority's opinion.

When cases are overturned, there are often other issues to be resolved. The wording at the end of the majority opinion may read "Reversed and **remanded**." This means the decision of the lower court is reversed, and the case is sent back to the lower court to resolve issues such as monetary damages or punishment. The Supreme Court usually does not deal with these administrative matters; as Justice Abe Fortas noted in *Tinker v. Des Moines School District* (1969): "We express no opinion as to the form of relief which should be granted, this being a matter for the lower courts to determine."

Justices who do not vote with the majority may issue a dissenting opinion, where they can voice their disagreement with the majority's ruling. They can use the dissent to make warnings or predictions about the problems the ruling presents. A dissenting Justice may cite just as many cases as a Justice writing a majority opinion. In fact, a dissenting Justice may even cite different parts of a decision cited by the opposing Justices.

An opinion of a lone dissenting Justice may actually represent the views of millions of Americans on a particular subject, anything from free speech to abortion. A dissent on a controversial case may in retrospect turn out to be the lone voice of reason. One example of this is Justice John Marshall Harlan's dissent in the *Plessy v. Ferguson* (1896) case, in which he argued against the doctrine of "separate but equal" while the rest of the Court ruled it was acceptable to restrict blacks and whites to separate rail cars. Complex cases may have more than one dissenting opinion.

Once the opinion is written and finalized, it goes to the Reporter of Decisions, who then writes a brief summary of what is often a pages-long decision. This summary is placed at the front of the opinion and is called the **syllabus.** The decisions eventually get published in a series of books called *United States Reports.* Cases are referred to by their name, but also by their number in the *United States Reports.* Until 1874, the citation began with the volume number, the name of the Reporter of Decisions, and the page number (3 Cranch 210). After 1874, the name of the Reporter is substituted with "U.S." (for example, 379 U.S. 536 was in 1965). Volumes are currently added at the rate of three to five per term and are about 800 to 1,200 pages each.

This system makes it easy for lawyers, judges, and law clerks to locate the complete text of a cited case in a law library or online database within minutes. Most Supreme Court decisions eventually wind up being cited in other future decisions.

INTERVIEW Arlen Specter

A U.S. Senator from Pennsylvania, Arlen Specter was selected as the Chairman of the Senate Judiciary Committee in January 2005. He was first elected to the Senate in 1980. Prior to that, he was District Attorney in Philadelphia and Assistant Attorney General of Pennsylvania. The Senate Judiciary Committee holds hearings for the Supreme Court Justice nominees before the nomination goes to the full Senate for a vote.

Q: *What is the role of the Chairman of the Senate Judiciary Committee?*

Specter: The Chairman sets the agenda for the Senate Judiciary Committee, deciding which issues within the Committee's jurisdiction are important for the Senate's consideration. The issues could include timely news topics, constitutional **Amendments**, or consideration of the President's judicial nominations. The Committee then hears testimony from experts and engages in robust debate on these subjects during hearings, which are scheduled and presided over by the Chairman. Once the Committee has ended debate, the Chairman oversees changes made to the legislation in the Committee "mark-up" before the Committee votes on the legislation and it is sent to the Senate floor for further debate.

Q: *Besides judicial appointments, what other issues does the Committee deal with?*

Specter: The Committee does play a key role in ushering the President's judicial nominations for the federal courts through the U.S. Senate, but it also has jurisdiction of a wide range of legal issues, civil liberty protections, and judicial and law enforcement oversight. It oversees criminal and civil judicial proceedings and the operations of governmental agencies within the Department of Justice. On the legislative end, the Committee debates and revises legislation on a variety of legal concerns—class action, bankruptcy, asbestos **litigation**, the Patriot Act, anti-trust, immigration and naturalization, constitutional Amendments, intellectual property—before it is sent to the Senate.

INTERVIEW   # James Sensenbrenner Jr.

James Sensenbrenner Jr. became the Chair of the House Committee on the Judiciary in 2001. He was first elected to the House of Representatives in 1978 as a Congressman from Wisconsin. In 1998, he was one of the managers appointed by the House of Representatives to conduct the impeachment hearings against President Clinton.

Q: *What are the differences in responsibility between the House and Senate Judiciary Committees?*

Sensenbrenner: The House and Senate Judiciary Committees have almost identical responsibilities. Only the Senate Judiciary Committee, though, decides whether to confirm people the President wants to serve as Attorney General, FBI director, [or as] a federal judge, including as a Supreme Court Justice, and other high-level positions.

Q: *What is the role of the Chairman?*

Sensenbrenner: The Chairman of the House Judiciary Committee helps prioritize what issues the Committee will address. With so many issues from crime, terrorism, drugs, lawsuit abuse, and abortion, to piracy, immigration, border security, and cloning, the Committee cannot work on every issue every individual wants to discuss. The Chairman also makes sure the rules of the Committee are fairly and consistently enforced. Rules help people get things done by putting some order and focus to the wishes of many people, including the 40 House Judiciary Committee members.

Q: *When the Supreme Court rules on an important issue, does the House Committee on the Judiciary examine the implications and effects of the decision?*

Sensenbrenner: When the Supreme Court rules on an issue, the members of the House Judiciary Committee read their opinion and consider it carefully. If the Supreme Court strikes down a law passed by Congress, Congress can change the law such that the Supreme Court supports it. Congress can also decide what sorts of issues the Supreme Court should not be able to decide at all, and leave those decisions to the States to decide. Congress can also impeach judges that commit "high crimes and misdemeanors." What "high crimes and misdemeanors" means is up to Congress. The Constitution is based in part on the idea of the "separation of powers." That means Congress has the power to make sure the Supreme Court behaves properly, just as the Supreme Court can say what it thinks about the laws Congress passes and the President signs into law.

Q: *The Subcommittee on the Constitution seems to be an extremely important group. What are some of the "hot issues" the subcommittee may face in coming years?*

Sensenbrenner: The Subcommittee on the Constitution helps decide whether the Constitution should be changed. The Constitution is the highest law in the United States, and all other laws must be consistent with it, or else they are invalid. In the coming years, one of the issues the Subcommittee will discuss is the importance of marriage between a man and a woman. The Subcommittee on the Constitution also makes sure other branches of government are enforcing laws that protect people's civil rights.

2

POLITICS AND POWER

The drafters of the Constitution made a noble effort to create a system of checks and balances to prevent abuse of power by the federal government. Still, states did not always recognize the authority of the federal government in the early days of the republic. The Supreme Court stepped in and helped define the boundaries of states' rights, using their authority to interpret the Constitution to establish where states' rights end and federal rights begin, and where they overlap. Over the years, there have also been questions on the limits of the powers of Congress, the President, and the judiciary. The Supreme Court has been the proving ground for battles of authority among the three branches of government. It has also made decisions that have had major political consequences.

One early sign that the newly created Supreme Court was willing to involve itself in political disputes was *Chisholm v. Georgia* (1793), in which the Supreme Court decided that an individual from one state could sue the government of another state. The individual states were wary of this decision, because they felt it left them too vulnerable. The Congress soon nullified this decision with the ratification of the Eleventh Amendment to the Constitution.

In a case called *Calder v. Bull* (1798), the Court ruled that when there was no federal issue or legal question at stake, the state court system was in fact the appropriate place to decide the legality of state laws.

JEFFERSON AND THE FEDERALISTS

Among the founding fathers, there was a growing rift over the way the young government should be run. Beginning with George Washington, the Federalists had introduced their ideas of a strong central government. When Washington finished his two terms in office, he was succeeded by another Federalist, John Adams.

The Republicans (later to become what we now call the Democrats) did not believe in an elite central government. They put their trust in the people, the common worker who toiled in the fields or the mills. The Republicans spoke ill of their Federalist counterparts. In response to this, the Federalist-controlled Congress passed the Sedition Act of 1798. This Act doled out penalties for anyone who wrote or spoke "false, scandalous and malicious" things about the government. Though supposedly aimed against foreigners, the Act was partly aimed at preventing the Republicans from talking negatively about the Feder-

alists. Several Republicans were convicted under the Act, causing anger against the Federalist judges who tried them.

Displeasure with the Sedition Act and other Federalist measures led the Republicans to fare very well in the 1800 elections. The Federalists were at last on their way out of the presidency and Congress. But before they left office, the Federalists passed the Judiciary Reform Bill of 1801. The judicial districts of the country were rearranged, and additional circuits were established. This rearrangement gave President John Adams the chance to appoint several new Federalist judges to various federal courts. On his last day in office, March 3, 1801, Adams made several hurried appointments. Known as the "Midnight Judges," their commissions were approved by the Senate, signed by Adams, and sealed with the seal of the United States. Another of Adams's acts in the weeks before he left office was to nominate his Secretary of State, John Marshall, for Chief Justice of the Supreme Court.

After the new President, Thomas Jefferson, took office on March 4, 1801, he and the new Congress nullified the Judiciary Act of 1801 and had the Supreme Court suspended from meeting for more than a year. During this time, the House also impeached (but the Senate did not convict) Associate Justice Samuel Chase because he expressed strong Federalist opinions on the bench. The Republicans wanted to scare the Federalist-led Court into believing they were not invincible.

One of the "midnight judges" appointed by John Adams, William Marbury, was to be a Justice of the

President John Adams.

Secretary of State James Madison.

Peace in Washington, D.C. Unfortunately for Marbury, this last-minute commission by Adams was not honored by the new President. The new Secretary of State, James Madison, simply refused to deliver Marbury and three other men their commission documents. Marbury contended that the commission was complete, while Jefferson countered that it was incomplete and worthless as long as it was undelivered.

The Supreme Court took up the case in its first session back after the hiatus. In *Marbury v. Madison* (1803), the Supreme Court had to deal with the thorny issue of its own authority. Marbury wanted to force Jefferson to appoint him by having the Supreme Court issue an order called a **writ of *mandamus*** (*mandamus* is Latin for "we order"), which is an order directing a public official to perform a certain duty. This power was authorized by the Judiciary Act that Congress had passed in 1789. However, the Supreme Court was hesitant to issue an order that it knew would be ignored by Jefferson's administration. If that happened, the authority of the Court would be undermined and its reputation damaged.

Chief Justice John Marshall knew about the "peculiar delicacy" of the case. In his decision, Marshall carefully examined the question of Marbury's appointment. Was his appointment official, even though the commission had not been delivered? Was he entitled to receive his commission?

The answers to those questions were yes. As Marshall put it, "A commission is transmitted to a person already appointed" and his serving office did not depend on whether the commission was delivered

safely or lost in the mail. Marbury was entitled to his commission.

But in a surprising turn of events, the Supreme Court decided that it did not have the constitutional authority to issue a writ of *mandamus*. Therefore, an act of Congress (the Judiciary Act of 1789) could be overturned if it was found to be unconstitutional. The decision did not force Jefferson and Madison to take any action, and Marbury gave up his fight for Justice of the Peace.

While not giving Marbury what he wanted, Marshall's Court established the principle of judicial review. In one bold move, the Court established that the Constitution was the highest law of the land and avoided an uncomfortable confrontation with the executive branch.

Instead of causing an embarrassment, Marshall's declaration that "a law repugnant to the Constitution is void" created the first and one of the most important landmark decisions in the Court's history.

As it turned out, John Marshall, last of the great Federalists, lasted well beyond his party's own lifetime. When he died in 1835, Marshall left behind a rich legacy of constitutional law grounded in Federalists beliefs about government.

Benjamin Civiletti

Benjamin Civiletti was the Attorney General of the United States from 1979 to 1981 under President Jimmy Carter.

Q: *How do you think a President's politics help shape the direction of the Justice Department during his term of office?*

Civiletti: I think it depends a great deal on the President, and it depends a great deal on the background, the nature, and characteristics of the Attorney General. In some instances, for example, the most blatant example are the Kennedy years, when there was such an intimate and close and shared relationship between the President and Robert Kennedy, and their philosophy and political judgment, that it would be hard to distinguish between the activities in the Department of Justice and the policies and directions of the President at that time.

Usually, in law enforcement matters and particularly in prosecutive matters, it doesn't make much difference who the President is. The Department of Justice is left to its own judgments on investigations and prosecutions, and the American public's confidence in those decisions being made independently and on the merits is so strong that few Presidents, and Nixon is the exception, risk interfering with, or seeming to interfere with, those responsibilities of the Department of Justice.

On the civil side, with taxation for example, or with environmental matters, or with regard to other policy matters under which the President has a responsibility to exercise either because of his campaign promises and philosophies, or because of his own basic set of principles, there the President, either directly or through agents, is able to influence the priorities of the Department of Justice and probably has a duty to try to do so in the most positive way . . . and most Attorneys General understand that and in taking the position are aware that the President is the Chief Executive Officer for domestic and foreign policy.

Q: *Do you feel that the President's selection of a Supreme Court Justice or an Attorney General is one of the more important selections that a President can make?*

Civiletti: Yes. I think it's important because I think the rule of law is important, and sound, independent decision making by people of capacity and ability are important to the public's faith in and honoring and treasuring of the rule of law.

STATE V. FEDERAL LAW

Martin v. Hunter's Lessee (1816)

Meanwhile, the individual states still struggled with the limits of their own powers. State law had a head-on collision with federal law in *Martin v. Hunter's Lessee*. A British-born man named Denny Fairfax owned land in Virginia that had been left to him in 1781. He never became a citizen of the United States and resided in England until his death around 1800. In his will, he left his land to a nephew named Thomas Bryan Martin, who was a citizen of Virginia. The treaties that the United States had entered into with Great Britain, beginning with the official end of the Revolutionary War in 1783, had provided for the protection of original rights of property.

But there was a problem—the state of Virginia had passed its own law regarding land that had been granted under royal control. In April 1789, the commonwealth of Virginia granted a parcel of land to a man named David Hunter, a lifelong resident of Virginia. This land was actually part of the tract that Thomas Martin had inherited. Both sides felt the land was legally theirs. The dispute was taken to court. In 1793, the District Court of Winchester, Virginia, ruled in favor of the defendant, Fairfax.

However, years later in 1810, the lower court's judgment was reversed in favor of Hunter. The case was appealed to the United States Supreme Court, which ruled in 1813 in favor of Fairfax and his heirs. The Virginia courts refused to follow the Supreme Court's ruling. The Virginia Supreme Court claimed it had

Justice Joseph Story in the early 1830s.

equal right to make the determination in the case, as did the federal court. In their opinion, the federal treaty did not bind the state. The case wound up back in the United States Supreme Court.

Justice Joseph Story wrote the opinion of the Court, in favor of Martin, in 1816. He said that the United States was not merely a confederacy of states like in ancient Greece; the states were unified under one powerful federal government.

He made two key points—that only the federal government could make treaties, and only the federal courts could interpret them. He realized that it would be chaos if the treaties the federal government made with other countries were ignored at will by the individual states. This would make the United States appear weak and untrustworthy in the eyes of foreign leaders. It might even lead to serious disagreements and war.

The bottom line was simple—where state courts had to deal with federal laws, the Supreme Court had the jurisdiction to make a ruling.

TAXING THE GOVERNMENT

McCulloch v. Maryland (1819)

Only three years later, another monumental case that pitted federal government against state government was on the docket of the Supreme Court—*McCulloch v. Maryland*. The United States Bank was originally created in 1791, at a time when the country's monetary system was in disarray. Branches of this new federal bank soon opened in various cities around the country. Instead of accepting local bank notes, the federal bank preferred nationally minted coin. People resented the banks and blamed them when their old local banks failed or when they could not secure a loan.

In 1818, the Maryland legislature passed a bill that called for federal banks to pay a lump-sum tax of $15,000 per year, or issue paper notes with a Maryland tax stamp. McCulloch, the cashier for the United States' bank in Baltimore, Maryland, heard about this new law and was outraged. There was no way he would pay any tax to the state.

When a customer of the federal bank spent some un-tax-stamped notes around Baltimore, the authorities got wind of it and traced the notes back to McCulloch. On May 8, 1818, McCulloch was in court, arguing his case before a judge. While he insisted that the state of Maryland had no authority to tax a federal bank, the judge was not moved, and fined McCulloch.

President James Monroe heard of the case and dispatched his Attorney General to argue for the federal government, on behalf of McCulloch, but the Court of Appeals upheld the lower court ruling.

The case was appealed to the United States Supreme Court. Both sides prepared their cases, hoping to sway the Justices with their arguments. The Attorney General and two other lawyers wanted to get across the point that it was very dangerous to let a state exert taxation powers over the federal government.

Maryland's 75-year-old Attorney General, Luther Martin, believed that the federal government had no right to create the bank in the first place, and that Maryland was within its rights to tax people and businesses located in the state.

The argument by one of the bank's lawyers, a man named William Pinkney, was so forceful, that Justice Story wrote afterward how brilliant the arguments were and how sparkling his language was, explaining that Pinkney spoke "like a great statesman and patriot." Story was not exaggerating. In his argument before the Court, Pinkney warned of the consequences of letting the states trample over federal authority and the Constitution. The bank's lawyer wondered aloud if the Constitution would become "a mere phantom of political power . . . a frail and tottering edifice . . . a creature half made up, without heart or brain, or nerve, or muscle—without protecting power or redeeming energy—or whether it is to be viewed as a competent guardian of all that is dear to us as a nation."

Chief Justice John Marshall examined the question in a methodical and logical way. The first question was basic—did Congress have the power and authority to incorporate a bank in the first place? Once he answered it with a resounding "yes," he could move on to additional questions about the power of the states to tax federal banks.

Marshall addressed the idea that the states created the Constitution, and that the ultimate power belonged to the states: "No political dreamer was ever wild enough to think of breaking down the lines which separate the States, and of compounding the

American people into one common mass . . . But the measures they adopt do not, on that account, cease to be the measures of the people themselves, or become the measures of the State governments."

He explained that when the states tax businesses, they are taxing their own citizens. However, when a state attempts to tax the federal government, it is acting upon "institutions created not by their own constituents, but by people over whom they claim no control." The whole can take action on the parts, but the parts (the states) cannot take action upon the whole. The federal government was "a Government declared to be supreme," while the state government "is not supreme" against federal laws.

Marshall summarized the argument by saying that, "the States have no power, by taxation or otherwise, to retard, impede, burden, or in any manner control the operations of the constitutional laws enacted by Congress to carry into execution the powers vested in the General Government."

The Supreme Court set a precedent for the power of federal government over state government and also helped cement the authority of the Supreme Court over the states at a time when there was still much uncertainty as to how much power the various states could exercise.

CHALLENGING THE FUGITIVE SLAVE LAW
Ableman v. Booth (1858)

During the 1850s, there was great tension over slavery. Northern anti-slavery states were furious with the lack of progress being made by the government. The Fugitive Slave Law of 1850 actually forced northern states to retrieve escaped slaves and return them to the slavery states. In 1854, one such escaped slave was known to be in Wisconsin. A Federal District Court judge issued a warrant for the slave's capture. An abolitionist named Sherman Booth was arrested for helping rescue a black fugitive from the marshal (Stephen Ableman) on March 11, 1854. Booth claimed that the Fugitive Slave Law was invalid and unconstitutional.

The marshal filed suit in the State Supreme Court of Wisconsin, but the court ruled in favor of Booth

Chief Justice John Marshall was one of the greatest Justices. Of the 1,106 opinions that were issued during his time as Chief Justice, Marshall himself wrote 519 of them.

and called the validity of the Fugitive Slave Law into question. They believed that Wisconsin could release the prisoner. Then the District Court tried Booth and found him guilty. Booth moved for a new trial, but was denied. He was sentenced to a month in prison and fined $1,000. Booth then filed with the State Supreme Court, claiming the District Court's trial was null and void, and that it had no authority to sentence him. The State Court ordered Booth released. It refused to recognize the authority of the federal government. It claimed that its decision was final and that it had jurisdiction over the federal courts since the Fugitive Slave Act was unconstitutional.

Now the federal government was furious. The Attorney General of the United States petitioned the Chief Justice of the Supreme Court to hear the case. The case eventually went to the United States Supreme Court as *Ableman v. Booth*.

Chief Justice Roger B. Taney explained that the Union could not have lasted a single year if offenses against the federal government "could not have been punished without the consent of the State in which the culprit was found."

Taney wondered where the state court could have gotten this new authority. It was a potentially dangerous situation. If the states indeed possessed the power that Wisconsin claimed to have, then each state's court system might rule differently on a similar case. This could not be allowed.

The Chief Justice also explained that the states had not been forced into the Union. They had all readily accepted the supremacy of the federal government and had done so for their own protection and good.

The states must therefore obey the Constitution and the laws of the United States. He maintained that no state judge or state court had the authority to release a prisoner of the United States government, for any reason. It did not matter what a state thought of a federal law; it was not for the states to pass judgment on federal laws.

Taney's goal was to "show plainly the grave errors into which the State court has fallen, and the consequences to which they would inevitably lead." He believed that allowing the state of Wisconsin to prevail "would subvert the very foundations of this Government."

Just three years after the *Ableman* decision, the country was plunged into the bloody four-year-long Civil War.

WHO DECIDES WHO CAN RUN FOR OFFICE?
U.S. Term Limits v. Thornton (1995)

Though the supremacy of the federal government had been fairly well established during the 19th century, occasional tests still arise in the Supreme Court. One recent example happened in 1995. The voters of Arkansas approved an amendment to the Arkansas State Constitution in 1992. The amendment prohibited a candidate for Congress from appearing on the ballot if that candidate had already served three terms in the House of Representatives (six years) or two terms in the Senate (12 years).

Make a Supreme Court Scrapbook

THE SUPREME COURT is constantly in the news, especially when it is hearing oral arguments. Some cases are instant landmarks, others are soon forgotten, and still others may grow in stature over time. In this activity you will keep a Court-related scrapbook.

YOU'LL NEED
- ✔ Newspapers
- ✔ News magazines
- ✔ Scissors
- ✔ Glue stick
- ✔ Blank scrapbook

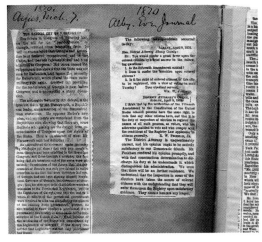

A page from Rufus Peckham's scrapbook. It contains more than 100 pages of newspaper clippings dating from 1863 to 1870.

Peruse at least two newspapers and two magazines over at least a one-month period (ideally, watch these periodicals for two to three months or longer) for anything pertaining to the Supreme Court, and cut out those articles. Categorize the articles by the type of case they discuss: civil rights, death penalty, abortion, business regulation, property rights, etc. Paste them neatly by type into a scrapbook, labeling each one at the top with the date and publication. When you are done, you will have a nice record of the cases and controversies of the Supreme Court. What themes emerge? How much coverage does each issue get? To calculate this, use your ruler to measure "column-inches" (the number of inches long a story is, measured by column in inches; for example, if it is two columns of four inches long each, then the story is eight column-inches long). Which issue got the most column-inches of coverage during your study period?

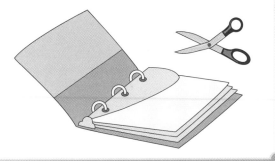

The amendment was challenged by Congressman Ray Thornton, and the Arkansas Supreme Court held that the amendment violated the federal Constitution. The state of Arkansas then appealed the case to the U.S. Supreme Court. The state argued that the Tenth Amendment applied to their case: "The powers not delegated to the United States by the Constitution, nor prohibited by it to the States, are reserved to the States respectively, or to the people."

The Supreme Court disagreed and ruled in favor of Thornton. The Court struck down the Arkansas provision as an unconstitutional attempt to add restrictions for congressional office beyond those found in the Constitution. The only way to change the requirements listed in the Constitution would be to ratify an Amendment. In its decision, the Court referred back to the words of both Alexander Hamilton and James Madison.

THE IMPEACHMENT OF PRESIDENT ANDREW JOHNSON

The Supreme Court sometimes finds itself at the center of a highly political conflict. The impeachment of President Andrew Johnson in 1868 was a divisive event for a nation still healing from the Civil War.

Vice President Andrew Johnson (a Democrat) assumed office after the assassination of Abraham Lincoln (a Republican) in 1865. The country had just ended a war that had split it in two and devastated the economy. Johnson had no popular consent to rule, as he was never elected President. President Johnson and the Congress disagreed on the nature of the reconstruction following the Civil War. The President said: "We have seen Congress gradually encroach, step by step, upon constitutional rights, and violate, day after day, and month after month, fundamental principles of government." On another occasion, he said: "I care not for their menaces, the taunts and the jeers. I do not intend to be bullied by my enemies, nor overawed by my friends; but God willing, with your help, I will veto their measures whenever they come to me."

The conflict rose to a head in March 1867, when Congress passed the Tenure of Office Act. This law stated that any presidential appointment requiring the Senate's approval must also pass the same test of Senate approval before the President could dismiss that person. Johnson wanted to remove his Secretary of War, Edwin Stanton, a radical Republican with whom he disagreed. The Senate refused to approve the firing of Stanton. The President refused to observe the Tenure of Office Act, calling it an unconstitutional law. He again told Stanton to leave. Stanton did not want to leave, but Johnson wanted to force him out.

The President wished to take the Tenure of Office Act before the Supreme Court for them to decide its constitutionality. Surely the Court would be sensible and decide in his favor, he thought. A firestorm brewed in Congress, and the House of Representatives then impeached Johnson, claiming that he had not followed his oath of office that called for him to execute the laws of the nation.

It would not matter what the Supreme Court said, according to many in Congress, because the President had broken the law. As provided in the Constitution, Johnson was then tried by the Senate in a divisive three-month-long trial. All the Democratic Senators voted against conviction, and they accused the Republicans of rushing to judgment and abolishing the right of appeal on important constitutional questions to the Supreme Court. A two-thirds majority was needed to convict the President, and in the end, the vote fell one man short. Still, Johnson finished out his term a weakened and disgraced President.

When President Bill Clinton was impeached 130 years later, there were also cries of unfair party politics and a "right-wing conspiracy" against the President. This time, beyond Chief Justice William H. Rehnquist presiding over the impeachment proceedings, the Supreme Court was not really a player in the political drama.

Court Packing

In the 1930s, the Supreme Court struck down several of President Franklin D. Roosevelt's New Deal policies (see page 151). President Roosevelt felt that the judicial branch of government had been gaining power for decades and had upset the balance among the three branches of government that the framers of the Constitution had in mind.

In response to the Court's annoying invalidation of his programs, the President developed an idea to add more Justices to the Supreme Court, as a way of "packing" the Court with those who favored his New Deal policies. He was frustrated that during his first four years in office, none of the Justices had resigned.

President Andrew Johnson.

Of the nine Justices in office at the time, three had been appointed by Herbert Hoover, one by Calvin Coolidge, two by Warren Harding, and one by William Howard Taft, for a total of seven Republican appointees.

President Roosevelt seemed to be stuck with a conservative, anti–New Deal Supreme Court. Roosevelt felt it was time to reform the Court. He planned to add up to five additional Justices to the existing nine, one for every Justice over the age of 70 who remained on the Court. It was a controversial plan, and one that did not have a lot of support.

He defended his plan in one of his Fireside Chat radio addresses to the American people in 1937:

If by that phrase "packing the Court" it is charged that I wish to place on the bench spineless puppets who would disregard the law and would decide specific cases as I wished them to be decided, I make this answer: that no President fit for his office would appoint, and no Senate of honorable men fit for their office would confirm, that kind of appointees to the Supreme Court.

Meanwhile, Chief Justice Charles Evans Hughes made it known to a prominent Senator that he felt the Justices were able to handle their workload just fine, thank you very much, and that the Roosevelt bill was unnecessary.

The measure did not gain much support, and eventually died a quiet death when the Senate voted against it overwhelmingly on July 22, 1937, by a margin of 70–20. Roosevelt's attempt at altering the composition of the Supreme Court was in a sense a demonstration of his commitment to the New Deal. Though not attacking the President directly, the Court had exerted its power and sided with business over the government.

If the President had been more patient, the whole embarrassment would have been avoided. As it turned out, Roosevelt got to "pack" the Supreme Court with hand-picked nominees anyway due to retirements. Between 1937 and 1943, he appointed eight new Justices to the Court, and a new Chief Justice in place of Hughes in 1941. In the end, Roosevelt may have had more of an impact on the long-term makeup of the Supreme Court than any other single President; his picks served a combined total of 136 years!

A President's Privacy
United States v. Nixon (1974)

The Supreme Court does not often come into direct conflict with the President, except during crises. In the Andrew Johnson impeachment crisis, a power struggle between the President and Congress nearly went to the Supreme Court, but instead wound up in the Senate as an impeachment hearing.

In the early 1970s, the country found itself in another presidential crisis. President Richard Nixon became embroiled in a scandal involving a break-in at the Democratic headquarters on June 17, 1972. The break-in occurred at the Watergate Hotel, which gave the scandal its infamous name.

Filming a newsreel about the Supreme Court during the Court-packing controversy.

Attorney General Elliot Richardson appointed a special prosecutor named Archibald Cox to investigate the scandal. When Cox found that there were secret tapes Nixon had made, he filed suit to have Nixon turn them over. Nixon in turn told Richardson to fire Cox, but Richardson refused. The duty then went to Deputy Attorney General William Ruckelshaus, who also refused. Both men resigned. Solicitor General Robert Bork was named Acting Attorney General, and he fired Cox. This infamous "Saturday Night Massacre" was the beginning of the end for Nixon.

On March 1, 1974, a District Court grand jury indicted seven people as part of the investigation into the Watergate scandal. Though the President himself was not specifically named, the grand jury called him an "unindicted coconspirator." The President's relevant documents and tape recordings were subpoenaed as part of the investigation. In April, Nixon released edited versions of his materials and portions of his tapes to the House Judiciary Committee. The District Court ordered him to release the original documents but the President refused to comply, citing his right to confidentiality.

The case went to the Supreme Court as *United States v. Nixon* (1974). It was argued on July 8, 1974, and the decision came down on July 24. The Justices had to weigh the value of the confidentiality and privacy of the President versus the need for information pertaining to potentially criminal activities. Chief Justice Warren Earl Burger wrote in his opinion:

A President and those who assist him must be free to explore alternatives in the process of shaping policies

and making decisions and to do so in a way many would be unwilling to express except privately . . . The privilege is fundamental to the operation of Government and inextricably rooted in the separation of powers under the Constitution.

But the Justices also felt that the President's interest in keeping communications confidential would not be violated by the disclosure of a limited number of conversations, especially since they had some connection to pending criminal cases.

The Chief Justice wrote that a President could not expect confidentiality in general. The "fundamental demands of **due process** of law" had to take precedence in a criminal justice case. In effect, a President was not untouchable. A President could not expect to get away with criminal behavior and keep records

Richard M. Nixon is sworn in as President by Chief Justice Warren Burger, 1973.

of that behavior secret, under the umbrella of so-called presidential privilege. If there was a specific need for evidence in a pending criminal trial, then the President must yield to any reasonable requests.

By the end of July, the House Judiciary Committee had adopted three articles of impeachment against Nixon. President Nixon resigned his office on August 9, 1974, before the impeachment process could progress any further.

But Nixon's dealings with the Supreme Court were not over yet. After he resigned, Nixon made an agreement with the General Services Administration (a government agency that acquires services and information for other government clients) to store 42 million pages of presidential documents and 880 tape recordings for a limited time. After three years had passed, Nixon would be allowed to remove and destroy documents. After five years, he could destroy tapes, and after 10 years or his death (whichever came first), all the tapes would be destroyed.

Then, later that same year, Congress passed the Presidential Recordings and Materials Preservation Act. The Act ordered that the GSA screen presidential materials, and that the President would have no say in what materials were marked as private and returned to him. There had already been some movement in the direction of more public access to government documents with the passage of the Freedom of Information Act in 1966.

On December 20, 1974, just one day after President Gerald Ford signed the bill, Nixon filed suit in District Court claiming that the Act was not legal. First of all, he claimed, it violated the separation of powers because Congress was trying to order the executive branch. He also claimed presidential privilege and a right to privacy regarding his documents.

The District Court did not put much stock into Nixon's arguments and ruled against him. The Supreme Court agreed with the lower court's ruling in *Nixon v. General Services Administration* (1977) and voted against Nixon 7–2. The Court shot down Nixon's claim that the Act violated the separation of powers. After all, once President Ford signed the measure, the executive branch was involved. In addition, the GSA, a part of the executive branch, was to conduct the screening of the materials. There was no conflict.

Nixon's claims were rejected by the Court. They referred back to their opinion in *Nixon v. United States* (1974) and also to the fact that Presidents Gerald Ford and Jimmy Carter did not agree with Nixon that it would be damaging to the presidency for his materials to be preserved. And who better to estimate the ramifications than another President? Nixon also claimed that having these papers stored and made available would be damaging because it would make future cabinet members and advisors less likely to give their honest advice to a President on controversial topics, for fear that their words would be used against them in the future. The Court countered that presidential materials had been screened for use in presidential libraries for many years, and that with time, even the most sensitive documents lose their need to be kept secret.

Nixon's brief complained that for the government to seize all his papers and personal materials for screening was akin to illegal search and seizure, outlawed by the Fourth Amendment. He was unhappy that his most personal and private communications would be reviewed and screened by people he never met, who would then decide which among those documents were personal enough to return to him.

The Court deflated this argument, too. It said that archivists were highly capable and had done this before, and that the only way to sort out the private papers from the rest would be through a screening process.

Justice William H. Rehnquist, a Nixon appointee, was one of the dissenters. He felt that the Act violated the separation of powers and would hamper communications within the White House. "I think that not only the Executive Branch of the Federal Government, but the Legislative and Judicial Branches as well, will come to regret this day when the Court has upheld an Act of Congress that trenches so significantly on the functioning of the Office of the President."

INTERVIEW

William Ruckelshaus

William Ruckelshaus served as the first head of the Environmental Protection Agency (EPA) in 1970, then as Acting Director of the Federal Bureau of Investigation (FBI). Next, he was appointed Deputy Attorney General under President Nixon. He had a role in the Saturday Night Massacre in 1973, when he resigned rather than obey Nixon's order to fire the Watergate Special Prosecutor Archibald Cox. In 1983, President Ronald Reagan asked him to once again head the EPA.

Q: *The Supreme Court upheld the independent counsel law in* Morrison v. Olson *[1988], though some people are still against an independent counsel. Do you think based on your experience with Nixon that such a law is necessary to keep the executive branch in check?*

Ruckelshaus: I do not think an independent counsel law is a good idea. If the Justice Department is not doing its job by investigating allegations about members of the executive branch, including the President, the recourse should be for the Congress to hold the Justice Department accountable. Creating a special counsel to perform this task only diminishes the accountability of the Department of Justice.

Q: *Should a President have the authority to keep certain documents private, no matter what? Was the Supreme Court right in ordering Nixon to turn over the tapes?*

Ruckelshaus: The President should have the authority to keep some documents private, no matter what. It is necessary for him as the head of state to keep private some information and not share it with the public. An example might be the decision by the President to invade Europe through Normandy in 1944. Certainly he would not want to share this decision or the documents backing it up until well after the event. I do think it was appropriate for the Supreme Court to order President Nixon to turn over the tapes. The essential public question was whether he participated in the cover-up of the Watergate crimes and these tapes were relevant information bearing on those allegations.

THE INDEPENDENT COUNSEL
Morrison v. Olson (1988)

The Ethics in Government Act of 1978 arose out of the Watergate scandal. Congress made sure that one of the Act's provisions allowed the Attorney General to recommend the appointment of an independent counsel to investigate alleged federal crimes by government officials.

On April 23, 1986, James C. McKay was appointed independent counsel to investigate testimony (regarding Department of Justice activities) given by Assistant Attorney General Theodore Olson before a House subcommittee in 1983. When McKay resigned as independent counsel, Alexia Morrison was appointed as his replacement.

Morrison served subpoenas on Olson and two other people, Edward Schmults and Carol Dinkins, who tried to get the subpoenas quashed, arguing that the independent counsel provision was unconstitutional and that Morrison therefore could not proceed with her investigation.

The District Court upheld the Act's constitutionality, but the Court of Appeals reversed, holding that the Act violated the principle of separation of powers by interfering with the President's authority. Morrison appealed and *Morrison v. Olson* (1988) went to the Supreme Court.

In a 7–1 decision, the Supreme Court upheld the constitutionality of the independent counsel. It found the separation of powers to be adequately preserved by the limits of the rules. Chief Justice Rehnquist said for the majority, "The Attorney General is not allowed to appoint the individual of his choice; he does not determine the counsel's jurisdiction; and his power to remove a counsel is limited. Nonetheless, the Act does give the Attorney General several means of supervising or controlling the prosecutorial powers that may be wielded by an independent counsel. Most importantly, the Attorney General retains the power to remove the counsel for "good cause," a power that . . . provides the Executive with substantial ability to ensure that the laws are 'faithfully executed' by an independent counsel."

The independent counsel law expired in 1992 but was renewed in 1994. In retrospect, the most important consequence of the Supreme Court decision was the investigation of President Bill Clinton by independent counsel Kenneth Starr. This investigation led to Clinton's impeachment. After the Clinton investigation, the law was allowed to expire again in 1999.

INTERVIEW

Kenneth Starr

Kenneth Starr was the Solicitor General of the United States from 1989 to 1993, under President George H. W. Bush. He served as a federal judge on the U.S. Court of Appeals for the District of Columbia Circuit from 1983 to 1989. In 1994, Starr became the independent counsel in the Whitewater investigation that led to President Clinton's impeachment. He has argued 25 cases before the Supreme Court. He is currently Dean of Pepperdine Law School.

Q: *Should the independent counsel law be reinstated or abolished?*

Starr: The short answer is no, it should not be preserved [reinstated]. But we should have a mechanism, and we do, for the Attorney General to appoint a special counsel or an independent counsel. That was the tried-and-true, time-honored way of handling sensitive investigations and sensitive prosecutions. But the reform Congress in 1978, at the insistence of President Carter, passed the law, notwithstanding thoughtful objections by senior lawyers in both political parties, indicating among other things that the creation of that particular mechanism, an independent counsel appointed by the federal Court, really eroded basic separation of powers principles. The Congress resisted that and ignored, or at least did not accept, the advice and guidance by very leading authorities.

We now have returned to the system that prevailed for many decades, going back to the administration of Ulysses S. Grant, which was the first administration that I know of that determined that someone outside of the President's appointees should be called in or asked to step in to handle a special investigation. But appointed by the Attorney General as opposed to appointed by the Court.

Q: *So then you disagree with* Morrison v. Olson [1988]?

Starr: Yes, I felt that *Morrison v. Olson* was wrongly decided, and that it had been rightly decided by the U.S. Court of Appeals, on which I was serving at the time, that struck the law down as unconstitutional, as a violation of separation of powers.

Q: *To what extent can and should executive privilege be invoked by a President, whether Nixon or Clinton or anyone, to protect the presidency and privacy?*

Starr: Well, the Supreme Court upheld the concept of executive privilege as necessary for the proper functioning of government, but it becomes a matter of practical wisdom and judgment as to when it should be invoked. My own view is that it should be invoked sparingly, but it is nonetheless an important principle and concept to the presidency.

THE LINE ITEM VETO
Clinton v. The City of New York (1998)

The Supreme Court plays an important role in ensuring the President and Congress follow the system of checks and balances ordered by the Constitution, but the only way the Court can pass judgment on a law is if it is brought before them in a case.

Laws are sometimes challenged by constituents who feel they are unfair, or by members of Congress who voted against a law. One recent example of a law that was challenged is the Line Item Veto. The President normally has the constitutional authority to reject, or veto, a bill that crosses his desk for signature. Congress may then override his veto with a two-thirds majority of votes. But what if that process is slightly modified?

In 1996, President Bill Clinton signed into law a special extension of presidential veto powers that allowed him to strike out only select parts of a bill. The Line Item Veto Act became effective as of January 1, 1997.

The President could use the Line Item Veto as long as its purpose was to reduce the federal budget deficit, and as long as it did not impair any essential government functions or harm the national interest.

For example, if a spending bill contained a provision for $45 million in federal funds to be spent on new roofs for post offices, the President could sign the overall bill, but veto only that particular item of the bill. Congress would then either approve or disapprove of the removed item by simple majority. If they did not agree, the Congress sent a "bill of disapproval" back to the President. The President could veto the disapproval bill. If Congress did not override his veto with a two-thirds majority, then the bill passed without the $45 million roof expenditure.

The day after the Line Item Veto Act took effect, six members of Congress who had voted against the Act filed suit in the District Court to challenge the Act's constitutionality. On April 10, 1997, the District Court found that the Act was unconstitutional. The case went to the Supreme Court on appeal, but the Court found that the six members of Congress had no **standing** to sue. They had not been injured by the Line Item Veto Act and so were not eligible to file suit. A challenge would have to come directly from an injured party.

Later that same year, a challenge did arise. Two separate suits were filed, one by the City of New

York, and one by a cooperative of Idaho potato growers, both claiming that a line item cancelation had caused them harm. The District Court combined the two cases into one and found that the Act "impermissibly disrupts the balance of powers among the three branches of government."

In *Clinton v. The City of New York,* the government, led by Solicitor General Seth Waxman, argued that the President had the right to decide not to spend certain money. In effect, he was not vetoing anything, he was only attempting to balance the budget by limiting spending. The Supreme Court, by a margin of 6–3, did not agree with that argument. They upheld the District Court ruling that the Line Item Veto Act was unconstitutional. The "Presentment Clause" of the Constitution outlined exactly how a bill became a law, and this Act unconstitutionally changed that process. A constitutional amendment would be needed to enact such a change to the lawmaking process.

In July 1998, the Office of Management and Budget announced that funding would be released for the few dozen line items that were canceled in 1997.

THE FLORIDA RECOUNTS
Bush v. Gore (2000)

Popular votes do not decide presidential elections in the United States. Instead, the people vote for electors, who then assemble and cast their votes as the people have dictated. The Constitution set up a system where the winner of the popular vote in each state would obtain all of that state's electoral votes (the number of Senators plus the number of Representatives in the House).

This system has resulted in some very close electoral victories that were actually popular-vote losses. It has also resulted in electoral landslides that were not actually popular-vote landslides.

In the contested election of 1876, the Democrat Samuel Tilden had 250,000 more popular votes than the Republican Rutherford Hayes, but lost the election by one electoral vote, 185–184. In 1984, the Democrat Walter Mondale got 2 percent of the electoral votes but 41 percent of the popular vote. In 1992, independent candidate Ross Perot received no electoral votes but got 19 percent of the popular vote.

In 2000, popular incumbent President Bill Clinton was leaving office after eight years, and his Vice President, Al Gore, sought election. The challenger was George W. Bush, the son of the 41st President, George H. W. Bush. Throughout a close race, both sides campaigned hard. On election night, it soon became clear that the race would be more than a simple nail-biter. Though Gore led nationwide in the popular vote, the election all came down to the 25 electoral votes held by the state of Florida. With Gore at 266 electoral votes and Bush at 246, Florida was the winner-take-all state. Its 25 electoral votes would give either candidate the 270 needed to win the election.

As the Florida results came in, it looked grim for Gore. Though Gore conceded to Bush at 3:00 A.M., he took it back when the results were still in question later in the morning. On that day, November 8, 2000,

Bush had 2,909,135 and Gore had 2,907,351 popular votes in Florida. The margin was 1,784 for Bush. It was still too close to call. Because Bush's margin of victory was less than one-half of one percent of the votes cast, an automatic machine recount was conducted as per the election code of Florida.

There were widespread allegations of various problems with the voting machines and the ballots. The complication of the Florida vote of 2000 had many dimensions. On the whole, the Florida election was marked by different counties using different types of ballots. Some counties used "butterfly" ballots. In these cases, voters were asked to poke holes in punch cards using a stylus (pointed instrument). Some voters were confused which "chad" they were supposed to punch for which candidate. When the ballots were counted, the examiners had trouble deciding which ballots counted. Some ballots were underpunched (the chad was not fully detached and was "hanging") while others looked to have had two selections made for President, with two chads missing. An unusual number of votes were registered for third-party candidates, leading Gore's supporters to believe that those votes had been mistakenly cast.

After the machine recount, Bush led by only 327 votes. As the days passed, America waited for resolution. Newspaper headlines each day told of the latest twists and turns in the contest. Both the Bush and Gore camps assembled various lawyers, advisors, and aides to spin their sides of the story and make a legal and emotional push for their candidate. As the seemingly endless legal battle played out in the courts, an actual deadline loomed ahead. The electors from each of the 50 states were scheduled to meet on December 18 and pledge their support for a candidate. According to the United States Code, any conflicts had to be settled by December 12.

Gore's lawyers wanted a hand recount in several counties where irregularities had been reported. This began a complicated legal battle between the Gore camp, which wanted hand recounts and examination of questionable ballots, and the Bush camp, which wanted to end all hand recounts. On December 8, the Florida Supreme Court ordered a hand recount of votes in certain counties. Bush's lawyers asked the U.S. Supreme Court to halt the recounts, which the Court did by a 5–4 vote on December 9. Two days later, the Court heard oral arguments to decide whether hand recounts could continue or should be ended for good. At that point, the tally left Bush with 537 more votes than Gore in Florida.

On December 12, the U.S. Supreme Court issued its two-part ruling. By a 7–2 margin, it decided that hand recounts could not be conducted selectively, and that there would have to be universal standards for recounting ballots throughout the state. Otherwise, the recounts would violate the Equal Protection clause of the Fourteenth Amendment. The reasoning was that the Florida Supreme Court ordered a recount throughout the state of Florida without taking any precaution that fair standards would be applied.

However, in the second part of the ruling, by a 5–4 margin, the Supreme Court Justices decided that any and all recounts would have to be completed by the legal deadline of midnight on December 12. Since there were only a few hours left until midnight, it appeared there would be no way to accomplish this. Bush had won the election. Whether intentionally or not, it was the most conservative Justices (Sandra Day O'Connor, Clarence Thomas, William H. Rehnquist, Antonin Scalia, and Anthony M. Kennedy) who had handed Bush a victory. The opinion, usually signed by a member of the majority, was instead issued as a **per curiam** (Latin for "by the Court"). This type of decision is usually reserved for unanimous rulings (9–0). Due to its time-sensitive nature, the case also progressed to the Supreme Court much faster than an ordinary case. The Court's decision read:

Upon due consideration of the difficulties identified to this point, it is obvious that the recount cannot be conducted in compliance with the requirements of equal protection and due process without substantial additional work. It would require not only the adoption . . . of adequate statewide standards for determining what is a legal vote . . . but also orderly judicial review of any disputed matters that might arise.

From Justice Stephen G. Breyer's dissent:

[T]here is no justification for the majority's remedy, which is simply to reverse the lower court and halt the recount entirely. An appropriate remedy would be, instead, to remand this case with instructions that, even at this late date, would permit the Florida Supreme Court to require recounting all under-counted votes in Florida.

From Justice Ruth Bader Ginsburg's dissent:

[T]he Court's conclusion that a constitutionally adequate recount is impractical is a prophecy the Court's own judgment will not allow to be tested. Such an untested prophecy should not decide the Presidency of the United States.

From Justice David H. Souter's dissent:

The [December 12 deadline] is not serious . . . no State is required to conform to [the deadline] if it cannot do that (for whatever reason) . . .

The decision instantly became controversial. Republicans believed the ruling had been logical and impartial. Democrats across the country decried the "stolen" election and the fact that Gore had won more popular votes. Some people even lashed out and blamed third-party candidate Ralph Nader for "stealing" votes from Gore in Florida. Some independent news investigations later showed that if recounts had been conducted, Gore would have been the winner of Florida and the presidency.

Gore conceded the election on December 13, and Bush was sworn in as President on January 20, 2001. Since then, there have been calls for reform of the electoral system. John B. Anderson, who ran for President in 1980 and received six million votes, is the Chairman of a group called FairVote. He believes that to prevent another case like *Bush v. Gore* in the future, the government must "abolish the Electoral College and go to direct popular vote." He feels this

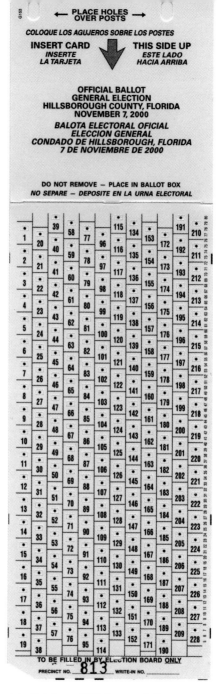

A ballot from Hillsborough County, Florida, November 7, 2000.

will prevent a "democracy deficit" by allowing everyone's vote to count equally in a nationwide tally, rather than a state-by-state vote for electors. The path to electoral reform may be tricky, however. Changing the over 200-year-old method for selection of our President could face challenges in Congress and perhaps eventually in the Supreme Court.

INTERVIEW James A. Baker III

James A. Baker III served as the nation's 61st Secretary of State from 1989 to 1992 under President George H. W. Bush and as the nation's 67th Secretary of the Treasury from 1985 to 1988 under President Ronald Reagan. He also served as White House Chief of Staff to President Reagan (1981 to 1985) and President Bush (1992 to 1993). A partner with the law firm Baker Botts, Baker headed the legal team that helped George W. Bush win the 2000 election dispute in Florida that was ultimately resolved by the U.S. Supreme Court in *Bush v. Gore* (2000).

Q: *Why should kids learn about the Supreme Court?*

Baker: The United States Supreme Court is one of the three political bodies that our founding fathers established to help guarantee the type of balance of power they sought for their new democracy. Thomas Jefferson, Alexander Hamilton, James Madison, and the other heroes who framed our Constitution understood that freedom can be jeopardized when power rests in the hands of too few.

The theory of the separation of powers goes back to the days of Aristotle, a critic of centralized power who believed that individuals require protection from abuse by the state. However, it was difficult to put the theory into practice because of the tendency of kings and rulers to consolidate power. Finally, the framers of our Constitution got it right. By establishing the Supreme Court at the top of the judicial branch, itself a separate branch to oversee our laws, they struck a balance between the judicial branch, the executive branch, and the legislative branch.

At times this system is cumbersome. It may promote inefficiency. But it distinguishes the United States from other countries and provides us with a framework that helps prevent corruption by one branch or another. Many of our individual freedoms can be traced to this separation of powers system.

Q: *How will* Bush v. Gore *be remembered 50 to 100 years from now?*

Baker: There are at least two important lessons that can be learned from *Bush v. Gore,* the case which led to the election of George W. Bush as President in 2000. The first is that the rule of law prevailed in the United States. While the case was a controversial one, our legal system determined the outcome. The most important ruling in the case, the one that said the recount process in Florida was unconstitutional on equal protection grounds, was made by seven of the nine Supreme Court Justices, including two appointed by Democrats. The second lesson learned is that our constitutional system in the United States worked. We had a smooth transfer of power despite a close election and emotional aftermath. However, there was no rioting in the streets, as there might have been in a country that lacks our stability.

INTERVIEW ## David Boies (part 1)

David Boies was lead counsel for Vice President Al Gore in the Florida election dispute in 2000 and argued before the Supreme Court in *Bush v. Gore* (2000). He has also been involved in several other high-profile cases, representing Napster and Microsoft.

Q: Why do you feel the Supreme Court made the wrong decision in **Bush v. Gore?**

Boies: First, the Court, in *Bush v. Gore,* departed from precedent. That is, it departed from the law that the Court had declared in prior cases. The Court was making new law, and that law was inconsistent, as the dissenting Justices pointed out, with the law that the majority Justices had previously declared.

Second, the Court said that this rule that it was announcing would in effect hold only for this case. In my view, what the Court should do is to declare principles of law that they are prepared to abide by in every case, regardless of the parties involved. It is almost an element of the rule of law that the outcome of a case should not depend on who the parties are or what the personal views are of individual judges as to who they would like to see win a particular case. An important safeguard for that is that when judges say what the law is, they have to say that that law applies to everybody now and in the future, because that constrains them from making decisions that benefit a particular party or a particular cause. And in *Bush v. Gore,* when the Court says in effect this decision is good for this case only, it is saying that it is not prepared to apply it in the future.

Third, this was the first time in the history of the country that the Supreme Court had intervened to decide or influence the decision of a presidential election. Our Constitution sets up checks and balances and one of those checks and balances is to try to keep the courts out of political decision making. I think that if you ever developed a precedent where the Court involves themselves in regular interventions in presidential elections that would have a bad effect. I think the Court recognizes it, which is why it says this is good for this case only. But I think what the Court really should have said is that because of that principle it should not have intervened in this case, or any other case with similar kinds of facts.

Q: How will Bush v. Gore be remembered 50 or 100 years from now in history books?

Boies: I think it will be remembered as a mistake.

Ralph Nader

Ralph Nader is a consumer advocate and past presidential candidate. For decades, Nader has been a crusader for government accountability and consumer protection. Nader ran for President on the Green Party ticket in 2000 and ran again in 2004.

Q: How should the Supreme Court have ruled in Bush v. Gore [2000]?

Nader: They should not have taken the case.

Q: You helped bring the Freedom of Information Act into existence. Why is it so important for Americans to have access to government documents? Is there a point at which too much access can become dangerous?

Nader: As has often been said, "Sunshine is the best disinfectant." Access to government held records is one of the most effective tools the American citizenry has to understand the workings of its government, at all levels. Without understanding the successes and failures of government actions, the citizenry cannot give informed consent to its Governors, the essence of our democracy. Too much access can be dangerous if narrowly crafted exemptions are not followed, for example, on national security or on personal privacy or on legal investigations. But access problems tend to come from too little, not too much disclosure.

Q: Is the Supreme Court most effective when it is balanced with conservative and liberal Justices?

Nader: No. The Supreme Court is most effective in the pursuit of justice and as a fully equal, independent branch of government, not tethered to electoral cycles.

THE FEDERALIST REVOLUTION

Under Chief Justice William H. Rehnquist, the Supreme Court moved in a direction that interpreted the Constitution as more limiting of federal powers over the states. In *Fry v. United States* (1975), the Court ruled that a federal law stabilizing the salaries states could pay to their employees was constitutional. Justice Rehnquist filed a dissent, claiming that the Court had gone too far in giving Congress power over the states.

This dissenting point of view became the Court's majority point of view as time passed. In *United States v. Lopez* (1995), the Court struck down as unconstitutional a federal law that banned handguns in school zones. In *United States v. Morrison* (2000), the Court struck down another federal law that gave abused women a federal remedy to sue their abusers. In both cases the Court held that regulating guns and violence against women were not matters of "interstate commerce," and so Congress had misused its authority by enacting them.

Only time will tell what direction the Court goes during Chief Justice John G. Roberts's reign and beyond.

3

FREE SPEECH

The Poverty of our Foreign Policy is Causing War

END THE DRAFT—
LET YOUNG MEN LIVE

I AM NOT A COMMUNIST AND I STILL OPPOSE THE WAR IN VIETNAM

STOP THE WAR NOW!

THE PEOPLE OF THE UNITED STATES WOULD LOOK OVER THEIR NATIONALISTIC, REAC-TIONARY PRIDE, THE WAR WOULD BE OVER. US CAN BE WRONG

BIG FI GET R GIs D

The right of free speech is one of the basic freedoms that sets our country apart from many other countries. It is addressed in the First Amendment to our Constitution. But is there a limit to free speech? How far is too far? Is it OK to take out an advertisement promoting the Communist Party? Is it illegal not to salute the flag or to set it on fire? Can you donate unlimited amounts to "buy" the election of a certain candidate? Can you say whatever you want, or should the government decide when enough is enough? Do laws such as the Patriot Act, which give the government new powers to monitor the activities of and detain American citizens, infringe on our civil liberties or place too many restrictions on our free speech? Can free speech really be free if there is a limit?

The Supreme Court has been the final proving ground on many free speech cases over the last 100 years, and each one depends on the unique details and circumstances of the case. Free speech has been most endangered during times of war.

Wars declared by governments are not always popular with the people who must fight them. During the Civil War, draft riots broke out in New York City because rich men could buy exemptions that poor men could not afford.

In April 1917, the United States declared war on Germany. At that point, World War I had already been raging in Europe for three years. In May 1917, the draft began. Soon after, Congress passed the Espionage Act of 1917, designed to protect the country against traitors and spies during wartime. The Act was reminiscent of the infamous Alien and Sedition Laws of 1798, which sought to suppress criticism of the government.

The Espionage Act made it illegal to make or convey false reports or false statements intending to interfere with military operations, to cause insubordination or disloyalty in the armed forces, or obstruct the recruitment of soldiers.

When the Act was amended in 1918, more illegal activities were added to the original three, including obstructing the sale of government bonds; writing, speaking, or publishing disloyal language that speaks of the Constitution, army or navy, or the flag; or publishing language that inspires resistance against the United States and loyalty to the enemy.

During World War I, nearly 2,000 court cases and proceedings came about that involved run-ins with the Espionage Act and claims of violation of First Amendment rights. Some of these cases made it all the way to the Supreme Court, but the first of them did not reach the Court until 1919, after the war had already ended.

An anti-war meeting, August 1914.

WARTIME WORDS
Schenck v. United States (1919)

After the United States entered the war in 1917, a new conscription law was passed and the government began to draft men into the armed forces. Though many Americans supported the war, and even joined the armed services voluntarily, there were dissenters. These dissenters felt the United States should stay out of the war.

A Socialist named Charles Schenck was one of the objectors. Since he felt so strongly about the issue, he decided to take action. Schenck mailed out flyers that condemned the war and called the draft illegal and unconstitutional. The flyer he created said, "Do not submit to intimidation," and claimed that anyone who did not let a person voice opposition to the draft violated the Constitution. The flyer went on: "If you do not assert and support your rights, you are helping to deny or disparage rights which it is the solemn duty of all citizens and residents of the United States to retain . . . You must do your share to maintain, support and uphold the rights of the people of this country."

He claimed it was his First Amendment right to distribute this flyer, but the Supreme Court decided that in times of war, different standards had to be applied; some things that might be harmless if said or written during peacetime could be dangerous or hinder the war effort. Justice Oliver Wendell Holmes wrote the unanimous opinion of the Court:

Words which, ordinarily and in many places, would be within the freedom of speech protected by the First Amendment may become subject to prohibition when of such a nature and used in such circumstances as to create a clear and present danger that they will bring about the substantive evils which Congress has a right to prevent.

But the character of every act depends upon the circumstances in which it is done. The most stringent protection of free speech would not protect a man in falsely shouting fire in a theatre and causing a panic.

Justice Holmes's point was simple; it depended what you said and where you said it. Yelling, "I hate this movie!" in a theater would be disruptive, but not dangerous such as yelling, "Fire!" On the other hand, yelling "Fire!" in your living room is quite different from yelling "Fire!" in a theater. Holmes also said that the flyers must have been intended to have some kind of effect, otherwise they would not have been sent at all. It was no accident. The Court upheld Schenck's conviction, and he spent six months in jail.

"GENTLEMEN, I ABHOR WAR"
Eugene Debs v. United States (1919)

Eugene V. Debs was a well-known labor organizer, Socialist, and pacifist who had run for President in 1900, 1904, 1908, and again in 1912, when he received 900,000 votes (6 percent of the popular vote), coming in fourth in a crowded field of three future or former Presidents: Woodrow Wilson, Theodore Roosevelt, and William Howard Taft. Debs spoke to an Ohio crowd on June 16, 1918, and told them about the future of Socialism. He explained that the upper class declared wars while the lower class fought the wars.

"You have your lives to lose; you certainly ought to have the right to declare war if you consider a war necessary," Debs told the audience.

Among other things, he also mentioned the cases of two women whom he felt had been wrongfully convicted of obstructing the recruiting service. Debs was accused of having "incited and attempted to cause and incite insubordination, disloyalty, mutiny and refusal of duty in the military and naval forces of the United States." At his trial, he addressed the jury and said: "I have been accused of obstructing the war. I admit it. Gentlemen, I abhor war. I would oppose the war if I stood alone." The jury found that Debs had specific intent to obstruct the recruiting service with his words, and he was found guilty of violating the Espionage Act and sentenced to prison for 10 years.

The Supreme Court upheld the lower court's decision, with Justice Oliver Wendell Holmes saying about the trial court, "We should add that the jury were most carefully instructed that they could not find the defendant guilty . . . unless the words used had as their natural tendency and reasonably probable effect to obstruct the recruiting service . . . and unless the defendant had the specific intent to do so in his mind."

Debs ran for President again, and received 919,000 votes in the 1920 election, while still in prison. President Warren Harding ordered his release in 1921 by presidential pardon. Debs died in 1926 at the age of 71.

After World War I, the government continued to focus on threats to the nation's security. The Russian Revolution of 1917 had been the catalyst in a worldwide increase in Socialism and Communism. These movements advocated that the common people revolt against the "system" and overthrow capitalism. In response to the presence of active Communists and Socialists in the United States, the government took legal action. Several political activists wound up in prison during the 1920s. A Communist publication of the time featured an essay that said, "When [the ruling class] saw the conditions for working class revolt developing here in the United States, they began to search for agitators to put in their jails. They wanted

to lock up their ideas . . . The Communists have an idea that the masters fear, therefore it is illegal and the persecution of the Communists continues."

Is Writing Incitement?
Gitlow v. New York (1925)

Benjamin Gitlow was a Socialist who distributed pamphlets titled *The Revolutionary Age* that contained part of his "Left Wing Manifesto," calling for the creation of a Socialist system and advocating labor strikes. He was indicted in the Supreme Court of New York for criminal anarchy. The jury in the case was instructed to consider the "ordinary" meaning of the words. Mentioning historical facts and describing economic trends was not in itself anarchy. Gitlow was found guilty and sentenced to prison.

The U.S. Supreme Court upheld the ruling of the lower courts to convict Gitlow. Justice Edward Terry Sanford said:

[The pamphlet] advocates and urges in fervent language mass action which shall progressively foment industrial disturbances and, through political mass strikes and revolutionary mass action, overthrow and destroy organized parliamentary government.

Freedom of speech and of the press, as secured by the Constitution, is not an absolute right to speak or publish without responsibility whatever one may choose or an immunity for every possible use of language.

The Supreme Court felt that caution should rule when dealing with potential anarchy, and that even a small spark could be the cause of a disastrous fire. The ruling was not unanimous, however. From the dissent, by Justice Oliver Wendell Holmes:

It is said that this manifesto was more than a theory, that it was an incitement. Every idea is an incitement . . . The only difference between the expression of an opinion and an incitement in the narrower sense is the speaker's enthusiasm for the result . . . But the indictment alleges the publication, and nothing more.

Holmes had been on the other side on the earlier incitement cases. This time he offered a looser inter-pretation of the Espionage Act. He explained that the act of writing was itself passionate, and that powerful writing could be stirring, but was not evidence enough that a piece of writing such as Gitlow's manifesto would be the trigger for violence. Anarchy had to be in the here and the now, and Gitlow could not be imprisoned for inciting something 20 years in the future.

DRAFT CARD PROTEST
United States v. O'Brien (1968)

The Vietnam conflict generated a great deal more dissent than World War I ever did. Many Americans were not sure why the government had involved the country in the war to begin with. Protest marches and demonstrations took place across the country. The draft was an especially controversial subject as many hundreds of thousands of young men were sent off to fight in the jungles of Vietnam. It only got worse as the casualties mounted.

On March 31, 1966, a 19-year-old named David O'Brien burned his two-inch by three-inch draft card on the steps of the South Boston courthouse in front of a crowd of people. The crowd began to harass him and he was taken to safety by an FBI agent, who then arrested him for breaking a federal law. The law made it illegal for anyone to change a draft card and made it a punishable offense for anyone "who forges, alters, *knowingly destroys, knowingly mutilates,* or in any manner changes any such certificate . . ." The words in italics had been added to the existing law in 1965,

IS IT PROTECTED SPEECH?

IN 1921, a publisher in Cleveland, Ohio, printed a magazine called *The Red Album—May Day 1921*. In this activity you will read an actual passage from the magazine and decide whether the words should be allowable as free speech. By today's standards the passage might seem fairly tame, and it would certainly be protected as free speech, but try to imagine you're a lawyer in 1921. How was society different then? What kinds of things are acceptable now that weren't back then? Compare what is said here to what Charles Schenck wrote in his flyer.

answer questions from the Justices. Then the Justices will confer and decide whether *The Red Album* is protected by the First Amendment or is illegal and incites violence. The Chief Justice should write an opinion that is two to three paragraphs long and read it before the class.

The Red Album, 1921.

THE RED ALBUM

YOU'LL NEED

✔ 9 index cards
✔ Classroom Supreme Court
✔ Lawyer for the Toiler
✔ Lawyer for the government
✔ Text of the opinion in *Gitlow v. New York* (1925) (go to: http://laws.findlaw.com/us/268/652.html)
✔ Text of the opinion in *Schenk v. United States* (1919) (go to: www.law.umkc.edu/faculty/projects/ftrials/conlaw/schenk.html)

Your classroom should split into two sides: those who will argue that the passages are harmless, and those who will find that the passages could incite anarchy and violence. Use passages from the *Gitlow* and *Schenk* cases to support your case. Each side will pick one lawyer to argue before the Supreme Court. Each side will have a maximum of 10 minutes to argue and

May Day, the Day of International Labor, has come! May Day, the Day of Revolution, is here, bringing its message of revolt—proletarian revolt! May Day, when the Workers in their millions, all over the world, assemble in the public squares and send forth words of challenge to the masters who hold them in chains! May Day, when men, women and children, grasping each other's hands, thrill with the songs of emancipation that Revolutionists who have lived and died for the Revolution, have written with their life's blood!

This year, May Day has come in the midst of bitter struggle. People are pitted against people. Workers are challenging their masters. Governments are crushing the ranks of Labor. The Workers, suspicious of one another, not knowing whither the struggle is leading, are fighting one another. Oppressed, deceived, and fettered, the Workers are pressing onward, urged by the dream of liberty, or freedom from exploitation.

For seven years, the Workers have lived in a world of sham. Surrendering to the wiles of their masters in August, 1914, they gave up their right to think and to act. Accepting the slogans that brought disaster to the entire world, they went out to the battlefields prepared by their masters, and slaughtered their fellow workers by the millions . . . But at last, the Workers have awakened. At last their eyes are opening. They are beginning to see—and **to see means the beginning of the Revolution!**

This is the era of the world revolution. The war is on and there will be no more peace until the Workers triumph everywhere.

A political prisoner depicted in *The Red Album.*

after Congress considered the "increasing incidences in which individuals and large groups of individuals openly defy and encourage others to defy the authority of their Government by destroying or mutilating their draft cards."

The U.S. District Court heard the case, since it was a federal offense, and convicted O'Brien. While he never denied burning the card, he did believe it was within his rights to do so, and that the federal law

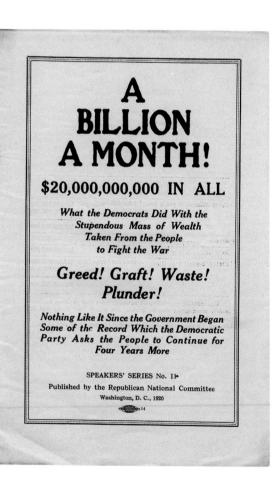

Free speech means that people are able to criticize their government. In this 1920 pamphlet, the Republican Party accused the Democrats of "silly Socialist prejudice."

A
BILLION
A MONTH!

$20,000,000,000 IN ALL

What the Democrats Did With the
Stupendous Mass of Wealth
Taken From the People
to Fight the War

Greed! Graft! Waste!
Plunder!

Nothing Like It Since the Government Began
Some of the Record Which the Democratic
Party Asks the People to Continue for
Four Years More

SPEAKERS' SERIES No. 14
Published by the Republican National Committee
Washington, D. C., 1920

barring him from doing it was unconstitutional. The District Court found that the law was an acceptable protection of the government's right to raise armies and therefore was constitutional.

Upon appeal, the case went to the U.S. Court of Appeals, where this time the court ruled in favor of O'Brien. Nonetheless, it upheld his conviction because he had violated another law in the process of destroying his draft card, which said that a draft card must be kept on your person at all times. So according to the Court of Appeals, the act of burning the card was not in itself a problem, but after it was burned, there was no card left, and that was a problem.

Even though the conviction was maintained, the U.S. attorneys were not happy that the Court of Appeals had called the draft card mutilation law unconstitutional. O'Brien was unhappy that his conviction had been maintained based on another crime he had not even been formally charged with. The case reached the Supreme Court in January 1968.

O'Brien argued that he had committed an act of symbolic speech that should have been protected under the First Amendment, and that Congress had intentionally written the law to try to suppress free speech.

The Supreme Court Justices in *United States v. O'Brien* (1968) listened to O'Brien's argument that once he received the card and was officially notified, it had served its purpose and was meaningless. The Justices did not agree. Chief Justice Earl Warren wrote for the majority: "[O'Brien] essentially adopts the position that such certificates are so many pieces of paper designed to notify registrants of their registration or classification, to be retained or tossed in the wastebasket according to the convenience or taste of the registrant."

Warren explained that the draft cards were indeed important and helped the government keep track of registrants. The Court felt that having the certificates available at all times "substantially furthers the smooth and proper functioning of the system that Congress has established to raise armies."

The Supreme Court upheld O'Brien's original conviction and therefore did not have to examine the issue of the Court of Appeals finding him guilty of a different offense. The case was decided in 7–1 (not all nine Justices have to be present for a case to be decided) against O'Brien.

INTERVIEW | **Morley Safer**

Born in Toronto, Canada, Morley Safer joined CBS News in 1964 and rose to national prominence for his coverage of the Vietnam War in the mid-1960s. He has been on the award-winning CBS television news magazine *60 Minutes* since 1970.

Q: Does the media play a big role in helping shape the public perception and image of the Supreme Court?

Safer: Not as big a role as it may have in other elements of public policy. Largely because, I think for the most part, journalists covering the Court have a greater awe of the institution than those covering other institutions, such as the House and the Senate. I think the coverage of the Supreme Court is pretty much down the middle. In terms of popular journalism—television, the *New York Times*—journalists and reporters may well affect policy in covering consequences of Supreme Court decisions. *Roe v. Wade* [1973] is a perfect example of this, as are most civil rights decisions. So it's more the consequences of the Supreme Court decision, rather than the Supreme Court decision itself.

Q: In New York Times Co. v. United States [1971], the Court said the government could not halt the publication of the Pentagon Papers [a 7,000-page government document on the history of United States–Vietnam relations]. Justice William Orville Douglas said: "Secrecy in government is fundamentally anti-democratic." Are there times when the government should exercise prior restraint?

Safer: It's all hypothetical, because it can't. It generally can't. Now the government does often step in and ask a journalist or newspaper or television program to please not publish a story and hold it, but they can't really do it. A journalist may have to face consequences. They may take a lot of heat or criticism. The government has every right to ask, and we have every right to say no, or say yes, if that's what the decision of the editor is.

On the Abu Ghraib [Iraqi prison] story, we held that story for about two weeks at the request of the Chairman of the Joint Chiefs of Staff. I think that was a fair decision, by the way, to hold the story.

Q: You held it until it wasn't a sensitive time to air it?

Safer: No, it wasn't a question of a sensitive time. The Chairman of the Joint Chiefs asked CBS to please hold the story while he looked into it. I think it was certainly a fair request and I think that we did the right thing. If only to be able to get a response out of them, to make the story at least balanced.

Q: More than 30 years ago, the Supreme Court said reporters are not shielded from testifying before a grand jury to reveal their sources. This issue has come up again recently. Reporters feel it will make it harder for them to do their job and find sources who will talk to them.

Safer: We have some important decisions on our side in this one. It depends to what degree the administration wants to pursue this. We have to maintain a common front that we must protect our sources, even if it means going to jail.

THE FLAG AND THE FIRST AMENDMENT

The U.S. flag is a very powerful symbol for many Americans, especially for those who fought for it in wars or who came to America to escape persecution in another country. Respect for the flag has always been important. But when the flag and free speech rights clash, the end result is often a Supreme Court case.

Street v. New York (1969)

World War II veteran Sidney Street was listening to the radio in his New York City apartment on June 6, 1966, when he heard of the fatal shooting in Mississippi of the civil rights leader James Meredith. This news made Street, an African American, angry. What kind of country was it where things like this could still happen?

Street found his American flag and took it outside with him. He walked to a street corner and lit a match and held it to the flag, then let the burning flag fall to the ground. A small crowd gathered to watch. A police officer arrived and heard Street say, "If they let that happen to Meredith, we don't need an American flag." Street was charged with violation of New York state law and was found guilty in criminal court. The Court of Appeals upheld the lower court's findings. When the case got to the Supreme Court, there was some confusion as to whether Street's words alone had got him convicted or his words and actions combined. The Court said, "Appellant's words, taken alone, did not urge anyone to do anything unlawful."

Justice John Marshall Harlan spoke for the majority, which ruled in favor of Street: "disrespect for our flag is to be deplored no less in these vexed times than in calmer periods of our history. Nevertheless, we are unable to sustain a conviction that may have rested on a form of expression, however distasteful, which the Constitution tolerates and protects."

Smith v. Goguen (1974)

In a case called *Smith v. Goguen,* a man named Valarie Goguen was observed by police officers in Leominster, Massachusetts, to be wearing pants with a small four-inch-by-six-inch American flag sewn onto the seat of the pants. He was arrested and charged under a local statute that said public mutilation or defacement of the American flag was a crime.

Goguen was sentenced to six months in prison. The District Court and Appeals Court both ruled that the statute was unconstitutional because it was too vague and too broad. Justice Lewis F. Powell Jr., speaking for the majority, said, "It could hardly be the purpose of the Massachusetts Legislature to make criminal every informal use of the flag."

The Supreme Court agreed and ruled in favor of Goguen. Justice William H. Rehnquist dissented. He explained that the Court had ruled in *Euclid v. Ambler Realty Co.* (1926) (see page 160) that a person's land could be subject to control by the state through zoning laws. It followed, then, that other personal property, such as a small flag, could also be subject to regulations by the state.

Spence v. Washington (1974)

A college student named Harold Spence got into trouble in 1970 when police noticed an upside-down flag suspended from his apartment window in Seattle, Washington. The flag had been altered by the addition of a peace symbol made of black tape. When police showed up at his door, he told them, "I suppose you are here about the flag. I didn't know there was anything wrong with it. I will take it down." They entered the apartment, seized the flag, and arrested him anyway.

He was charged with violating a law that forbade the alteration of "any flag, standard, color, ensign or shield of the United States or of this state." At his trial, he explained that his action was a protest against the recent American invasion of Cambodia and also the killings at Kent State University.

He told the court: "I felt there had been so much killing and that this was not what America stood for. I felt that the flag stood for America and I wanted people to know that I thought America stood for peace."

Spence also explained that he purposely used black tape since he knew it could be removed without harming the flag. The jury was told that his intent did not matter; he altered the flag and that was enough to convict him. So he was found guilty and sentenced to 10 days and a fine of $75.

While the Washington Court of Appeals reversed Spence's conviction, the Washington Supreme Court reinstated his conviction. The case was appealed to the U.S. Supreme Court, which ruled in favor of

Spence. The *per curiam* opinion noted that the flag itself was private property and was displayed on private property. Spence did not break the peace or draw any extraordinary attention to his display. The flag was not permanently damaged, and Spence was trying to communicate a message by his action. It was within his First Amendment rights to do so.

The Court recognized that the flag can evoke a wide variety of feelings, depending on the person. The Justices repeatedly cited a case called a landmark case about the right not to salute the flag (*West Virginia Board of Education v. Barnette* [1943]—see page 78), where the majority opinion stated, "A person gets from a symbol the meaning he puts into it, and what is one man's comfort and inspiration is another's jest and scorn."

Chief Justice Warren Earl Burger dissented. He felt that Court was playing a role it wasn't supposed to play by striking down "unwise laws." He said, "That is not our function, however, and it should be left to each State and ultimately the common sense of its people to decide how the flag . . . should be protected."

SYMBOLIC PROTEST
Tinker v. Des Moines Independent Community School District (**1969**)

One day in December 1965, a small group of teenage students in Des Moines, Iowa, decided to go to school wearing black armbands bearing the peace symbol. They planned to wear the armbands as a protest of America's involvement in Vietnam. The Des Moines school principals found out about the students' plan and decided that anyone who came to school wearing one of the armbands would be asked to remove it or risk expulsion.

On December 16, 16-year-old Christopher Eckhardt wore his armband to high school and 13-year-old Mary Beth Tinker wore hers to junior high school. The next day, 15-year-old John Tinker (Mary Beth's brother) wore an armband to high school. All three were suspended from school until they were willing to return without the armbands.

The case went to the District Court, which ruled against the students. The Court felt it was acceptable for the school district to prevent disturbances by forbidding armbands. The Court of Appeals was split in its opinion, and so the ruling of the lower court stood.

The case reached the Supreme Court in November 1968, and a ruling was issued in February 1969. The Court returned a decision in favor of the students, 7–2. The Justices cited *West Virginia Board of Education v. Barnette* in their decision. One had to be careful when dealing with limiting school freedoms, otherwise there was a risk of closing young minds rather than opening them. It would be bad to "strangle the free mind at its source."

Justice Abe Fortas wrote for the majority:

It is also relevant that the school authorities did not purport to prohibit the wearing of all symbols of political or controversial significance. The record shows that students in some of the schools wore but-

tons relating to national political campaigns, and some even wore the Iron Cross, traditionally a symbol of Nazism. . . . School officials do not possess absolute authority over their students. Students in school as well as out of school are "persons" under our Constitution.

After all, anything that a student said that was different from what another student believed could start an argument or cause a disturbance in school. Fortas wrote, "Our Constitution says we must take this risk."

Most importantly, Justice Fortas wrote that students and teachers do not "shed their constitutional rights to freedom of speech or expression at the schoolhouse gate." Only "reasonable regulation" of speech could be imposed in "carefully restricted circumstances." The decision was another in a series of rulings on how far schools can go in attempting to control or limit their students' speech or compel them to commit an act of speech (see chapter 4 for more examples).

see chapter 4 for more examples

INTERVIEW

John Tinker (*Tinker v. Des Moines Independent Community School District*, 1969)

John Tinker was 15 years old when he decided to wear a black armband with a peace symbol to school, in protest of American involvement in the Vietnam War.

Q: *What do you remember most about that day in December 1965?*

Tinker: It was a memorable day. Many of the details of my experience are still clear in my memory. I had to hurry to school and felt too exposed to wear the armband on the street, so I didn't put it on until just before my first class. A friend saw me in the restroom struggling to pin it on. So he helped do that. The morning classes were weird, because only the students sitting near me in class could see that I had the armband on. The teachers apparently did not notice it. Or, if they did, they did not make an issue of it. I realized that the armband did not stand out well against the dark suit coat that I was wearing. So after gym class I put the armband on over my white dress shirt, and I did not wear my suit coat. Then the armband stood out pretty well.

Someone from the office saw me wearing it in the lunchroom, and she reported me to the principal. When I went to my first afternoon class there was a phone call and I was told to go to the office. The principal took a paternal attitude and warned me that I would be ruining my chances of getting into college if I did not take the armband off. He also said that it was important to support our government during times of war. He said that I might have been influenced by Communist propaganda. He told me about his experience in the military service during the Korean War.

But I told him that I had already thought about what I was doing, and that I was not going to remove the armband. So then he told me that I would have to leave the school and not come back with the armband on. But he said that he was not going to formally suspend me. He treated me with a certain degree of respect, but he said that he had no choice, and was doing what he must do.

Q: Did the case change your life?

Tinker: The case did change my life. I'll never know exactly how it changed it, of course. But my involvement in the case has resulted in many opportunities to speak to students and to correspond with them about peace and about the importance of freedom of speech in our democracy.

Q: Justice Abe Fortas wrote for the majority: "There is no indication that the work of the schools or any class was disrupted." Justice Hugo Lafayette Black wrote in his *dissent: "Even a casual reading of the record shows that this armband did divert students' minds from their regular lessons." How can anyone determine what is disruptive if the Justices cannot even agree? Isn't a bright orange shirt disruptive too, or a tattoo, or a jacket with political buttons?*

Tinker: I cannot fully explain Justice Black's attitude. But it was very interesting to me that he misunderstood several things about what happened. I realized that Supreme Court Justices are not infallible. Regarding possible disruption to the educational process, there really was not any significant disruption that I was aware of. And besides, during my years in school it was not uncommon for teachers to occasionally go off on extended tangents about subject matter that they were interested in, but which was not particularly related to the lesson plan. The idea that the minute or so during which students were noticing the armbands was a distraction from some critical educational experience is a little silly.

Justice Black was also quite mistaken in his belief that our parents had put us up to wearing the armbands in the first place.

FREEDOM OF THE PRESS

America's treasured freedom of the press goes all the way back to 1733, when a German-born printer named John Peter Zenger was arrested in New York for printing a journal that criticized the Governor. He was charged with seditious libel, which meant he was publishing scandalous things. Zenger's lawyer was able to convince the jury that Zenger did nothing wrong by printing the stories, because they were true. The case established that truth did not equal libel.

New York Times Co. v. Sullivan (1964)

The issue of libel came up again in a landmark Supreme Court case called *New York Times Co. v. Sullivan*. There, the Court examined an advertisement that had been published in the *New York Times* in 1960. This ad made claims about the activities of the police in Montgomery, Alabama, against participants in a civil rights demonstration.

The Circuit Court ruled in favor of Commissioner L. B. Sullivan, the Montgomery official who oversaw the police department. The Alabama Supreme Court upheld the lower court's ruling. The U.S. Supreme Court reversed the decision, ruling that the test for libel should be "actual malice"—whether a controversial statement was made with knowledge of its falsity or with reckless disregard of whether it was true or false. Justice William J. Brennan wrote for the majority, "Raising as it does the possibility that a good-faith critic of government will be penalized for his criticism, the proposition relied on by the Alabama courts strikes at the very center of the constitutionally protected area of free expression."

Hazelwood v. Kuhlmeier (1988)

One of the most important freedom of the press cases in recent history dealt with whether a school-sponsored newspaper can be censored or whether such censorship will interfere with students' First Amendment rights.

Like many other high schools, Hazelwood East High School in the St. Louis, Missouri, area offered

USE SYMBOLIC SPEECH

NOT ALL "free speech" is actually spoken or written. Sometimes, it is a symbolic gesture that comes in conflict with authority.

YOU'LL NEED
- ✔ 2 white wristbands
- ✔ 1 fabric marker in a dark color
- ✔ Your classroom attorney
- ✔ Government's classroom attorney
- ✔ Classroom Supreme Court
- ✔ Text of the opinion in *Tinker v. Des Moines Independent Community School District* (1969) for lawyers and Justices to cite (go to: http://laws.findlaw.com/us/393/503.html)

Draw a peace symbol (or some other symbol) on your wristbands with the fabric marker. Bring the wristbands to school and wear them in class that day, with the teacher's permission. (This is only for the activity, so do not wear or show this symbol anywhere else in the school.) Does your gesture surpass free speech in the school setting? Is it distracting to the rest of the class? What rights do kids have in school? Use the *Tinker* case and other cases in this chapter as guidelines. The two lawyers will have 10 minutes each to argue their sides before the Supreme Court. The Justices will then confer and make their ruling.

a class in journalism. The journalism course was taught by a teacher named Robert Stergos for most of the 1982–1983 academic year. But at the end of April 1983, and before the students had been able to put out all their issues, Stergos left Hazelwood East to take another job. The students said their good-byes, and their lives went on. A teacher named Howard Emerson took Stergos's place as the journalism teacher and advisor to the newspaper while the May 13 edition of *Spectrum* was nearing its publication date.

The students were planning some interesting articles in that issue. One topic was divorce among the parents of high school students. Another article topic was teen pregnancy. In both cases, the staff writers had talked to students who shared their experiences for the article.

The journalism teacher typically showed the pages to the principal for his review before publication. On May 10, Principal Robert Reynolds read the proofs (laid-out newspaper pages ready to go to the printer) of the May 13 edition and did not like what he saw. Though the newspaper staff writers had changed the names of the girls interviewed for the pregnancy story, he felt that it still might be too easy for readers of the newspaper to figure out their identities. He also thought that some of the issues about sex and pregnancy mentioned in the story might be too sensitive for the Hazelwood East students to read about.

The principal felt that it was his responsibility to monitor the newspaper's content to make sure nobody would be offended or hurt by anything in any of the articles. In addition, the $4,600 for printing the paper, the money for supplies, and the journalism teacher's salary were all paid for by the Board of Education. The *Spectrum* was by no means an independent newspaper.

Unbeknownst to the students who had worked hard to write and edit the articles and put the newspaper together, the principal cut six articles from the paper (two full pages) before it went to the printer. He felt that there was no time to try to re-layout the newspaper without the two offending articles, and that in order to get it to the printer on time, cutting the entire two pages containing the articles was the only solution.

Reynolds told his superiors and the teacher what he planned to do. The final printed newspaper was four pages instead of six. The journalism students were outraged when the finished product arrived from the printer. When they found out what had happened, some of them contacted their old journalism teacher, Robert Stergos, and asked his advice. He told them to contact the American Civil Liberties Union (ACLU). With the help of the ACLU, three of the newspaper staffers, Cathy Kuhlmeier, Leslie Smart, and Leann Tippett, filed a lawsuit against the school.

The first stop for the case was District Court. The court found that Principal Reynolds had acted within his authority, and that the printing of the articles could be halted on the grounds that the issues were too mature and too sensitive, and would also invade the privacy of some of the students interviewed.

The Court of Appeals, however, relied heavily upon the decision in *Tinker v. Des Moines Independent Community School District* and decided that it was indeed a violation of the students' First Amendment rights for the principal to hold back two pages from publication. The school's lawyers appealed the decision, and the Supreme Court granted *certiorari,* meaning it agreed to hear the case, called *Hazelwood v. Kuhlmeier.*

In considering the case, the Justices had to look back to *Tinker,* in which the Supreme Court had decided in favor of student expression that did not harm anyone. They made a big distinction between *Tinker* and this case. They saw *Tinker* as a case where the Court had refused to allow the school to punish a student's independent speech. They saw the *Hazelwood* case as different because it dealt with school-sponsored student expression.

The Supreme Court vote was 5–3 in favor of the principal and the school, reversing the Court of Appeals. The students felt they had the right to print whatever they wanted and that their right to do so had been violated. The Court pointed out that the journalism teacher's function was to edit the articles, select letters to the editor, and make other decisions about the content of the paper and selection of the staff.

Justice Byron White wrote the opinion for the majority. Justice White felt that just as the school could reject poorly written articles, it could reject topics that were inappropriate for school audiences.

A school must be able to set high standards for the student speech that is disseminated under its auspices—standards that may be higher than those demanded by some newspaper publishers or theatrical producers in the "real" world—and may refuse to disseminate [publish] student speech that does not meet those standards. In addition, a school must be able to take into account the emotional maturity of the intended audience in determining whether to disseminate student speech on potentially sensitive topics . . .

In sum, we cannot reject as unreasonable Principal Reynolds's conclusion that neither the pregnancy article nor the divorce article was suitable for publication in Spectrum *. . . we conclude that the principal's decision to delete two pages of* Spectrum, *rather than to delete only the offending articles or to require that they be modified, was reasonable under the circumstances as he understood them. Accordingly, no violation of First Amendment rights occurred.*

The dissenting Justices felt that the majority's decision was a mistake. From Justice William J. Brennan:

He [the principal] objected to some material in two articles, but excised six entire articles. He did not so much as inquire into obvious alternatives, such as precise deletions or additions (one of which had already been made), rearranging the layout, or delaying publication. Such unthinking contempt for individual rights is intolerable from any state official. It is particularly insidious from one to whom the public entrusts the task of inculcating in its youth an appreciation for the cherished democratic liberties that our Constitution guarantees.

In closing, Justice Brennan wrote: "The young men and women of Hazelwood East expected a civics lesson, but not the one the Court teaches them today."

Cathy Kuhlmeier Frey (*Hazlewood v. Kuhlmeier*, 1988)

Cathy Kuhlmeier was the layout editor, one of several students working on their high school newspaper, the *Spectrum*, in 1983. Cathy was one of three students who filed suit against the school.

Q: Where did you get the idea for the articles?

Frey: We took the ideas for the stories from our classroom morgue of past issues. A few years earlier, and under a different principal, the same story ideas were printed. One of the stories we had written was on the problems of teenagers, which included hotline numbers for help. Perhaps if the stories were published they would have touched one person from our school and made a difference. As it turns out, an individual from our class ran away and ended up committing suicide. Could the articles have made a difference for his life choice? It is a question that I will always wonder about.

Q: What gave you the courage to stand up and fight for your rights?

Frey: I had the courage to stand up for my rights because of our teacher Robert Stergos. We had just finished our Journalism 1 class, which taught us about press law and rights. We learned that even as youth, we were entitled to rights.

Q: The Court has examined free speech in many cases over the last 100 years, with varying results. How do we determine when speech goes too far to be considered protected?

Frey: I feel that it needs to be examined on a case-by-case basis. Our principal fully admitted to not reading all of the stories which were submitted to him. Perhaps if he had taken the time to do so, the entire situation could have been avoided. The articles state that all names had been changed to protect the identities of those interviewed. All of the students interviewed in the divorce article also had to have parental consent before we would accept their statements.

Q: What should kids today learn from your case?

Frey: I would hope that kids would learn to have the courage to make a difference in the world. If kids would learn to speak up more often and question things that they may not necessarily agree with rather than always just accepting things the way they are, the world could become a different place.

OBSCENITY AND INDECENCY

Free speech in America is something we enjoy every day. Americans have the freedom to say or write anything they want—almost. What happens when people speak, write, or depict something obscene or deeply offensive? Where does our right to free speech end? What happens when some people consider something "indecent," and others do not?

Board of Educ., Island Trees Union Free School District v. Pico (1982)

In 1976, the Board of Education in Island Trees, New York, created a list of books that they believed to be "anti-American, anti-Christian, anti-[Semitic], and just plain filthy." The board decided that these books were candidates to be removed from the junior high school and high school libraries. The board appointed a book review committee made up of four parents and four members of the school staff. The committee's job was to review the books and determine whether they should be kept or removed from the school libraries.

Upon examination, the committee recommended that five of the listed books should be kept and that one, *Slaughterhouse-Five*, should be made available with parental consent. The board rejected the committee's work and decided that all but one of the "offensive" books should be removed. The banned books were: *Slaughterhouse-Five*, by Kurt Vonnegut Jr.; *The Naked Ape*, by Desmond Morris; *Down These Mean Streets*, by Piri Thomas; *The Best Short Stories of Negro Writers*, edited by Langston Hughes; *Go Ask Alice*, by anonymous; *Laughing Boy*, by Oliver LaFarge; *Black Boy*, by Richard Wright; *A Hero Ain't Nothin' But A Sandwich*, by Alice Childress; *Soul on Ice*, by Eldridge Cleaver; and *A Reader for Writers*, edited by Jerome Archer.

Students Steven Pico, Jacqueline Gold, Glenn Yarris, Russell Rieger, and Paul Sochinski brought a lawsuit against the school district because they felt their First Amendment rights were being abused. The U.S. District Court ruled in favor of the school board, saying that while the removal of books may have been misguided, it was not unconstitutional. The students appealed and their case went to the Court of Appeals, where the three-judge panel reversed the lower court's ruling and found in favor of the students.

This time, the school district appealed and the case reached the Supreme Court as *Board of Educ., Island Trees Union Free School District v. Pico*. The Court ruled in favor of the students, explaining that while

A 1942 poster denouncing book burning in Germany. Ironically, many books have been banned in the United States since the 1940s.

school boards may freely choose which books to add to their libraries, once they have those books, the situation changes and, "local school boards may not remove books from school library shelves simply because they dislike the ideas contained in those books." As Justice William J. Brennan Jr. wrote for the majority, "If a Democratic school board, motivated by party affiliation, ordered the removal of all books written by or in favor of Republicans, few would doubt that the order violated the constitutional rights of the students denied access to those books."

Once again citing *West Virginia State Board of Education v. Barnette*, Brennan said that school boards had to be careful not to "strangle the free mind at its source" by overregulating the flow of ideas and thought within the school setting. Schools are not simply machines of the government designed to implant only certain ideas and philosophies. Singling out certain books was simply unacceptable.

While schools must exercise control over their students in many areas, school library books are not textbooks. Visiting libraries is optional; they are supposed to serve as centers where knowledge and ideas can be shared and spread. To enact censorship in that setting sends a contradictory message to students about free thought and free speech.

Kurt Vonnegut Jr.

Born in 1922, Kurt Vonnegut is one of the country's most popular novelists. His books include *Mother Night* (1962), *Cat's Cradle* (1963), *Slaughterhouse-Five* (1969), *Breakfast of Champions* (1973), *Galapagos* (1985), and *Bluebeard* (1987). His books often use black humor and science fiction plots to point out some of the horrors of 20th-century history. *Slaughterhouse-Five*, about the firebombing of Dresden, Germany, during World War II, was one of the books banned by the school district in *Board of Educ., Island Trees Union Free School District v. Pico* (1982).

(Answers copyright Kurt Vonnegut Jr.)

Q: *You once said that man's worst folly is attempting to adjust "smoothly, rationally, to the unthinkable, the unbearable." Your books seem to magnify these adjustments to the unthinkable. Do you think that this is at the heart of why some people want to censor your work?*

Vonnegut: No, I think that the people who censor books, people who get excited about one thing or another, rally, and get together, are responding to loneliness, and a lack of power, and not to the books themselves. And the protests that you get on campus, I don't care what the hell they're about . . . [their function] is that people have got an extended family. Suddenly surrounded with people chanting the same thing. Human beings need this, and get too little of it in the course of their lives . . . So these rallies that form are in response to loneliness, not to common sense.

The people who censor books commonly are proud to say, "I haven't read the whole thing, I didn't have to."

And, what they object to is to my being a humanist, and they're defending God and Jesus against the anti-Christ. But again, they're doing it out of loneliness. It's not a rational thing, except it is rational to seek a solution to loneliness. They object to my being a Democrat, my being a First Amendment person. All of which are offensive to certain Christians. But again it's lonely people who have very likely not read my books.

There's a list of banned books, many of which are out of print now, it started to be circulated in 1971, I'm not certain where, but in the age of [the] Xerox machine, this list continues to arrive in the mail to school committee members. You know, "This is why your daughter is pregnant, this is why your son is blowing dope." And so they're going to look for the books in the library, to see whether this is what's making kids crazy. But a lot of these books are out of print. So it's not serious, it's not based on anything. *Slaughterhouse-Five!* It's just lonely people raising hell.

Q: Do you think you fit in more easily today than you fit in in 1964 or 1974? Do you think people accept you more today?

Vonnegut: I always had quite a wide acceptance because I attracted a following early on . . . in the form of paperbacks, not hardcovers. For sale in bus stations, drugstores, and PXs [stores on military bases]. People liked the books, that's all.

Reno v. ACLU (1997)

Unlike the limited number of channels available on television or radio, the Internet features millions of Web pages that are posted by different individuals and companies. In 1996, Congress passed a federal Communications Decency Act that attempted to limit the availability of indecent material on the Internet to minors under the age of 18. The law was challenged by the American Civil Liberties Union, on the grounds that it violated the First Amendment, in a case called *Reno v. ACLU.*

In his oral argument for the U.S. government, Deputy Solicitor General Seth Waxman tried to explain the need for the provisions. "With as many as 8,000 sexually explicit sites on the World Wide Web alone at the time of the hearing, and the number estimated to double every nine months, the Internet threatens to render irrelevant all prior efforts to protect children from indecent material," he told the Justices.

The Supreme Court was concerned with the lack of a reliable and effective way to screen for age and felt the Act was too broad, did not clearly define "indecent," and would unfairly curtail First Amendment rights. Justice John Paul Stevens wrote for the majority: "The interest in encouraging freedom of expression in a democratic society outweighs any theoretical but unproven benefit of censorship."

United States v. American Library Assn., Inc. (2003)

In 2003, the Court was faced with a new Internet-related challenge. Congress had passed a law called the Children's Internet Protection Act (CIPA), which prevented public libraries from getting federal money for Internet access unless they installed software to block obscene images and to prevent children from accessing this material. The law was challenged by a group of libraries and other interested groups in a case called *United States v. American Library Assn., Inc.*

This time, the Supreme Court sided with the government. The Justices, by a margin of 6–3, felt that CIPA was not a violation of library patrons' First Amendment rights. They noted that most libraries exclude pornography from their collections to begin with and should be allowed to exclude it from their Internet access as well. They believed Congress had the authority to pass the bill.

Chief Justice William H. Rehnquist noted in his opinion that there was no punishment or penalty for libraries that did not want to apply the filter:

CIPA does not 'penalize' libraries that choose not to install such software, or deny them the right to provide their patrons with unfiltered Internet access. Rather, CIPA simply reflects Congress' decision not to subsidize their doing so. To the extent that libraries wish to offer unfiltered access, they are free to do so without federal assistance.

National Endowment for the Arts v. Finley (1998)

A similar funding case had occurred a few years earlier. *National Endowment for the Arts v. Finley* involved a performance artist named Karen Finley and three other artists, all of whom were unable to get federal funding from the National Endowment for the Arts (NEA) because it considered their art to be indecent. The artists claimed that their First Amendment rights to freedom of expression were being discriminated against by the application of standards by a government agency. The District Court and Appellate Court both ruled in the artists' favor.

The United States appealed and the case went to the Supreme Court. In a reversal of the lower courts' rulings, the highest court ruled in favor of the NEA by an 8–1 margin. The Court decided that the NEA could spend its money subjectively, and noted that the whole funding process was subjective to begin with.

Justice Sandra Day O'Connor wrote for the majority:

Any content-based considerations that may be taken into account in the grant-making process are a consequence of the nature of arts funding. The NEA has limited resources and it must deny the majority of the grant applications that it receives, including many that propose 'artistically excellent' projects.

Tim Miller (*National Endowment for the Arts v. Finley,* 1998)

Tim Miller is a performance artist who was one of the "NEA Four" whose case went to the Supreme Court.

Q: *The original law creating the NEA sought "a climate encouraging freedom of thought, imagination, and inquiry." What does that mean to you?*

Miller: To me that means a vigorous and risk-taking kind of creativity that challenges clichés, dishonesty, and silence. This kind of boldness is within the very best of our American traditions under the First Amendement. Sadly such creativity is no longer encouraged in the arts and sciences in the U.S.

Q: *Do you remember the day the Supreme Court decision was announced?*

Miller: Vividly! I was in Texas performing. At first it made me very depressed, but then I decided I would rather get pissed off and feisty and look forward to the day when this particular decision would seem as absurd and embarrassing as *Plessy v. Ferguson* does to us today.

I will look forward to the time (in the not-too-distant future, I hope) when a teacher will step before a community college class exploring late-20th-century social movements and say, "Now, students, I know it is shocking to believe this, but there was once a time as recent as the late 1990s and early years of the 21st century when lesbian and gay men were actually denied certain civil rights within our democratic society. The Supreme Court even upheld a series of laws that constitutionally discriminated against them!" Until that day in school, I'm in it for the long haul.

Q: *The Supreme Court majority opinion said that all government grants and scholarships are in some way subjective, and that lines of some sort can be drawn without it being "constitutionally vague." Obviously, you disagree?*

Miller: Well it is interesting that the art that gets defunded is almost always by lesbian and gay artists! The so-called chilling effect—that the limits on freedom of speech since the NEA battles have dampened expression—is very real. I travel and perform a lot at universities all over the country. Hundreds of young artists have told me they no longer imagine cultural freedom exists in the U.S. in terms of funding for the arts and humanities, and that influences how they imagine their creativity and future.

FREEDOM OF ASSEMBLY

Do you and a couple of friends ever go to the park and hang out? What if 20 friends gathered? What if your friends wanted to organize a rally against unfair final exam policies in your school? The First Amendment of the Constitution proclaims the right to freedom of assembly, but at what point can the government step in and regulate your rally?

Hague v. Committee for Industrial Organization (1939)

The right to assemble freely was put to the test in *Hague v. Committee for Industrial Organization*. In Jersey City, New Jersey, a permit was needed for speaking in parks or on the streets. The permit had to be obtained three days in advance from the Director of Public Safety. According to a local ordi-

Industrial Workers of the World, 1914.

nance, if the Director felt that refusing a permit would prevent riots or disturbances, he could do so. The Committee for Industrial Organization was denied a permit on the grounds that they were a Communist organization. They filed suit against the Mayor, the Director of Public Safety, and the Chief of Police of Jersey City, New Jersey, and the Board of Commissioners.

The members of the group felt that being denied a permit was unfair. They argued that their purpose was not to advocate the destruction or overthrow of the government, but rather to explain to workers the purposes of the National Labor Relations Act. They claimed that their activities were peaceful and in no way could be considered unlawful.

The Court ruled in favor of the committee, stating that it was the right of Americans to use parks and streets to assemble. This right could be regulated, but only carefully. Regulation could not be absolute; it had to be relative. The committee was free to hold meetings without a permit and without regard to the terms of the ordinance, which was ruled void.

Cox v. Louisiana (1965)

In 1961 a man named B. Elton Cox was arrested for violating a "breach of peace" statute when he said "inflammatory" words to a crowd at a civil rights demonstration in Baton Rouge, Louisiana. He urged the crowd of university students to stage a sit-in at a segregated lunch counter. The sheriff then announced: "Now, you have been allowed to demonstrate. Up until now, your demonstration has been more or less peaceful, but what you are doing now is a direct violation of the law, a disturbance of the peace, and it has got to be broken up immediately."

Cox was convicted and sentenced to serve jail time and pay fines. On appeal, the Supreme Court ruled that the breach of peace law was too broad and that Cox's right to due process had been violated.

Freedom of assembly almost always comes up against the right of the local government to exercise its police powers. The Supreme Court must take each freedom of assembly decision on a case-by-case basis.

CAMPAIGN DONATIONS
Another Type of Free Speech?

Free speech can be applied to so many different activities. This even includes the freedom of people to donate money as they see fit. In a case called *Buckley v. Valeo* (1976), the Federal Election Campaign Act of 1971 was challenged. The Act limited the donation of "hard" money (money that is given directly to candidates running for office), and its opponents claimed that was a violation of their First Amendment rights. The case featured two opposite viewpoints. Secretary of the Senate Francis Valeo defended the law, contending that the Act regulated conduct and did not affect free speech. The candidates who challenged the law said that contributions and expenditures are at the "very core of political speech," and so limited First Amendment rights.

The opinion of the Court stated that the donation of money was a form of speech since "virtually every means of communicating ideas in today's mass society requires the expenditure of money." The Supreme Court ruled that the limits on campaign contributions were valid, but limits on overall campaign spending were invalid.

As campaign spending ballooned during the 1990s, many people were wary of the fairness of the whole election process. The fear was that those with the most money possessed too much influence on elections. Senators John McCain (Republican) and Russell Feingold (Democrat) introduced a piece of legislation called the Bipartisan Campaign Reform Act (BCRA for short, but also known as McCain–Feingold). Campaign contributors had been exploiting **loopholes** in existing laws upheld in *Buckley v. Valeo* that allowed them to make unregulated "soft-money" donations (contributions to candidates indirectly, through political parties).

The McCain–Feingold bill passed in the Senate and was signed into law by President George W. Bush in March 2002. The bill was designed to regulate the amount of "soft" campaign money that corporations or individuals can give to political parties. Republican Senator Mitch McConnell immediately challenged the bill in a lawsuit. Eventually, there were numerous plaintiffs against the bill, including the National Rifle Association, the American Civil Liberties Union, the AFL-CIO (a labor union), and the Republican National Committee. It was an unusual alliance of both conservative and liberal groups; the influential lobbyist groups did not want to see their power limited, and the ACLU did not want to see the right to free speech limited.

In May 2003, a District Court in Washington, D.C., struck down some of the bill's provisions. The ruling was appealed and was argued in the Supreme Court in September 2003. A total of eight high-profile attorneys were involved in the case (the normal protocol is two).

On the side of the challengers to BCRA was Kenneth Starr, former Solicitor General and independent counsel on the Whitewater investigation. On the side of the defenders was Theodore Olson, the Solicitor General under President George W. Bush, and Seth Waxman, former Solicitor General under President Bill Clinton. The case, known as *McConnell v. Federal Election Commission* (2003), was argued in a special four-hour session (as opposed to the one hour normally allotted for oral arguments).

In December 2003, the Court announced its 5–4 decision upholding the major provisions of the bill. Justice John Paul Stevens and Justice Sandra Day O'Connor wrote the majority opinion that "there is substantial evidence to support Congress' determination that large soft-money contributions to national political parties give rise to corruption and the appearance of corruption." In the Court's opinion, the bill did not violate the First Amendment.

Justice Antonin Scalia wrote sarcastically in his dissent:

If the Bill of Rights had intended an exception to the freedom of speech in order to combat this [evil tendency] of the officeholder to agree with those who agree with him, and to speak more with his supporters than his opponents, it would surely have said so.

Seth Waxman (part 1)

Seth Waxman was the 41st Solicitor General of the United States, serving under President Bill Clinton (1997 to 2001). The position of Solicitor General was first created in 1870. Since then, the list of Solicitors General has included several future Supreme Court Justices. Waxman has argued 45 cases before the Supreme Court.

Q: How would you summarize the Solicitor General's role?

Waxman: The Solicitor General represents the United States in the Supreme Court. The SG, as he's called, is also the government's chief courtroom strategist. Ordinarily in trial and regular appellate courts, the United States is represented by a lawyer in the Department of Justice, but the SG is responsible for making strategic judgments about what positions to take, what cases to appeal, etc. Except in unusual cases, though, the SG usually appears personally only in the Supreme Court.

Q: You argued in McConnell v. Federal Election Commission [2003] that the McCain–Feingold campaign reform bill was constitutionally acceptable. Is the First Amendment being applied too broadly as a shield for things such as making a political contribution?

Waxman: The people who challenged the law argued that the First Amendment rendered the law unconstitutional. I thought that it did not. The Supreme Court agreed that the First Amendment doesn't prohibit the kind of campaign finance regulation that the McCain–Feingold law embodied. The law's opponents, for example, argued that the law's prohibition against corporate campaign speech in the 30 [primary] or 60 [general election] days before an election, and the prohibition against soft-money donations, are inconsistent with the First Amendment right to engage in political speech. The Court disagreed.

4

FREEDOM OF RELIGION

William Thomas Cain/Getty Images

For hundreds of years, the Roman Catholic Church was the most powerful religious organization in the world. By the time of the Renaissance, there was disdain across Europe for what people felt had become a corrupt and too-powerful Catholic Church.

In England, the government had broken away from the Catholic Church under King Henry VIII and formed the Church of England in the 1500s. Parliament approved a Book of Common Prayer that was to be the official guidebook for religious services in response to the inconsistencies in the way services were being said across the country. It gave specific instructions as to which prayers and what instruction was to be said on what occasion. It also laid out penalties for any minister who did not follow the book's direction and to any person who spoke in a derogatory fashion about it.

People who felt left out by the way the book was written had no recourse. Many of the first settlers who arrived in the New World were trying to escape religious persecution. The Puritans settled in New England because they believed the Church of England to be corrupt and did not wish to be forced to follow its ways. The Shakers also came to America to avoid persecution.

Religion was a big part of the lives of the earliest settlers. The Pilgrims' Mayflower Compact of 1620 began with the words "In the name of God, Amen," and later continued, "having undertaken, for the glory of God, and advancement of the Christian faith . . . a voyage to plant the first colony . . ."

These settlers, in spite of their enthusiasm for their own faiths, did not want the colonies to become too restrictive, like England. In 1649, Maryland devised the Toleration Act, which said that no citizen of Maryland "shall from henceforth be any ways troubled, molested, or discountenanced for or in respect of his or her religion, nor in free exercise thereof . . ." The Act went on to explain that anyone who wronged someone on account of their religion was to pay a fine.

The spirit of religious tolerance was contagious. As the colonies grew, Americans wanted the government to guarantee neutrality in all matters dealing with religion. Roger Williams (founder of Rhode Island) and William Penn (founder of Pennsylvania) both fought for religious toleration.

After the Revolution, the young republic continued to push for tolerance. In 1786, some of the founding fathers successfully pushed for a Virginia Bill for Religious Liberty to be passed in the Virginia legislature, which declared all religions equal under the eyes of the law. In this bill, Thomas Jefferson wrote:

"Our civil rights have no dependence on our religious opinions, any more than our opinions in physics or geometry . . ."

In 1787, the U.S. Constitution was written. Article VI of the Constitution read "no religious Test shall ever be required as a Qualification to any Office or public Trust under the United States." Soon after that, separation of church and state was written into the Bill of Rights for that very reason, to ensure the government did not interfere with religion. The First Amendment forbade Congress from making any laws "respecting an establishment of religion, or prohibiting the free exercise thereof."

Yet our money says "In God we trust," our Pledge of Allegiance says "one nation, under God," and Presidents often conclude major speeches with the words "God bless America."

In 1875, President Ulysses S. Grant said: "Leave the matter of religion to the family altar, the church, and the private school, supported entirely by private contributions. Keep the church and state forever separated."

Americans, for the most part, have always been a religious people. The mainly Protestant Christian nation that was born out of the American Revolution has changed over the years. By the turn of the 20th century, Jews, Catholics, Mormons, Jehovah's Witnesses, and members of other faiths were common. Atheists, or nonbelievers in God, were also a part of the American fabric.

★ ★ ★ ★ ★ ★ ★ ★ ★

Are Religions Above the Law?
Reynolds v. United States (1878)

The Mormon religion was founded in 1830 by Joseph Smith in New York. After being persecuted, Mormons fled New York and settled in Utah Territory in 1847. One of the hallmarks of their social life was the practice of bigamy (being married to more than one person at a time). The United States had passed a law forbidding bigamy, and a case called *Reynolds v. United States* brought the issue of government regulation of religion to the Supreme Court.

A Mormon man named George Reynolds was married to Mary Ann Tuddenham and then later married a woman named Amelia Jane Schofield while his first wife was still alive. Reynolds felt that the government could not tell him how many wives to have since it

A Mormon man with six wives, 1885.

was his religion that promoted multiple marriages. In fact, he claimed that according to the Mormon customs at the time, God would punish men who had the opportunity to take more than one wife but did not. The District Court of Utah Territory was not swayed; it found him guilty of bigamy and sentenced him to two years of hard labor and a $500 fine. The Utah Supreme Court upheld the lower court's judgment.

When the case reached the United States Supreme Court, Chief Justice Morrison Remick Waite agreed with Reynolds on the point that Congress could not stop the free exercise of religion, but he drew the line in this case, explaining that marriage was something that could in fact be regulated. Religion could not be an excuse for something that the government considered to be a crime.

"Marriage, while from its very nature a sacred obligation, is nevertheless, in most civilized nations, a civil contract, and usually regulated by law," the Chief Justice said.

The Chief Justice wondered hypothetically if Mormons were allowed to practice polygamy because of their religion, and exempted from the criminal law, what would happen to those men who were not Mormons who married more than one wife? Would they be punished, while Mormons doing the same thing went free? If that were the case, then criminal law would become very complicated because it would be unequally applied. "Suppose one believed that human sacrifices were a necessary part of religious worship; could it be seriously contended that the civil government . . . could not interfere to prevent a sacrifice?"

That Goes Against My Religion

Minersville School District v. Gobitis (1940)

Many freedom of religion cases have dealt with the government's ability to "compel" speech or make people do certain things even when they go against one's religion. Billy and Lillian Gobitas were pupils in the Minersville, Pennsylvania, school district in the mid-1930s. They also happened to be Jehovah's Witnesses. When one day Billy decided to stop saluting the flag and was followed by his sister the next day, it was trouble for the Gobitas children. They objected to the flag salute based on several Bible passages, including Exodus 20 of the Old Testament.

The school board let two weeks go by before setting up a meeting with Billy and Lillian's parents. The end result was that Billy and Lillian were expelled from school because even after being warned, they would not resume saluting the flag and reciting the pledge.

Their father, Walter Gobitas (a spelling error in legal documents memorialized the name in the Court records as *Gobitis*), decided to take legal action. Meanwhile, the children were being home schooled. After a while the school district sent a letter to the Gobitas family saying that the children had to be taught by an accredited teacher. The children were then sent to a new school for Jehovah's Witnesses 30 miles away in the home of a man named Paul Jones.

It was a one-hour trip on winding roads to get to the school. They lived at the school Monday through Friday before returning home for the weekend. They missed their parents, but they really had no choice, since they did not want to give in and salute the flag.

The first judge to hear the case, Albert Maris, ruled in favor of the Gobitas family. The school district appealed and again the decision went in the Gobitas' favor. Unsatisfied to leave it at that, Minersville took the case to the Supreme Court and it was heard in 1940, nearly five years after the children had been expelled. By this time, the war raging in Europe was already several months old and patriotic emotions were running high. The Supreme Court reversed the ruling of the lower courts and ruled against the Gobitas family, by an overwhelming margin of 8–1.

Justice Felix Frankfurter delivered the opinion of the Court:

The wisdom of training children in patriotic impulses by those compulsions which necessarily pervade so much of the educational process is not for our independent judgment. Even were we convinced of the folly of such a measure, such belief would be no proof of its unconstitutionality . . . the court-room is not the arena for debating issues of educational policy . . . [this] would in effect make us the school board for the country. That authority has not been given to this Court, nor should we assume it.

But for us to insist that, though the ceremony may be required, exceptional immunity must be given to dissidents, is to maintain that there is no basis for a legislative judgment that such an exemption might introduce elements of difficulty into the school discipline, might cast doubts in the minds of the other children which would themselves weaken the effect of the exercise.

The lone dissenting Justice, Harlan Fiske Stone, said about the Gobitas children:

They and their father are citizens and have not exhibited by any action or statement of opinion, any disloyalty to the Government of the United States. They are ready and willing to obey all its laws that do not conflict with what they sincerely believe to be the higher commandments of God. It is not doubted that these convictions are religious, that they are genuine, or that the refusal to yield to the compulsion of the law is in good faith and with all sincerity.

He wrote that this was a small group who shared these opinions, and that accommodating them would not be disruptive, nor would it threaten discipline in schools. He saw no reason to trample upon their rights—rights that should be protected by the Constitution.

The ruling had two different effects in America. On the one hand there was increased violence against Jehovah's Witnesses nationwide after the ruling. More than 3,000 arrests were made in 1940 alone for violence against Witnesses. Property was destroyed and Witnesses were injured. On the other hand, there was also outcry among newspapers across the nation against the ruling. Even First Lady Eleanor Roosevelt made her opinion against the *Gobitis* ruling known in a newspaper column in June 1940.

Jehovah's Witness children were taught at the home of Paul and Verna Jones of New Ringgold, Pennsylvania.

Lillian Gobitas Klose (*Minersville School District v. Gobitis*, 1940)

Lillian Gobitas was 12 years old in October 1935 when she and her brother stopped saluting the flag and reciting the Pledge of Allegiance. Their actions got them expelled from school two weeks later and their case eventually went all the way to the Supreme Court.

Q: *What do you remember about that day in 1935 when you refused to salute the flag?*

Klose: That I was dying. I was a big chicken. My brother and I had felt that we were doing something wrong. Our parents did not urge us, or push us, or anything. We did discuss things as a family, but we were never urged by them to take a stand. I want to make that very clear. I was always such a chicken, that when the teacher would look my way [during the pledge], I would kind of move my lips and put out my hand right away. And finally, Carlton Nichols [a Jehovah's Witness] in Lynn, Massachusetts, took a stand and it was on the national news.

And so Joseph Rutherford, who was at that time the president of the Watchtower Society, gave a talk on the radio about saluting a flag. He said we feel it's in violation of Exodus 20, the Ten Commandments, where it says not to have any other God before me or any image of anything in the earth beneath or the sky above . . . we very definitely feel that the flag is an emblem, and to perform a ritual would classify that as idolatry. But as I said I was a big chicken.

After the Nichols case came into prominence, my brother came home one day and said, "I stopped saluting the flag, and the teacher tried to put my hand up and I held on to my pants pocket." So I thought, oh, I can't go on like this. I didn't even tell my family I was going to take a stand too. And the next morning, I went to my teacher, who was a doll, and I went to her before class and I said, "I want to tell you this, I'm not going to salute the flag anymore, and this is the reason." And she listened, and she was not angry. She put her arm around me and said, "Oh, Lillian, you are a dear." Is it right to stand up, is it right to sit down? And I sat down, and the class all looked at me, like "Aghh! What's happening to Lillian!" And they were very hostile after that. Not everyone. Some girls were very nice, they came to me one on one; "How come you're not saluting? Ah, OK." And they were quite nice, but otherwise every day when I'd come to school these guys would throw pebbles at me. "Here comes Jehovah! Ha ha!"

Q: *Did you ever dream in your wildest dreams that it would reach the Supreme Court?*

Klose: No, not in my wildest dreams. And to have the notoriety that it does now, not in my wildest dreams. My father sued the school board, and he was helped by the lawyer of the [Jehovah's Witnesses]. Different ones were trying to take it to court and it never was accepted. But finally, Judge Albert Maris in Philadelphia accepted the case. And he was a Quaker, and I often wonder if he was sympathetic because of that or what.

Billy Gobitas's letter to the school directors, 1935.

Anyway, he did accept the case, and so we went to Philadelphia. It was the United States District Court, and he decided favorably. And the school board was furious, they said, "Don't even think about coming back, we're appealing the case." And they did. And so it went to the Circuit Court of Appeals again in Philadelphia, and this time there were three judges. And our school superintendent said that these children are being indoctrinated—in other words we would say brainwashed today—and [he didn't] believe it was their idea at all . . . the three judges decided, it was unanimous, they decided that it was again in our favor.

We felt so good about that. We just felt, we won, we won, we'll win again . . . When it went to the Supreme Court, we felt so confident, but then in June of 1940, we had a grocery store downstairs, and we lived on the second floor and the third floor. Bill was working with daddy, and I was working with mother in the kitchen, with the radio on.

"The Supreme Court today announced on the flag salute issue, 8–1 against us." Oh, we could have just fallen over. That was really, really a blow. Justice Stone was the only one in our favor. And that's when it was like open season on Jehovah's Witnesses.

Oh, the things that started up. Now that was a scary time. Like, we got a call at three o'clock in the morning, a telephone threat that if you don't call the *Philadelphia Enquirer* and say that you'll now salute the flag, and in time for the morning edition, a mob will come to your store and we're not responsible for what will happen to your family. Well, the store was for sure our livelihood. By now we were six children. Mom and Dad said, Bill, you take the four little ones out to Grandma and Grandpa's house, and then Bill and I stayed in the store.

And Dad went to the chief of police, and he said "No, they're not going to do that in my town," and parked a police car in front of the store all day. So we went about our work, and oh, every time a group of three or four people got together, we thought, uh-oh, is this it? But it turned out that nothing happened. Maybe in the light of day they cooled down.

RECONSIDERING *GOBITIS*
West Virginia State Board of Education v. Barnette (1943)

The *Gobitis* case was far from the final word on the subject. Only three short years later, another case arose that allowed the Court to reexamine the issue. It arose as a direct result of the ruling in *Gobitis*. On January 9, 1942, the West Virginia Board of Education officially adopted a resolution that ordered that the flag salute and pledge become part of the school day.

Later that year, Walter Barnette filed suit against the West Virginia School Board because they had expelled his daughters, Gathie and Marie, for not saluting the flag. Eleven-year-old Gathie and her family were aware of the *Gobitis* ruling, but that did not stop them from trying to fight.

The West Virginia Supreme Court ruled in favor of the Barnette family, but the *Gobitis* case had begun in the same positive way, and it had ended badly for the Gobitas family in the nation's highest court.

Upon further appeal, *West Virginia State Board of Education v. Barnette* reached the U.S. Supreme Court at the height of World War II. It was argued in March 1943 and decided in June 1943. Though it would seem that the war would only make the *Barnette* case more difficult to win, things had changed on the Supreme Court. By now there were two new Justices on the Court, Wiley Blount Rutledge and Robert Houghwout Jackson (appointed by President Franklin D. Roosevelt). The lone dissenting Justice in *Gobitis,* Harlan Fiske Stone, had since become the Chief Justice, and three other Justices had reconsidered their *Gobitis* ruling. In *Barnette,* the Justices ruled in favor of Barnette by a margin of 6–3.

Overturning such a recent precedent as *Gobitis* was not a simple matter. The Court would have to carefully deconstruct the *Gobitis* decision to explain why their lopsided 8–1 decision should be negated and why their points of three years earlier were invalid. In *Gobitis,* the Court had questioned their own competence to decide such a case and pointed at legislatures as the proper forum for it. In *Barnette,* the Court said that fundamental rights are not to be decided by elected officials. They said that you don't need forced ceremonies to keep patriotism alive.

When the *Barnette* decision came down, it had been eight years since the Gobitas children were expelled from school. The Minersville School District sent a notice telling the Gobitas children they were now allowed to return. Lillian was now 20 and her brother was 18. It was too late for them to return to public school, but their four younger siblings got to go back.

INTERVIEW   Gathie Barnette Edmonds (*West Virginia State Board of Education v. Barnette,* 1943)

Gathie Barnette was 11 years old when she and her sister were expelled from school for refusing to salute the flag and their case went to the Supreme Court.

Q: *Was it your idea or your parents' idea not to salute?*

Edmonds: No, it was our idea. We did it for our conscience. We did not want to salute anything or worship anything that wasn't our God.

Q: *Did people realize that just because you didn't salute the flag it didn't mean you weren't patriotic?*

Edmonds: No, they didn't realize it, because of the war [World War II].

Q: How did the other kids treat you in school?

Edmonds: We were in a little country school. They weren't too bad. They were kind of calling us names. One name they called us was 'Jap' because of the war.

Q: You just ignored it?

Edmonds: Yeah. We didn't say anything back.

Q: Did you go to school at all between the time you were expelled and the time the case was decided in the Supreme Court?

Edmonds: We got to go that following fall [1942], because the West Virginia Supreme Court ruled in our favor. But it wasn't settled until the next summer [1943].

Q: You actually went while it was still under appeal?

Edmonds: Yeah. The school board appealed it and took it to the Supreme Court, but we went to school that following fall, after it was settled in the West Virginia Supreme Court. We were just out a half a year.

Q: When did the teacher notice you weren't saluting the flag?

Edmonds: Well, I don't know when she noticed it. After the war started in December, after the Christmas vacation was over and we went back to school, that was when the principal told us that the teacher had noticed that we weren't saluting the flag. He told us, he said, "Well, if it was left up to me, I wouldn't send you home." But he had orders from the school board; he had to obey them.

Schoolchildren saluting the American flag, circa 1900.

RELIGIOUS EDUCATION

Since the country's earliest days, learning the Bible has been a part of millions of children's education. Religious education was a big part of 19th-century life. Public school students did not receive religious instruction, so many attended Sunday school, a special class where kids learn about the history, customs, and rites of their particular religion. This weekend learning was not enough for some religious leaders, however. They wanted to experiment and try to give religious instruction during regular school hours.

McCollum v. Board of Education (1948)

One of the early experiments with religious education in school happened in Gary, Indiana, in 1914. Children could either attend religious instruction classes or be excused for recreation.

In 1940, members of the Jewish, Catholic, and Protestant faiths in Champaign, Illinois, formed a group called the Champaign Council on Religious Education. They received permission from the Board of Education to offer classes in religious instruction to public school pupils in the fourth through ninth grades. Parents had the option of deciding whether or not to allow their children to attend this "released-time" program. The classes were held once a week for 30 to 45 minutes, depending on the age of the student. The schools did not pay for the religion teachers, but did approve and supervise the activities. Classes were broken up by religion and held inside the normal classrooms of the schools. Any pupils who did not participate in the religious education program went elsewhere in the building to continue their school day.

Almost two million students in 2,200 different communities participated in released-time programs during 1947. But trouble was brewing in Champaign, Illinois. A woman named Vashti McCollum was unhappy that her son was forced to be in a position to accept or reject this religious education. She felt it was a violation of the separation of church and state for public school buildings to be used for religious education during mandatory school hours. She filed suit on behalf of her son, but the Circuit Court and the State Supreme Court both ruled that the released-time program was constitutional.

The case reached the U.S. Supreme Court in December 1947 and was decided in March 1948, 8–1 in favor of McCollum. The main problem was that this was definitely a case of a "tax-established and tax-supported public school system" helping religious groups spread their faith.

"Separation is a requirement to abstain from fusing functions of Government and of religious sects, not merely to treat them all equally." The Court noted that not all of the practicing sects in Champaign were willing or able to provide religious instruc-

Vashti McCollum and her son Jim McCollum.

tion in the schools. Children who belonged to those religions would feel excluded.

"Separation means separation, not something less."

The Court argued that by offering religious education classes, the public school system of Champaign helped kids of certain faiths obtain a stronger religious identity. It created a situation where one religion was being favored over another (those not offering classes). The classes also helped define the differences between the religions. That might promote the government becoming "embroiled, however innocently, in the destructive religious conflicts of which the history of even this country records some dark pages."

Jim McCollum (*McCollum v. Board of Education*, 1948)

Jim McCollum was the child at the center of the landmark *McCollum v. Board of Education* case that involved religious education during school hours. He went on to become an attorney.

Q: What do you remember about the day the decision was announced?

McCollum: I was living with my maternal grandparents at the time, in Rochester, New York, since the school environment in Champaign at the time was somewhat difficult. As I recollect, it was a Monday, March 8, 1948, when the U.S. Supreme Court handed down its decision. I found out when I came home from school. Needless to say, I was elated! It was, indeed, an occasion to celebrate, as we, at last, had been vindicated by an 8–1 decision of the U.S. Supreme Court.

Years later, in 1966, when I was being admitted to practice before the high court, I was privileged to have an audience with Justice Hugo L. Black, the Justice who wrote the majority opinion for the Court on that historic occasion.

Q: How has your case changed your life?

McCollum: I don't know for sure. I think I still would have gone to law school and become an attorney. However, it has given me a perspective on religious issues I probably would not have had otherwise. I have also dedicated much of my energies to a defense of the religion clauses of the First Amendment to the U.S. Constitution—probably more than if I had not been involved in this case.

Q: Is religion still too much a part of government? For example, should the phrase "In God We Trust" be struck from our money?

McCollum: Unquestionably, it is. This, in large part, is the result of a backlash to the controversies emanating from the Vietnam War and the natural rise in religiosity attendant to a wartime mentality, in this case, perpetrated by the Bush administration and his NeoCon [Neoconservative] associates. The motto, "In God We Trust," came out of the Civil War and became the national motto during the Eisenhower administration, as a result of the fear generated by the Cold War. It doesn't belong on our money and has no business being the national motto. Indeed, when my fraternity brother, Francis Bellamy, a Baptist minister, wrote the pledge, he specifically left out any mention of a supreme being. Again, this was introduced during the same period as the aforementioned motto and for the same reasons. I am sure Bellamy would not have approved.

Engel v. Vitale (1962)

The setting of the next major religion in education case was the New Hyde Park School district in New York, where, as in many other school districts in the state, the prayer led by a teacher at the start of each school day went as follows:

"Almighty God, we acknowledge our dependence upon Thee, and we beg Thy blessings upon us, our parents, our teachers and our Country."

Authorized by the New York State Board of Regents, the prayer did not mention Jesus. It was known as the Regents' prayer. Students who did not wish to participate could be excused from the room during the prayer with a note from their parents. The parents of 10 children in the New Hyde Park District protested, claiming that the prayer was against their and their children's beliefs and was also unconstitutional. Steven Engel was one of the plaintiff parents and the case took his name. Despite the parents' arguments, both the lower courts and the New York Court of Appeals found that it was OK for prayers to be recited in school, as long as pupils were not forced to participate.

The Attorneys General of 22 states filed a brief of *amicus curiae* (Latin for "friends of the court") in support of the school district. They wanted to show their support for the authority of public schools. Nonetheless, the Court was unmoved. The Justices felt strongly that allowing prayer in schools was not an acceptable practice. It did not matter how general in nature the prayer might be, or whether it was unbiased toward one religion or another.

Justice Hugo Lafayette Black wrote for the majority:

We think that by using its public school system to encourage recitation of the Regents' prayer, the State of New York has adopted a practice wholly inconsistent with the Establishment Clause.

He went on to explain that this type of involvement was the very reason that the first settlers came to America, to escape religious interference by the government.

The First Amendment was added to the Constitution to stand as a guarantee that neither the power nor the prestige of the Federal Government would be used to control, support or influence the kind of prayer the American people can say . . .

The founding fathers had written the Constitution and the First Amendment with the knowledge that "governments of the past had shackled men's tongues to make them speak only the religious thoughts that government wanted them to speak and to pray only to the God that government wanted them to pray to."

Steven Engel (*Engel v. Vitale*, 1962)

Steven Engel was the parent plaintiff for whom the landmark case *Engel v. Vitale* was named.

Q: *Do you still feel as strongly about the issue today as you did in 1958?*

Engel: Stronger. The very Constitution is at risk. These days, religion itself is at peril.

Q: *How do you feel about the continuing controversy surrounding creationism in the schools?*

Engel: Without evolution, there is no science, no biology. You want to go back to the Dark Ages, start teaching creationism. Where would medicine be today if we all adhered to creationism?

Q: *Is that issue related to the school prayer issue?*

Engel: Yes, all of these issues are the same. The same with vouchers [an experimental program paying families directly to allow them to decide to which school they will send their children].

Q: *What is the main problem with school prayer?*

Engel: God is a personal thing. It's personal. Nothing I want to force on anyone else.

Q: *Including your own children?*

Engel: Including my own children. They have freedom of choice. Prayer is the very essence of man's communication with his God. You can't create one that fits all people.

Q: *Why do you suppose there was such an outcry against the decision?*

Engel: It's simple. This was never about religion at all. This was always about money. [The ruling meant bad news for religion trying to get government subsidies.] The Hasidim [orthodox Jews] attacked [the decision] just as badly as any other religious group.

Abington School Dist. v. Schempp (1963)

Following close on the heels of the *Engel* decision was another very similar case (though the events leading to the case actually began before those in *Engel*).

The year was 1956. A man named Edward Schempp lived in Pennsylvania with his wife Sidney and their children Roger, Donna, and Ellery. Every morning at Abington Senior High School, 16-year-old Ellery Schempp heard 10 verses from the Bible read over the intercom system and broadcast throughout the school as per Pennsylvania law. After the reading, the Lord's Prayer was recited. The law allowed that a child could be excused from the Bible readings with a note from a parent or guardian.

This was not good enough for Mr. Schempp. He felt that a note excusing his children might create tension between them and the teachers and fellow students. The teacher might resent having to excuse the children every day, and the other children might tease the "different" kids who needed to leave the room during the readings. Mr. Schempp also felt that his children's classmates might tend to view any kind of religious objections as a sign of atheism, and that they would then be connected with Communism. They would be seen as un-American. Why should his children have to be made the center of attention over something that was actually a violation of their constitutional rights?

Mr. Schempp and his family brought suit against the school district, and besides their own testimony at the trial, they introduced experts who testified that some parts of the New Testament might be offensive to Jewish children if not put into context and explained properly to those who might be present. The Schempps were not Jewish; they were Unitarian, yet they felt that some of the passages in the Bible were contradictory to what they believed and taught their children. The trial court found that since the Schempp children were required to attend school and that reading of the 10 verses from the Bible was also required by law, this was indeed a violation. The Abington School District appealed the *Schempp* ruling.

When the *Schempp* case got to the Supreme Court, it was combined with a similar case from Maryland whose plaintiff was an atheist named Madalyn Murray. Attorneys General from 19 states joined in the *amicus curiae* brief that was filed urging that the lower court's ruling against the Murrays in the Maryland case be upheld. These Attorneys General were standing up for the rights of public schools to decide how and what students are taught. Briefs of *amicus curiae* for both cases were filed by the American Jewish Committee, the Synagogue Council of America, and the American Ethical Union.

In their decision, the Supreme Court Justices cited a case from the 1940s called *Everson v. Board of Education* (1947). In the opinion for that case, Justice Wiley Blount Rutledge explained that the First Amendment did not mean simply to stop the government from creating a religious sect or promoting a particular religious faith. It also meant "to create a complete and permanent separation of the spheres of religious activity and civil authority by comprehensively forbidding every form of public aid or support

"In God We Trust" on the back of a 1900 dollar coin.

for religion." The Justices also cited *McCollum* and *Engel* as examples of the Court's position on religious freedom over the years.

The majority opinion said in part: "While the Free Exercise Clause clearly prohibits the use of state action to deny the rights of free exercise to anyone, it has never meant that a majority could use the machinery of the State to practice its beliefs . . . In the relationship between man and religion, the State is firmly committed to a position of neutrality."

The *Engel* and *Schempp* cases were a one-two punch that made the Court's stance on the issue very clear—religion and public school did not mix. Times had certainly changed since the *Gobitis* case.

INTERVIEW   **Donna Schempp and Ellery Schempp**
(*Abington School Dist. v. Schempp, 1963*)

Ellery Schempp was 16 years old when he objected to the reading of the Bible in his classroom. His younger sister Donna lived through the notoriety that the case brought the family. Ellery is still very active in issues of separation of church and state.

Q: What was your reaction when the Supreme Court handed down the decision?

Ellery: My family and I always felt a strong loyalty to the ideals of the United States, and we were delighted that we won a strong 8–1 decision. We felt that this decision supported all Americans, from all our different backgrounds. We were particularly pleased that Justices from Catholic, Protestant, and Jewish traditions concurred in the Supreme Court opinions. We felt validated that our government and Constitution gives us a Supreme Court where ordinary citizens could bring such a case and have it considered—that even as a high school student I could have ideas and, with the support of my parents and the ACLU, valid ideas would win.

By the time when the Supreme Court decision was announced in June 1963, I was almost 23 years old and in grad school. I had learned many new viewpoints during my college years, including how many different versions of the Bible and differing beliefs existed: Coptic Christians, Mandeans, Eastern Orthodox, freethinkers, and all the views that had been suppressed by a dominant church. I saw that the reaction to the decision would be complex, but I gained a new awareness that religious freedom was important, and the Supreme Court decision affirmed my conviction that public recognition of only one religious view was unfair.

Some people said we were only looking for publicity. I was glad that a teenager could be recognized for having thoughts, ideas, and feelings, and not be merely judged on athletics. I had a little success in running track, but I thought my mind was as good as my legs. My high school promoted that athletes and pretty girls were stars. I was glad that being a "brain," and having friends who were "brains," gave equality for thought. I think the mind is more important overall in life.

Donna: The decision came out on the Monday after I graduated from high school. I was very relieved, thinking I had not gone through all of this struggle in vain. My brother Roger and I went to school the next morning and stood in the hallway to see what they would say over the loudspeaker. They announced there would be no Bible reading that morning and then asked students to stand for the Pledge of Allegiance. I was nervous but happy.

Q: Why do you suppose there was such an outcry against the decision?

Ellery: I realized that some people considered this as an attack on their beliefs and wanted to condemn anyone who thought differently. But I had seen my classmates being put in an uncomfortable position undergoing "morning devotions," reciting one version of the "Lord's Prayer," in being made to conform and express beliefs that were not their own. I thought, "Good people will see, when they have considered all the issues, that this was about being fair and that it is not fair to impose one religious idea on others." This is eventually what happened when many religious leaders spoke to support the Supreme Court's decision.

We did not see that anything was lost by ending Bible reading and ritual prayer. If families and kids want to pray, why can't they do this at home or in church? Every family can freely pray at breakfast. Why is there a need to pray again at school? I noticed that prayer was asked for at school and football games; I thought this was peculiar. We do not have to pray when entering a shopping mall or to get a driver's license.

Donna: Remember, this was the height of the Cold War. We separated ourselves from the "Godless Communists" by not suppressing religion. I think people were genuinely scared of a nuclear attack, we still had air raid drills. Taking "God" out of the schools I think threatened people about whether "we would win" or "the Communists would win." People are still upset about this decision, 40 years later. It wasn't just then. There is still the thought that the magic of Bible reading and prayer will make the world a safer and more moral place. The events of 9-11 [September 11, 2001] increased the fear and hope for something that will help people to feel reassured. It is hard for people to live in a scary and uncertain world and they cling to things like this to give themselves comfort.

Q: Did the case change your life? What about the rest of your family?

Donna: I think the Bible reading case put a lot of strain on our family. It was the center of our lives for many years, between letters from people, phone calls, etc. It put a lot of strain on Roger and me, who were attending school and being taunted by kids because of it. I, in particular, was embarrassed by it. It was a time when I wanted to be just like everyone else and this, by definition, singled me out. So, although I supported it intellectually, I hated it emotionally.

I Don't Want to Pledge

 Many of the cases in this chapter feature kids who did not want to participate in school-sponsored prayer, pledges, or salutes. Often, there was an opportunity for kids not to participate, but this was not good enough. Why do you think that was the case? In this activity, you will see for yourself. You will need your teacher's participation beforehand for the first part of the activity.

One morning, if your class normally says the Pledge of Allegiance, try purposely standing at attention, but don't repeat the words. How does that feel? How might it feel every day? Would other kids notice? Another time, try sitting down while the other kids stand. How does that feel?

The next step is to have the teacher excuse you just before the pledge, to stand outside the room. (You can do this even if your class does not say the pledge. Just have the teacher excuse you in the morning for about a minute, and stand outside the door.) How do you feel leaving the room? How do you feel coming back in? Are the other kids looking at you? Would this be comfortable to do every day?

Now assume that you believe your constitutional rights have been violated. You will next take your case to the classroom Supreme Court.

YOU'LL NEED

✔ Lawyer(s) for student
✔ Lawyer(s) for school
✔ Classroom Supreme Court
✔ Text of the opinions from the following cases:

Minersville School District v. Gobitis (1940)
(go to: http://supct.law.cornell.edu/supct/html/historics/USSC_CR_0310_0586_ZS.html)

West Virginia Board of Education v. Barnette (1943)
(go to: http://supct.law.cornell.edu/supct/html/historics/USSC_CR_0319_0624_ZS.html)

Engel v. Vitale (1962)
(go to: http://supct.law.cornell.edu/supct/html/historics/USSC_CR_0370_0421_ZS.html)

Abington School Dist. v. Schempp (1963)
(go to: http://supct.law.cornell.edu/supct/html/historics/USSC_CR_0374_0203_ZS.html)

McCollum v. Board of Education (1948)
(go to: http://laws.findlaw.com/us/333/203.html)

The lawyer for the student should argue that the student's rights have been violated, and the student should not have to feel excluded. The school's lawyer should argue that the school has made arrangements for the students who do not wish to participate, and this should be sufficient. You should refer to the *Gobitis*, *Barnette*, *Engel*, *Schempp*, and *McCollum* cases in making your arguments.

The classroom Supreme Court should then decide the case, using previous cases as precedents. Is it OK for the pledge to be said? Is it enough for students to be allowed not to say it? Or not to be in the room? Pull key quotes from these earlier decisions, and don't be afraid to create your own important quotes on the subject—you are the Supreme Court, after all.

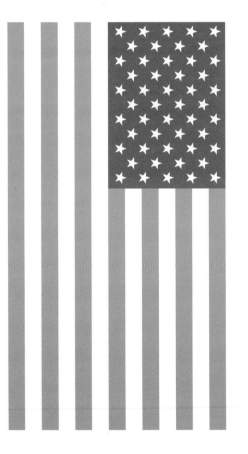

FREEDOM OF RELIGION TODAY

The struggle between church and state is not over. Even today, the courts hear cases about religion in schools. In a case called *Agostini v. Felton* (1997), the Court overruled an earlier decision in *Aguilar v. Felton* (1985) and said that public school teachers could also teach classes in religious schools. The Court felt that there was no danger that state-sponsored religion would infiltrate public schools just because some public school teachers spent time on the side teaching in religious schools.

There are also other cases involving religion and government. One notable instance was when the ACLU sued Judge Roy Moore to have him remove a monument to the Ten Commandments from the rotunda of the Alabama Judicial Building. He refused, even after a District Court judge ordered it removed, and Moore was then removed from office. Though Judge Moore appealed the decision in November 2003, the Supreme Court refused without comment to hear the appeal, thus letting the District Court's ruling stand.

Other controversial issues that may make their way to the Supreme Court in the future include the teaching of creationism in schools alongside Charles Darwin's theory of evolution. Some schools today favor the discussion of "intelligent design," an acknowledgment of some higher being's input. A federal judge ruled in 2005 that a Pennsylvania school board could not teach intelligent design in science class because it broke the boundary between church and state.

INTERVIEW | **Walter Dellinger**

Walter Dellinger was the Solicitor General of the United States from 1996 to 1997 under President Bill Clinton. Prior to that, he was Assistant Attorney General from 1993 to 1996. He has argued a total of 18 cases before the Supreme Court and was law clerk to Justice Hugo Lafayette Black from 1968 to 1969.

Q: How did being clerk to Justice Black help inspire you in your career? What were your duties as a clerk?

Dellinger: My duties were to help Justice Black to decide what cases the U.S. Supreme Court ought to hear. The Court only hears a very small portion of the cases that people ask the Court to hear. One of the important functions of a law clerk is to go through all the cases that people want the Supreme Court to hear and help the Justice pick out a relatively few cases, 100 out of thousands, that the Court will actually hear and decide. Also, Justice Black loved to talk to and argue with his law clerks about how cases ought to be decided, and at the end of the day this was not a democracy in Justice Black's chambers nor should it have been. In the end his vote was the one that mattered, because he was the one that had been nominated by the President and confirmed by the Senate as a Justice, and the two young law clerks had not. But we would have lively discussions and arguments about the cases. And then on the less important cases, we would help on the drafting of the opinions. Justice Black took the drafting of the most important cases each month for himself.

Q: *In Agostini v. Felton [1997], the Court overturned its ruling in Aguilar v. Felton [1985]. Is the Court still evolving in its views on the separation of church and state?*

Dellinger: Well I think the Court has got it just about right at the moment. And I hope it doesn't evolve in either direction. Basically, the Court's position is that private religion is good and government religion is bad. That's a simple statement, but there's a lot of truth in it. I think the Court is willing to admit religious groups to participate in pub-

lic programs with all other groups, as long as they're not given favoritism. They shouldn't be discriminated against.

So in the case of remedial services—reading, helping kids who are having trouble learning to read—the federal program in question was intended to reach low-income children with learning difficulties, wherever they were during the school day, with special teachers to help instruct them. The Court ruled you could do that inside a religious school as well as inside a public school. I think that was right. In the Court's other decisions, they're really walking a very fine line in which if private people are praying it's just fine, even if they're on government property or using some government resources, as long as the decision to pray is really the decision of the people themselves. But what is wrong is when the government gets into the business of sponsoring prayer or other religious activity. I think the Court has stuck with that line and is in a pretty good place, though by a fairly narrow margin. It's often 5–4 in many cases.

5

CIVIL RIGHTS

*W*hile the Constitution has been amended to give equal freedom and protection to all peoples, interpretation of that protection has changed over the years. What constitutes discrimination? Can and should diversity be forced? Is the policy of **affirmative action** necessary?

Civil rights are not just about the rights of minorities. Battles have also been fought in the Supreme Court over issues of discrimination based on gender and, more recently, sexual orientation.

What do our rights to "life" and "liberty" really mean? Civil rights cases have also encompassed issues of personal privacy and liberty. They have both granted and challenged certain guarantees about how we choose to live our lives.

AMERICA'S FIRST CIVIL RIGHTS CASE

The United States v. The Amistad (1841)

One of the biggest civil inequalities in our history has been the treatment of African Americans. The enslavement of African-born people dates back to the early 1600s, when the first European settlers arrived in the New World. The first civil rights case heard by

Joseph Cinquez, an African slave on the *Amistad.*

the Supreme Court did not even have anything to do with Americans. Instead it dealt with Spaniards and Africans. The complicated tale began on June 27, 1839, when the schooner *Amistad* sailed from Havana, Cuba, for Puerto Principe, Cuba. The ship was Spanish owned. Onboard were about 50 African slaves owned by three Spaniards who were also onboard the ship.

While sailing to Puerto Principe, the Africans staged a mutiny, killed the captain and a crew member, and gained control of the *Amistad.* Two other crew members escaped during the mutiny, and two of the slave-owning Spaniards, named Jose Ruiz and Pedro Montez, were kept alive and ordered to steer the ship toward Africa or else be killed. During the day the Spaniards obeyed, but at night they would change course and head for the American coast.

The Spaniards' plan worked. On August 26 the ship was found, anchored about half a mile from the shore of Long Island, by a U.S. lieutenant named Thomas Gedney. Ruiz and Montez begged for American assistance. Lieutenant Gedney seized the ship and its contents, including the slaves, brought them to Connecticut, and began salvage proceedings.

Ruiz and Montez filed claims for their slaves and other possessions. The Spanish government also filed a claim for the ship itself. After all, the treaty of 1795 between the United States and Spain had discussed just this sort of situation. The ship, cargo, and Africans were all documented as belonging to Spanish subjects.

The Africans protested, explaining that they had been kidnapped from their homes in Africa around

April 15, 1839, and brought to Cuba against their will. There, they were purchased by the Spaniards and placed aboard the *Amistad*. The slaves felt that they should therefore go free.

Representing the slaves was former President John Quincy Adams, who was by this time nearly 75 years old, but nonetheless a forceful attorney. The treaty could not be valid if there was evidence of fraud. The Court had to navigate the tricky waters involving both slavery and international treaties. In the end, the Court ruled that the slaves could not be considered merchandise according to the treaty, since the laws of Spain had made the slavery trade an illegal and punishable offense. The Africans were not pirates or robbers, since they were attempting to recapture the freedom that had been taken from them against their will. The slaves had to be set free.

From the opinion by Justice Joseph Story:

It is plain beyond controversy, if we examine the evidence, that these negroes never were the lawful slaves of Ruiz or Montez, or of any other Spanish subjects . . . It is also a most important consideration in the present case, which ought not to be lost sight of, that, supposing these African negroes not to be slaves, but kidnapped, and free negroes, the treaty with Spain cannot be obligatory upon them; and the United States are bound to respect their rights as much as those of Spanish subjects.

Through the 1840s and 1850s, slavery became the most sensitive issue in the United States. The North and South disagreed vehemently about it.

WINNING FREEDOM
Dred Scott v. Sandford (1857)

Though an important decision, the *Amistad* case did not actually make any statement about the slavery situation in the United States. As slavery threatened to rip the country in two, the Supreme Court was faced with another complex slavery case, this time about a fugitive slave.

By the time the Supreme Court heard the *Dred Scott* case in 1856, it had been argued in the lower courts for 10 years. The complicated case revolved around a slave named Dred Scott. Back in 1830, a military doctor named John Emerson purchased Scott in Missouri (a slave state) and brought Scott with him to Illinois, which was a free state. Scott was then taken to the Wisconsin Territory, which was also free, based on the Missouri Compromise of 1820. For several years, Scott lived in places that outlawed slavery.

Scott returned to the St. Louis area with Emerson, who died in 1843. In 1846, Scott sued Emerson's widow for his freedom, claiming that living on free soil had given him the right to be free. In 1847, the Circuit Court ruled in favor of Mrs. Irene Emerson, but allowed Scott to refile. This time, the jury found in favor of Scott, ordering him set free based on his residence in free territories.

Mrs. Emerson appealed to the Missouri Supreme Court, which ruled in her favor. The case was next appealed to the federal courts, against John Sanford (Mrs. Emerson's brother, who was now handling the estate of John Emerson). The federal court ruled in favor of Sanford, and the case *Dred Scott v. Sandford* (an error recorded Sanford's name incorrectly) was finally appealed to the U.S. Supreme Court.

The case was first argued in February 1856, and then again in December 1856, in order to clear up additional legal questions. Scott's lawyers argued that "naturalization was not limited to the whites by the Constitution, and it has been extended repeatedly by treaty and Act of Congress to Indians and negroes." The lawyers, Montgomery Blair and George Ticknor Curtis, continued by saying that, "the Constitution of the United States recognizes but two kinds of free persons, citizens and aliens. Nobody supposes that free negroes are aliens. They must therefore be citizens."

Chief Justice Robert B. Taney, by this time 80 years old, wrote the decision of the majority, in favor of Sanford and Mrs. Emerson. He did not believe that the framers of the Constitution intended to give any rights to African Americans.

It becomes necessary, therefore, to determine who were citizens of the Several States when the Constitution was adopted. And in order to do this, we must recur to the governments and institutions of the thirteen colonies . . . In the opinion of the court, the legislation and histories of the time, and the language used in the Declaration of Independence, show, that neither the class of persons who had been imported as slaves, nor their descendants, whether they had become free or not, were acknowledged as a part of the people.

Chief Justice Taney tried to back his argument by citing many instances where blacks had been excluded from language in important documents and laws. In 1792, the Militia Law was passed by Congress. This law stated that every "free able-bodied white male citizen" had to enroll in the militia. Because Africans were excluded from the language, they were "repudiated, and rejected from the duties and obligations of citizenship in marked language." The Chief Justice cited another Act from 1813 that stated that ocean vessels were not allowed to employ anyone except "citizens of the United States, or persons of color," noting that according to that Act, a person could be one or the other, but not both. Taney felt that "this class of persons [blacks] were governed by special legislation" that did not apply to white people.

He argued that if Africans could be considered citizens of one state, and then traveled to another state, then two members of the same race could theoretically have two different legal statuses. This would produce "discontent and insubordination among them, and endangering the peace and safety of the state." He added that "the state may give the right to free negroes and mulattoes, but that does not make them citizens of the state."

Because he was not a citizen, Scott could not file a suit in either the state or federal courts. Because slaves were not citizens, they were to be considered property.

Next came another controversial argument. According to the Fifth Amendment, slave owners could not be restricted in their right to hold property depending on where they lived. They could not be limited based on an Act of Congress that delineated territories to be "free" areas. Importantly, the Supreme Court said that the Missouri Compromise of 1820 was, in effect, unconstitutional. It was not up to Congress to designate certain territories as "free."

The decision was extremely unpopular among the northern states. It did not show any hint of compromise or create any hope of agreement on the issue of slavery. What it seemed to indicate was that as long as there was slavery, there would be strife between north and south.

Ironically, when Mrs. Emerson remarried in 1857, her new husband was opposed to slavery, so she returned Scott to the family that had owned him before 1830. That family, the Blows, granted Scott his freedom. Unfortunately, Dred Scott's newfound freedom was short-lived, as he died in 1858.

EMANCIPATION

The tension surrounding the *Dred Scott* decision only escalated, and the slavery issue finally propelled the nation into a terrible Civil War that began in 1861. In 1863, President Abraham Lincoln signed the Emancipation Proclamation, which freed all slaves in the rebel states. It was really the end of the Civil War that brought freedom to these slaves throughout the former Confederacy. The end of the war also began a tense period of healing known as the "Reconstruction Era." After President Lincoln was assassinated in 1865, Andrew Johnson became President.

In 1867, the population of the Southern states was roughly 40 percent black. Resentment among Southerners was high, but even many Northerners were uneasy. An Albany, New York, newspaper published an editorial in 1867 that proclaimed:

The people of the Union do not want the Southern States to be reconstructed entirely by blacks. They are not willing that the balance of political power shall be controlled by the hands of negroes. They do not enjoy the prospect of having colored officials, elected by the votes of those who have barely emerged from a condition of barbarism in slavery, making and administering laws for vast communities.

ABOVE: Advertisement offering reward for a runaway slave, 1838. BELOW: Lincoln signs the Emancipation Proclamation.

The Thirteenth Amendment (December 1865) ended slavery, and the Fourteenth Amendment (June 1866) gave African Americans the right of full citizenship. The Fourteenth Amendment also made the first thirteen Amendments applicable to the states as well as the federal government.

The Fifteenth Amendment (March 1870) gave blacks the right to vote. But although African Americans now had constitutional rights, their struggle for equality was far from over. In fact, though the constitutional Amendments made them citizens, it did not force whites to treat them fairly.

Even after slavery was abolished, the country struggled to integrate African Americans into society. The doctrine of "separate but equal" was applied in many locations around the country. This segregation of blacks from whites was the law through much of the South.

Cases dealing with the newly granted rights of ex-slaves began to appear before the Supreme Court. In a case called *Strauder v. The State of West Virginia* (1879), the Supreme Court ruled that a state could not exclude someone from a jury because of color.

FIGHTING SEGREGATION
Plessy v. Ferguson (1896)

In June 1892, a man named Homer Plessy was found guilty of refusing to leave a whites-only train car. Plessy was actually seven-eighths white and one-eighth black, meaning only one of his eight great-grandparents was African American. He bought a first-class train ticket on the East Louisiana Railway, for a trip from New Orleans, Louisiana, to Covington, Louisiana. The state had passed a law two years earlier that allowed railways to maintain separate cars for whites and blacks. The law stated that "any passenger insisting on going into a coach or compartment to which by race he does not belong, shall be liable to a fine of twenty-five dollars, or in lieu thereof to imprisonment for a period of not more than twenty days in the parish prison."

When Plessy entered the car where whites were accommodated, the conductor told him that he had to ride in a coloreds-only car. Plessy refused and was promptly ejected by a police officer and thrown in jail.

The Supreme Court first of all brushed off Plessy's argument that he was white and should be treated as such, based on his seven-eighths-white blood. The Court said that it was really up to each state to determine what mix of white and black blood would equal a black.

The Justices took a very limited view of the intentions of the Fourteenth Amendment. They agreed that it had been passed in order to give blacks a certain measure of equality as citizens of the country, but "it could not have been intended to abolish distinctions based upon color, or to enforce social, as distinguished from political, equality."

The Supreme Court ruling, written by Justice Henry Billings Brown, continued:

We cannot say that a law which authorizes or even requires the separation of two races in public conveyances is unreasonable, or more obnoxious to the

Fourteenth Amendment than the acts of Congress requiring separate schools for colored children in the District of Columbia, the constitutionality of which does not seem to have been questioned.

The Justices also felt that separation did not mean anything socially. It was not a stigma, or anything of which to be ashamed: "We consider the underlying fallacy of the plaintiff's argument to consist in the assumption that the enforced separation of the two races stamps the colored race with a badge of inferiority."

In the dissent, the forward-thinking Justice John Marshall Harlan wondered where the government could draw the line. Could blacks be forced to keep to one side of the street while whites keep to the other side? Should Protestants and Catholics be segregated into separate rail cars as well?

"Our Constitution is color-blind, and neither knows nor tolerates classes among citizens. In respect of civil rights, all citizens are equal before the law," Harlan wrote. He also pointed out that a Chinese man who was not even a citizen could get on a whites-only train car, while a black man who had fought and risked his life to preserve the Union during the Civil War could not.

Separate but Unequal
Brown v. Board of Education (1954)

The doctrine of "separate but equal" reigned for many years after *Plessy.* Segregation was rampant across America, especially in the South. Blacks and whites lived in the same cities and towns, but had completely different life experiences. One of the problems was that blacks' schools were fewer in number than whites' schools, so African American children were more likely to have to travel greater distances to get to school. Another problem was that their school experiences were not likely to be "equal" to that of white children, since they might not have had access to the same textbooks and resources.

Civil rights marchers on Washington, D.C., in 1963 express their views.

97

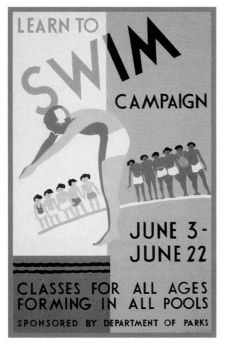

A poster for swimming lessons shows segregated classes.

The National Association for the Advancement of Colored People (NAACP) began to organize lawsuits to fight segregation. They believed that segregation could never be "equal" and that it violated the Fourteenth Amendment, which promised equal protection under the law to all.

In the fall of 1950, NAACP members in Topeka, Kansas, strategized on how they could change the system. They signed on 13 parents as plaintiffs in a suit against the Topeka Board of Education. This case, filed in February 1951 under the name of one of the parent plaintiffs, became known as *Brown v. Board of Education.*

Meanwhile, in Washington, D.C., a group of 11 African American children set another lawsuit in motion. Led by a concerned citizen named Gardner Bishop, the children went to Washington's new whites-only Sousa High School and asked to be admitted as students. The request was refused because the students were black, and a lawsuit began to take shape. Bishop wanted his friends' and neighbors' children to have a facility that was equal to the new whites-only school. The case reached the U.S. District Court as *Bolling v. Sharpe* (1951).

Another case arose when 117 African American high school students called a strike at their blacks-only high school in Richmond, Virginia. Requests to replace their crumbling school went ignored, and student leader Barbara Johns organized a strike on April 23, 1951. The students stood outside their building, some carrying signs, and protested the unfair and unequal conditions they had to put up with. Johns and her schoolmate Carrie Stokes asked for

advice from the local NAACP chapter. After 10 days on strike, work began on a lawsuit that became known as *Davis v. County School Board of Prince Edward County* (1952).

In Delaware, there was further unrest. African American students and their parents were unhappy at their 10-mile trip to and from school when there was a roomy whites-only school in their own neighborhood. Also in Delaware, an African American mother named Sarah Bulah wanted her daughter to get a ride on a school bus that passed her house every day, filled with white children on their way to their school. She felt this would be much easier than her driving her daughter to the blacks-only school two miles down the road. Her requests were denied because a black child could not share a bus with white children. These cases were known as *Bolton v. Gebhart* and *Bulah v. Gebhart.*

The District Court rulings acknowledged inequality, but did not condemn or outlaw segregation. For example, in the *Davis* case in Virginia, the three-judge District Court ruled that the African Americans' school did need to be repaired, but it forbade the children from attending the whites-only school while repairs were being made. In the *Brown* case in Kansas, the judges found that while segregation had a negative effect on African American children, the existing school facilities were equal enough to remain in effect.

Upon appeal to the Supreme Court, most of these cases were combined into one case, called *Brown v. Board of Education.* On May 17, 1954, the Supreme Court announced its landmark decision. The lower courts were overruled. Segregated public schools were declared unconstitutional. No longer could African American children (or any other race of children, for that matter) be kept out of schools because of their color. They would share. Importantly, the Court decided that one could not simply compare "tangible" aspects such as building size, qualifications of teachers, or the curriculum being taught. The effect of segregation upon the black students had to be considered as well. A key victory had been won for civil rights, a struggle that would hit full steam during the mid-1960s.

The main argument of the plaintiffs had been that segregated schools were not "equal" and could not be made equal. Chief Justice Earl Warren wrote for the majority:

We conclude that in the field of public education the doctrine of "separate but equal" has no place. Separate educational facilities are inherently unequal. Therefore, we hold that the plaintiffs and others similarly situated for whom the actions have been brought are, by reason of the segregation complained of, deprived of the equal protection of the laws guaranteed by the Fourteenth Amendment.

Desegregation was a slow process and took many years to accomplish. The last of the desegregation cases before the Supreme Court was *United States v. Fordice* (1992).

(d) To promote the value of maintaining the existing social structure in North Carolina in which two distinct races heretofore have lived as separate groups, and the value of educating the different races in separate schools.

(e) To promote loyalty to the traditions of the State and to appeal to all loyal and patriotic citizens for their wholehearted support in maintaining the integrity of those traditions.

(f) To promote the right of the State of North Carolina to regulate its own internal affairs in the manner it believes to be most conducive to the happiness and welfare of its citizens.

(g) To cooperate with and support our State and local civil authorities, agencies and committees, including State and local school boards and officials, to the extent that they are favorable to the objects and purposes herein set forth.

Annual membership dues—$1.00. Payable September 1st of each year.

Contributions in addition to membership fee will be gratefully received.

A racist society membership card dated 1957 still promoted segregation.

INTERVIEW   Victoria Jean Benson (*Brown v. Board of Education*, 1954)

Victoria Jean Benson is the daughter of Maude Lawton, one of the plaintiffs of the Kansas case that became part of *Brown v. Board of Education*. Victoria was eight years old when the decision was handed down in 1953. Though there was an elementary school a block away, Victoria could not go there because it was whites-only. Victoria's mother was a close friend of McKinley Burnett, the president of the Topeka branch of the NAACP and one of the initiators of the Kansas case.

Q: *What is the most important thing kids should understand about* Brown v. Board of Education?

Benson: Everybody should know their history. We should always build on history in a positive manner and not relive or repeat it. Education, outside of God and family, is the most important thing. There will be suffering and sacrifice, but you have to persevere. You cannot be a negative person and succeed. No one wants to help a child who is negative. My mother taught me, don't be intimidated by anyone.

Benson: She was proud of the part she played. When we were children she did not discuss it. She always fought for the underdog. We should learn to love one another. People won't like you all the time and that's because of their ignorance of other cultures.

Q: *What was the situation that led your mother to become involved in the Kansas case?*

Benson: My mother and older sister Gloria used to go to the five-and-dime stores and pound on counters and say, "I want to be served!" We lived in an integrated neighborhood, and we were never mishandled. We went to all-black elementary schools. When the decision came down, I was eight years old. After the decision, my mother chose to finish my education there. My younger brother was the first in the family to go to an integrated elementary school.

Japanese Internment

African Americans were not the only ethnic group to experience the harsh reality of discrimination. Cloaked in the pretense of national defense, laws were enacted that restricted the freedom of Japanese Americans. These laws were challenged as being biased and unjustifiable.

America entered World War II when the Japanese bombed Pearl Harbor, Hawaii, in a surprise attack on December 7, 1941. The nation was shocked and angered. How could Pearl Harbor have been so vulnerable? What if the Japanese tried to attack the mainland? The long coast of California seemed especially vulnerable. An additional worry to the government was the presence of more than 100,000 Japanese Americans on the West Coast, mainly in California. Though most were certainly loyal Americans, the government felt it was possible that some Japanese Americans were plotting against the country.

Through a series of executive orders and proclamations, it was decided that all persons of Japanese ancestry living near the Pacific Coast would be relocated to internment camps. Anyone who disobeyed would be charged with a crime and fined or imprisoned.

A pair of cases that made it to the Supreme Court were *Hirabayashi v. United States* (1943) and *Korematsu v. United States* (1944). Both the men in these cases had been convicted of failing to obey military orders. Gordon Hirabayashi had not obeyed a curfew that required him to be at home between the hours of 8:00 P.M. and 6:00 A.M. He argued that while a curfew in and of itself might be used during wartime, the application of the curfew only to Japanese Americans was in violation of his Fifth Amendment rights to equal protection. Fred Korematsu had remained in San Leandro, California, contrary to an order to evacuate. He argued in part that the danger of Japanese invasion had disappeared by May 1942.

The Supreme Court struck down both arguments. The Justices in *Hirabayashi* and *Korematsu* felt that the government was acting in the best interests of the country when it decided to isolate the Japanese Americans, and that the government believed there was a serious threat of espionage by people of Japanese descent. In *Hirabayashi,* Justice Harlan Fiske Stone said that it was possible the government did feel that Japanese Americans "constituted a menace to the national defense and safety which demanded that prompt and adequate measures be taken to guard against it."

In *Korematsu,* Justice Hugo Lafayette Black explained that Korematsu was not excluded from his home because of hostility to his race, but simply because the military authorities had to take "proper security measures" due to the "military urgency of the situation." Years later, facts emerged that showed the government's case against both men was based on false and misleading information. Korematsu's case was retried in 1983 and his conviction overturned. Hirabayashi's case was retried and his conviction overturned in 1987. In 1988 Congress apologized for the internment of Japanese Americans during World War II and gave $20,000 to each survivor.

Japanese American teenagers walk to school in the Manzanar War Relocation Center, Owens Valley, California, 1943.

DISCRIMINATION THROUGH APPORTIONMENT

Baker v. Carr (1962)

The U.S. House of Representatives is composed of elected representatives from all the states of the union. Each state receives a different number of representatives as the population of the state changes. If California gains population while New York loses population, then California will have more representatives in Congress and New York will have fewer.

But during the first half of the 20th century, state legislatures were a different story. There was a wide range of practices in place according to each state's constitution. New York assured every county, regardless of the number of its inhabitants, at least one seat in their respective Houses. Missouri gave each of its counties, however minimally populated they were, one representative. In Pennsylvania, the basis of **apportionment** (the method of dividing up the total number of elected officials among all the counties) in both Houses was taxable inhabitants, and in the House, every county of at least 3,500 taxable inhabitants had a representative. Rhode Island gave one Senator to each of its towns or cities, and New Jersey gave one to each of its counties.

As the country grew in population, some of the inequities of the apportionment systems began to be noticed. Voters in Illinois complained that their heavily populated congressional districts were underrepresented. In the case that resulted, *Colegrove v. Green*

(1946), the Supreme Court decided that reapportionment was not within their jurisdiction. There, the Justices claimed that the Constitution left many legal matters to be decided by the executive and legislative branches of government. It would be almost 15 years before the Supreme Court Justices changed their mind about reapportionment.

A case called *Gomillion v. Lightfoot* (1960) concerned an African American man who was a resident of Tuskegee, Alabama, until the boundaries of the city were changed. Most African Americans suddenly found themselves outside the city's new boundaries and therefore they could no longer vote in city elections. There the Court ruled that though states were normally to be in control of their own municipal boundaries, the guarantees in the Constitution could not be "manipulated out of existence" by an action a state takes.

Just a year later, a similar case was heard. In Tennessee, apportionment of members of the state assembly from the different counties was to be made every ten years.

But in 1901, the Apportionment Act had been passed. Between 1901 and 1961, there was no reapportionment in Tennessee. In those 60 years, the population grew from 2,000,000 to 3,500,000. Some counties gained in population while others decreased in population, but the number of members of the state assembly from each county remained fixed at the same ratio it was in 1901.

The areas that were experiencing the most population growth were the cities, while rural areas were stagnant. Many of these new inhabitants were African

Americans. For example, due to the outdated apportionment of elected officials, a representative from the city of Memphis might represent 10 times as many people as one from the countryside represented. This meant that a vote in Memphis did not count equally compared to a vote in a rural area. A voter in the country had more power in determining the election of his representative than a voter in Memphis did.

A group of people filed suit, with Charles Baker being the name at the top of the list, against the Secretary of State of Tennessee, Joe Carr, who was in charge of elections. The case, *Baker v. Carr,* was a landmark case.

Justice William J. Brennan Jr. ruled: "When a state exercises power wholly within the domain of state interest, it is insulated from federal judicial review. But such insulation is not carried over when state power is used as an instrument for circumventing a federally protected right."

In his dissent, Justice Felix Frankfurter pointed out how the 50 states had many different ways of dealing with apportionment, and that it was an extremely complex matter. Colebrook, Connecticut—population 592—elects two House representatives; Hartford—population 177,397—also elects two.

In 2005, the Supreme Court agreed to hear a group of cases challenging a 2003 Republican effort in Texas to redraw voting districts in a way that Democrats feel favors Republican candidates and weakens minorities' voting power. Cases such as this are important because they could affect standards for redistricting around the country.

AFFIRMATIVE ACTION

During the mid- to late 20th century, "affirmative action" programs began to spring up across the country. These programs were designed to give minorities, who had long been excluded from many activities, a fair chance to get a foothold. The goal was to make discrimination, a longstanding problem in the United States, nearly impossible. This included everything from businesses to education.

A government contract, for example, may have to include at least 10 percent minority-owned firms. The courts have to consider if affirmative action actually works and what the situation would be like for minorities if it did not exist.

One complaint about affirmative action is that it has served its purpose and should be dismantled. If minorities have made inroads in business and higher education, do they still need help?

Regents of Univ. of Cal. v. Bakke (1978)

Universities have given special consideration to minorities to ensure that they are adequately represented in the student body. This can result in different standards being applied to students of different racial backgrounds. Perhaps the most famous affirmative action case is *Regents of Univ. of Cal. v. Bakke.*

Allan Bakke was a white student who applied for admission to the Medical School of the University of California at Davis in 1973 and 1974 and was rejected both years. On both occasions, the university admitted students with significantly lower admissions scores than Bakke.

After the second rejection, Bakke filed suit in the Superior Court of California. The court ruled in favor of Bakke, but did not order the university to admit him. The court said that Bakke had never proved that he would have been admitted in the first place, even if the university did not have a special admissions program. So Bakke sued in protest of that part of the decision that barred him from admission, and the university sued to try to overturn the ruling on the unconstitutionality of their admissions policy.

The California Supreme Court agreed that the school's policies did violate the Constitution. It also decided that Bakke had done his job in proving that he was unfairly discriminated against. It was now up to the university to prove that Bakke would not have been accepted anyway. The university could not prove this concretely, so the university was ordered to admit Bakke. At that point, the university filed a petition with the U.S. Supreme Court. Bakke's University of California education was put on hold. He would have to wait until the case was decided to start school.

The case was controversial, and dozens of *amicus* briefs were filed for both sides. Not only had the policy violated the Equal Protection Clause of the Fourteenth Amendment, the argument for Bakke went, it had violated Title VI of the Civil Rights Act of 1964. This section said: "No person in the United States shall, on the ground of race, color, or national origin, be excluded from participation in, be denied the ben-efits of, or be subjected to discrimination under any program or activity receiving Federal financial assistance."

The Supreme Court decided in favor of Bakke, and the school was ordered to admit him. The Court said that it was OK to use race as *one* of the factors when considering admission, but that race played too big a part in the school's admissions policy. It was a predominant factor, rather than just one of several.

"Preferring members of any one group for no reason other than race or ethnic origin is discrimination for its own sake. This the Constitution forbids." Justice Powell felt that the university's attempt to bring diversity was different from what the Court ordered in *Brown v. Board of Education*. In that case's ruling, the goal was "to redress the wrongs worked by specific instances of racial discrimination." Trying to stop racial discrimination against one traditionally discriminated against group while putting another group at a disadvantage was not in the spirit of what *Brown* was trying to accomplish.

The Supreme Court did something that it did not often do. It issued a mixed ruling. The judgment of the lower court was upheld in part and reversed in part. The Court ruled that Bakke should be admitted and that the University of California—Davis's special admissions program violated the Constitution. However, the Court still allowed race to be taken into account as a factor in future admissions decisions. Justice Powell felt that race could be considered so long as there was no blatant use of quotas or true discrimination in deciding who was admitted.

Griffin B. Bell

Griffin Bell was the 72nd Attorney General of the United States (1977 to 1979) under President Jimmy Carter. He campaigned for John F. Kennedy in 1960, and was appointed by President Kennedy as a Circuit Court of Appeals judge. During his 14 years as a judge, he participated in nearly 3,000 cases. Many of his cases dealt with civil rights.

Q: *In* United States v. Hinds County School Board *[1969], the United States Supreme Court ordered the Fifth Circuit Court to implement immediate desegregation plans in Mississippi. You were placed in charge of these efforts. Why do you suppose the Supreme Court wanted to rush the process? Can you describe your experience?*

Bell: This was a group of 32 local school district cases which had been heard by the District Court in Mississippi. In an unprecedented move, the Supreme Court reversed the panel decision of the Fifth Circuit with direction. Part of the direction was that the case be administered at the Circuit Court level and not in the District Court. I think that the Supreme Court had lost patience with the many delays in carrying out the edict of *Brown v. Board of Education.* I was not on the original Fifth Circuit panel, but was assigned to preside over the panel which took over the cases after the Supreme Court decision. It was our panel that implemented the Supreme Court order.

Q: *When the* Bakke *decision was announced you called it a "great victory for affirmative action." Do you still feel that affirmative action is morally and constitutionally right?*

Bell: I referred to *Bakke* as a great victory for affirmative action because of the opinion of Justice Lewis F. Powell Jr., which made sense out of the affirmative action movement. His idea was that a goal was proper but not a quota, and that the goal would allow the consideration of race among other factors in deciding admissions. It was quite different from affirmative action, which places a set-aside based on race.

Gratz v. Bollinger (2003)

In 2003, the Supreme Court took on two major cases that dealt with affirmative action in the admissions at the University of Michigan. These cases challenged the use of quotas to determine how many black students were admitted to the school. The most exclusive colleges in the country sometimes apply goals in order to give disadvantaged minority students a better chance to gain admission.

Be a Courtroom Artist

PHOTOGRAPHY is not allowed in the Supreme Court. The only way to capture the action is in a drawing. Courtroom artists work quickly to capture a lawyer making his or her case or a Justice speaking from the bench. The idea is similar to court reporting; you want to capture the essentials and then later you can flesh out the detail. In this activity, you will sketch a friend as the friend is speaking.

YOU'LL NEED

✔ Sketchbook or pad of white paper that is at least 8" x 10"
✔ Charcoal pencil (or a regular pencil if you cannot find a charcoal pencil)
✔ A friend
✔ Stopwatch

Set the stopwatch to one minute. Ask your friend to stand up, raise his or her arm, and hold up a finger as if making a point. Begin to sketch. After the minute is up, your friend can relax, your time to sketch is up. Courtroom artists often have only seconds to sketch a gesture or position, but can still observe the person's features after they have moved. Try again with the watch set to 45 seconds.

Some helpful tips on quick sketching:

Capture the general shape of the person's face with an oval

Capture the direction your friend's face is turned by positioning the eyes, nose, and mouth properly

Capture the gesture your friend is making with his or her arm by drawing quick lines

If you have time, capture more of the general appearance: Is your friend wearing short sleeves? Does the shirt have a collar? What color is his or her hair, etc.? You can either sketch these details or write a brief note on the bottom of the paper that says "short sleeves, dark shirt." After your friend has relaxed, you can fill in the details of your drawing. When you are done, see if you have captured the moment.

High school student Jennifer Gratz applied for undergraduate admission to the University of Michigan's College of Literature, Science, and the Arts for the fall of 1995. She had a grade point average of 3.8. Patrick Hamacher applied for admission in the fall of 1997. The students were both disappointed to find out that they had been rejected. They filed suit against the school because they felt that they had been passed over in favor of minority students who actually had lower grades. The University of Michigan had an admissions system in place that gave bonus points to minority applicants. For example, in 1998, an applicant was entitled to 20 points, out of a total possible score of 150, based upon his or her membership in an underrepresented racial or ethnic minority group.

The university's system changed slightly over the years since Jennifer Gratz originally applied for admission. The District Court ruled that the university's undergraduate admissions minority policy had not been "narrowly tailored" to allow for race as a factor (but not the deciding factor) during 1995–98, but that in 1999 and 2000 the policy had changed to qualify it as narrowly tailored.

The students believed that the school's use of race as a factor in admissions violated Title VI of the Civil Rights Act of 1964 and the Equal Protection Clause of the Fourteenth Amendment. One of the students' lawyers argued that the university "flagrantly discriminated on the basis of race." While admitting that the university was trying to create a more diverse student body, the lawyer explained that diversity depended on "the standardless discretion of educators."

U.S. Solicitor General Theodore Olson also argued during the half-hour allotted for the plaintiffs. He told the Justices that the university had created two doors for admission, one for preferred minorities and one for all others. Though the university had made changes in its admissions system in the years since the students were rejected, Olson said that the changes were only "cosmetic" and that the school was using a "thinly disguised quota" system.

The school pointed to the opinion of Justice Lewis F. Powell Jr. in the *Bakke* case to respond to students' arguments. The university's lawyer explained that there were educational benefits that came from having a diverse student body, and that there needed to be a meaningful number of African American students on campus, not simply a token few who would feel isolated and out of place.

Chief Justice William H. Rehnquist wrote for the majority:

Nothing in Justice Powell's opinion in Bakke *signaled that a university may employ whatever means it desires to achieve the stated goal of diversity without regard to the limits imposed by our strict scrutiny analysis. We conclude, therefore, that because the University's use of race in its current freshman admissions policy is not narrowly tailored to achieve respondents' asserted compelling interest in diversity, the admissions policy violates the Equal Protection Clause of the Fourteenth Amendment.*

Grutter v. Bollinger (2003)

Another case, called *Grutter v. Bollinger,* alleged discrimination in the University of Michigan Law School. An applicant named Barbara Grutter was rejected, and she sued claiming discrimination based on the admissions policy. In this case, however, the Supreme Court found in a 5–4 ruling that the Law School admissions policy was sufficiently "narrowly tailored" and ruled in favor of the university.

In *Grutter,* Justice Sandra Day O'Connor said, "The Law School's goal of attaining a critical mass of underrepresented minority students does not transform its program into a quota." An individual had to be evaluated in such a way that race was not the "defining feature of his or her application."

In a separate opinion, Justice Clarence Thomas quoted a speech in which the abolitionist Fredrick Douglass begged white people, "What I ask for the negro is not benevolence, not pity, not sympathy, but simply justice . . . Do nothing with us!"

STRIDES IN WOMEN'S RIGHTS

Women have struggled for many years to gain the same basic rights men have enjoyed. It wasn't until 1920, after a 70-year struggle, that women won the right to vote, and other struggles against discrimination have been ongoing since then. A case in the 1930s called *West Coast Hotel Co. v. Parrish* (1937) (see page 152) dealt with a woman suing to get wages that were owed to her under a state minimum wage law, but the modern women's rights movement did not really hit full steam until the 1960s and 1970s.

One early case arose when Sally and Cecil Reed's adopted son Richard died in 1967, and the separated parents both asked to be appointed as administrator of his estate (he had no will). The lower court ruled in favor of Cecil Reed because an Idaho law said that, all other things being equal, if two parties had equal claims to manage an estate, "males must be preferred to females."

Sally Reed filed an appeal and it was heard in the District Court, which ruled that the Idaho law was in violation of the Equal Protection Clause of the Constitution. At this point, Cecil Reed filed an appeal in the Idaho Supreme Court, which overturned the District Court's decision. Sally Reed took the case to the U.S. Supreme Court, where it was known as *Reed v. Reed* (1971).

The Court noted that state laws were allowed to make certain differentiations among different classes of people when deciding upon their legal rights (for example, it was OK if parents had more rights than grandparents). However, upon examination of the particular issue in the case at hand, the Court ruled that the Idaho law was unconstitutional because Sally and Cecil Reed were both members of the same class—they were both parents who should have an equal chance of becoming administrator of their son's estate. Chief Justice Warren Earl Burger said: "To give a mandatory preference to members of either sex over members of the other, merely to accomplish the elimination of hearings on the merits, is to make the very kind of arbitrary legislative choice forbidden by the Equal Protection Clause of the Fourteenth Amendment."

The Supreme Court has dealt with many different issues pertaining to women's rights over the years. In *Corning Glass Works v. Brennan* (1974), the Court ruled that a company that made glass had violated a law called the Equal Pay Act by not paying female workers the same as male workers doing the same exact job.

In *Meritor Savings Bank v. Vinson* (1986), the Court ruled that sexual harassment in the workplace could be considered a violation of the Civil Rights Act of 1964. Michelle Vinson had first been hired at Meritor Savings Bank in 1974. By 1978, she had been promoted to Assistant Branch Manager. When she took an extended sick leave in the fall of 1978, she was fired. She filed a lawsuit, claiming that for more than two years she had been sexually harassed in the workplace by her supervisor, a vice president named Sidney Taylor.

After much contradictory testimony from both sides, the District Court found that if there was a romantic relationship between the two, it had been voluntary, and had nothing to do with Vinson's continued employment at the bank. Therefore, her rights had not been violated. Vinson appealed, and the Court of Appeals reversed the lower court's decision, saying that Vinson had been harassed, that sexual harassment created a hostile work environment, and that qualified as a violation of Title VII of the Civil Rights Act.

The bank took the case to the U.S. Supreme Court. The bank claimed that Title VII of the Civil Rights Act prohibited discrimination in the workplace only when it resulted in economic loss to the worker, and had nothing to do with preventing psychological damage or a hostile work environment. The Supreme Court disagreed, stating that Congress intended "to strike at the entire spectrum of disparate [unequal] treatment of men and women" in employment, and ruled in favor of Vinson.

Women continue to break down the barriers that have kept them from exercising rights guaranteed them by the Constitution. In an important case called *United States v. Virginia* (1996), the Supreme Court ruled that the government-funded, all-male Virginia Military Institute (a training school for military cadets) was in violation of women's equal protection rights because it did not allow women to be admitted.

Over the years, the American Civil Liberties Union has submitted briefs and argued in many women's rights and civil rights cases (as it has in cases pertaining to free speech and other important issues). Civil rights cases, whether for minorities, gays, or women, continue to come before the Supreme Court often because there are still many inequalities to be challenged.

RIGHT TO PRIVACY
Roe v. Wade (1973)

Civil rights cases have revolved around not only questions of discrimination, but also around the right to personal privacy. The most notorious such case is undoubtedly *Roe v. Wade*.

Jane Roe (aka Norma McCorvey) was a single woman living in Texas. She already had a young child who was in the care of her mother. She became pregnant again and wished to terminate her pregnancy. However, abortion was illegal in Texas at the time, except when the life of the mother was in danger. Through her lawyer, she claimed that her right of personal privacy (through the First, Fourth, Fifth, Ninth, and Fourteenth Amendments) had been violated by the Texas law. She claimed it was her right to have a safe abortion performed by competent medical staff. Her case reached the Supreme Court as *Roe v. Wade*.

A Texas physician named James Hallford joined Roe in the suit. Hallford had been arrested before for performing abortions and at the time had two prosecutions pending against him. It did not matter that Roe was no longer pregnant once the suit reached the Supreme Court. The opinion noted that the normal nine-month gestation period for a baby was too short for the usual appellate period of a case. It should not exclude any pregnancy case from ever reaching the Supreme Court.

Though the ancient Greek Hippocratic Oath included a line that said, "I will not give a woman an abortive remedy," the Court pointed out that abortion before the "quickening" (when the baby can be felt moving) was not always considered criminal. Clinical abortion procedures had also become safer over the years, with proper care. On the other hand, illegal, back-alley abortions were still dangerous and had high mortality rates.

So what exactly was this "privacy" that Roe claimed protected her right to an abortion? "The Constitution does not explicitly mention any right of privacy. In a line of decisions, however . . . the Court has rec-

ognized that a right of personal privacy, or a guarantee of certain areas or zones of privacy, does exist under the Constitution."

The Court agreed that the right of privacy should include a woman's decision to continue or terminate her pregnancy. In a controversial explanation of the Court's position, Justice Harry A. Blackmun continued, "Maternity, or additional offspring, may force upon the woman a distressful life and future. Psychological harm may be imminent. Mental and physical health may be taxed by an unwanted child."

The state of Texas argued that life began at conception and that the fetus was a person and should be protected. "If this suggestion of personhood is established, the appellant's case, of course, collapses, for the fetus's right to life would then be guaranteed specifically by the Amendment." However, the Court found no legal precedent that gave such status to a fetus. Instead, it found that unborn children "have never been recognized in the law as persons in the whole sense."

The Court acknowledged that Texas had "one theory of life," but that did not mean it could override a woman's right to an abortion. Still, there were limits to when the abortion could be performed. The Court reasoned that although a state could not interfere with a woman's right to terminate her pregnancy if she desired, it did have an interest in protecting the mother's health and the potential of human life. The Court felt that once the fetus was mature enough to

Pro-choice protesters at the 1976 Democratic National Convention.

be able to survive on its own, it must be protected. Thus the Court ruled that during the first three months of pregnancy, abortion could be decided upon by a woman and her doctor. After that, the state could regulate abortions. After the fetus became viable, the state could prohibit abortion except when the mother's life was in danger.

Justice William H. Rehnquist, in his dissent, argued that the "right to an abortion is not so universally accepted as the appellant would have us believe."

Some Supreme Court decisions have little influence on the average person's life, but the effect of *Roe v. Wade* on Americans was profound. It opened the doors for legalized abortion and polarized the nation. *Roe v. Wade* was perhaps the most divisive Supreme Court decision of the 20th century.

The issue of a woman's right to choose, her right to control her own body, has clashed with the idea of the sanctity of life and with the way we define what life is and when it begins. Many people on the pro-choice side also argue that the issue is one of public health and safety. After *Roe v. Wade*, women could get safe medical treatment and avoid back-alley procedures and even death. There are few people who have no opinion on the subject. Many have extreme opinions. There are numerous groups in favor of abortion rights and many groups against abortion rights. Protests and even violence have been part of the painful national debate on this difficult subject.

Since the appointment of conservative Reagan and Bush Justices, anti-abortion supporters have been waiting for legalized abortion to be overturned. Perhaps more so than any other landmark case that has confronted the Supreme Court, *Roe v. Wade* has a chance of being overturned depending on the makeup of the Court in coming years. If it is overturned, then it will once again be up to the individual states to decide whether to make performing an abortion a criminal act.

Justice William Rehnquist, who dissented in *Roe v. Wade* (1973), in 1976.

Q: *How did it feel to become the center of attention on this difficult issue the first time, back in the 1970s?*

McCorvey: It was hard in many ways. I never felt that I was accepted by the pro-abortion side. They simply needed someone to use as a pawn to advance abortion in the courts. I was the guinea pig.

Q: *You have come out against the very decision you have come to stand for. How has your life changed since you became a vocal pro-life supporter? How important is it for people to speak out on their beliefs?*

McCorvey: My life has been changed so much since I worked in the abortion clinics. I saw the crying women, the baby parts, the pain. I am glad I gave my life to Jesus and He has forgiven me for my role though I was used in legalizing abortion. We must also seek the truth.

Q: *Do you think that Roe v. Wade will be reversed one day soon? What steps are you taking to make that happen?*

McCorvey: Yes, I am speaking out around the world. Now women who have had abortions are beginning to tell the world abortion hurts women. You can't kill your own child and not suffer.

Mario Cuomo

Mario Cuomo was the Governor of New York from 1983 to 1995. He rose to national prominence at the 1984 Democratic National Convention. He is the author of several books, including *Why Lincoln Matters*.

Q: *At a speech during the 1984 Democratic National Convention, you said, "The nation must think of this— what kind of Supreme Court will we have [if Reagan is elected]?" In retrospect, how have the Reagan and Bush appointees performed?*

Cuomo: I think the Supreme Court should be left to do the judicial work of the country and should assiduously avoid becoming simply an expression of the political governance of the country. There's a big difference between political judgments and judicial judgments, and the design of the founding fathers brilliantly separated them. What happened especially in the Reagan and Bush years, and has happened with some Democratic administrations as well (the Roosevelt administration comes to mind), is the political side tries desperately hard to use the judicial side to do the work it can't get done politically. And so the judges are converted into politicians who instead of waiting for a set of facts to be developed on a trial and to be reviewed by intermediate courts, and then limiting themselves to the facts that are in that case, and to the rules of law, make judgments in advance, whether it's on abortion or other subjects, deciding that *Roe v. Wade* is good or is bad in advance because they're asked to. So that has been distinctly the characteristic, I believe, more of the Reagan/Bush bench, than of benches before it.

Q: *Do you think* Roe v. Wade *will be reversed anytime soon?*

Cuomo: I think despite the fact that there has been a heavy attempt at politicization of the Court, probably, the political judgment by judges will be not to overturn *Roe v. Wade,* because it leaves you in a more difficult political position. If you don't have *Roe v. Wade,* the case gets decided by 50 [state] courts, all of them arriving at their own conclusions. Considering that our President [George W. Bush] said recently there should be a constitutional amendment on the subject of same-sex marriage, if he's going to be consistent, then President Bush would have to say now that we shouldn't overturn *Roe v. Wade* until we have a constitutional amendment that's going to give

us a federal position. Because if you take down *Roe v. Wade,* you have no federal position, and it'll be reduced to 50 states. So I think politically, ironically, it will work out so there is an avoidance of having to overrule *Roe v. Wade* despite what Republicans and conservatives may be suggesting to the voters.

Q: *Is it true that you were once considered as a possible nominee for Supreme Court Justice?*

Cuomo: Actually, it's true that I was twice considered, or at least two times it appeared that the President [Bill Clinton] was willing to offer my name.

Q: *Have you argued any cases before the Supreme Court?*

Cuomo: No. As a very young man I was in the Supreme Court a number of times, and in some cases, like *Goldblatt v. the Town of Hempstead* [1962] and in a couple of cases, I wrote the briefs, wrote the briefs in their entirety in every court that preceded the Supreme Court, and then in the Supreme Court I attended the arguments, but I was an associate in a firm, not yet a partner, and I did not have the opportunity to argue the cases.

GAY RIGHTS

Toward the end of the 20th century, cases about gay rights and discrimination against homosexuals began to appear in the Supreme Court. In a case called *Romer v. Evans* (1996), the Court struck down an amendment to Colorado's state constitution because it prevented lawmakers from protecting gays against discrimination. As some politicians push for a constitutional amendment defining marriage as a bond between two people of the opposite sex only, gay rights cases will likely continue to appear before the Court in the near future.

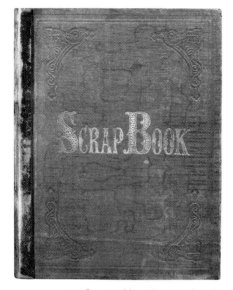

Rufus Peckham's scrapbook.

A Justice's Scrapbook

Often, a Supreme Court Justice's personality is best seen through the opinions he or she writes while on the bench, and through the way he or she votes. Rufus W. Peckham (1838–1909) served as an Associate Justice from 1896 to 1909. He wrote the opinion of the Court in the famous *Lochner v. New York* (1905) case and was also on the bench when *Plessy v. Ferguson* was decided. He was born to a father who was a District Attorney, and he practiced law in Albany, New York, before becoming a District Attorney himself in 1872. He next served on the New York Supreme Court, then the New York Court of Appeals. His older brother Wheeler was nominated to the Supreme Court by President Grover Cleveland, but the nomination was rejected for political reasons. When another seat on the Court opened up in 1895, Cleveland nominated Rufus.

As a young lawyer, Peckham assembled a personal scrapbook. It contains more than 100 pages of newspaper clippings dating from 1863 to 1870. Most of the articles Peckham cut and pasted into the book deal with the politics of the day, including the impeachment of President Andrew Johnson, the Civil War, and subsequent reconstruction.

Peckham's scrapbook contains several clippings that provide insight into the issue of civil rights. One clipping features a letter written by President Abraham Lincoln dated April 4, 1864: "I am naturally anti-slavery. If slavery is not wrong, nothing is wrong." Another is an article about President Johnson speaking with a delegation of representatives from South Carolina in June 1865: "The slaves went into the war as slaves and came out free men of color . . . the loyal men who were compelled to bow and submit to rebellion, should, now that the rebellion is ended, stand equal to loyal men everywhere."

Finally, there is a letter from an African American received by Peckham a week after the Fifteenth Amendment to the Constitution passed. The man, named William Johnson, asked District Attorney Peckham if it was true that blacks could now vote. Peckham replied that it was, and that "colored persons have the same right to vote that any other citizens have, and that it is the duty of inspectors of election to register the names of all such persons, as voters, who are otherwise qualified to vote . . ."

CRIMINAL JUSTICE AND THE RIGHT TO PRIVACY

*I*n colonial times, Americans endured invasive searches by British officials. Once the colonies gained their freedom from Britain, they made sure to include language about unreasonable search and seizure in the **Bill of Rights** (the first 10 Amendments to the Constitution). Other related rights guaranteed by the Amendments include the right not to testify about a crime of which you have been accused, to not be tried twice for the same offense, and the right to a "speedy and public" trial. If convicted, you also have protection against "cruel and unusual punishment."

Because they are expressed in general terms in the Constitution, the interpretation of the actual words has been subject to change over the years. Each situation is unique, and the Supreme Court must ultimately decide the outcome. The first major test of criminal justice issues came in a time of great turbulence.

On September 24, 1862, in the midst of the Civil War, President Abraham Lincoln issued a proclamation that said all rebels or anyone who discouraged enlistment, resisted drafts, or helped rebels would be subject to martial law and liable to trial and punishment by the military. The proclamation also suspended the **writ of *habeas corpus*** (*habeas corpus* is Latin for "you have/hold the body"), which meant people could be arrested arbitrarily, without showing definite cause or reason. The Constitution allowed this suspension "in Cases of Rebellion or Invasion."

Lincoln believed this was a necessity in order to swiftly and firmly deal with any traitors. With the chaos of a Civil War, the enemy was always close at hand. There was no time to send suspected traitors through the regular justice system. Such persons would be better off separated from society in special prisons, Lincoln felt. As Senator Stephen Douglas said when the war started, "There can be no neutrals in this war, only patriots or traitors."

Lamdin P. Milligan was arrested in 1864 by order of the military commandant of the District of Indiana and was taken to a military prison in Indianapolis. He was charged with several serious crimes, including joining a secret society whose purpose was to overthrow the government of the United States; communicating with the enemy; conspiring to seize munitions of war stored in the arsenals; conspiring to free prisoners of war; and resisting the draft. Milligan objected to the authority of the military to try him, but his objection was overruled. The military court found him guilty as charged and sentenced him to death. In May 1865, a week before he was scheduled to die, Milligan filed an appeal with the Circuit Court. The Circuit Court's opinion was split, and the case went to the Supreme Court.

The Justices in ***Ex Parte Milligan*** (1866) believed that there was no need for the defendant to have been tried in a military court. Indiana had been a loyal state during the Civil War, and there had been no question of its patriotism. The regular court system was not in jeopardy, so there was no good reason to hold a military trial: "Why was he not delivered to the Circuit Court of Indiana to be proceeded against according to law?"

The Court did recognize the need for exceptions, but also recognized that there was no need in this case for the writ of *habeus corpus* to be suspended in the peaceful state of Indiana, where the court system was not in upheaval due to the war. Chief Justice Salmon P. Chase wrote: "But whatever his . . . punishment may be, it is more important to the country and to every citizen that he should not be punished under an illegal sentence, sanctioned by this court of last resort, than that he should be punished at all" by "unauthorized though merited justice." The Court overruled the government's treatment of Milligan, showing its willingness to become involved in matters of criminal justice.

THE WIRE TAP CASE
Olmstead v. United States (1928)

During the mid-1920s, more than 70 people in Washington state were indicted for violating the National Prohibition Act by unlawfully possessing, transporting, and selling intoxicating liquors. Seventy-two others in addition to the petitioners were indicted. Some were not apprehended, some were acquitted, and others pleaded guilty. Roy Olmstead was the leader of the alcohol smuggling ring, which had offices in Seattle. The main office had three telephone lines.

Some of the men also used phones in their homes to conduct company business. The telephones were used to receive orders and organize the filling of those orders. When the government found out about this operation, it decided to catch Olmstead and his associates red-handed. Federal prohibition officers inserted wire taps along the telephone wires near the residences of four of the suspects and also in the basement of the office building.

Federal agents transcribed many hours of conversations over the course of several months. Taken together, those conversations provided damning evidence of the illegal transactions and activities of Olmstead's business and proved sufficient to convict him in District Court. The case was appealed to the Supreme Court as *Olmstead v. United States.*

Olmstead claimed his Fourth Amendment rights protecting against unreasonable search and seizure had been violated. He also claimed that his Fifth Amendment rights not to be a witness against himself had been violated by the wire taps. The government argued that the taps were conducted without entering the defendants' homes or offices, so the evidence should be admissible. The Court felt that the search and seizure referred to in the Fourth Amendment meant material things, not intangible things such as telephone conversations.

Chief Justice William Howard Taft wrote for the majority:

The Amendment does not forbid what was done here. There was no searching. There was no seizure. The evidence was secured by the use of the sense of hearing, and that only. There was no entry of the houses or offices of the defendants . . . The language of the Amendment cannot be extended and expanded to include telephone wires reaching to the whole world from the defendant's house or office.

SEARCH AND SEIZURE

The things you do in the privacy of your own home are nobody's business, right? Suppose a police officer comes to your door wanting to search your home because someone with the same hair color as you was seen committing a crime the night before?

Fortunately for you, the U.S. Constitution protects against illegal search and seizure, and the Supreme Court affirmed this right in two key cases, *Weeks v. United States* (1914) and *Mapp v. Ohio* (1961).

Weeks v. United States (1914)

In December 1911, while Fremont Weeks was at work, federal agents entered and searched his home in Kansas City, Missouri, without a search warrant. A neighbor had told them where Weeks kept the key. Once inside, the agents seized books, letters, money, papers, stocks, insurance policies, and other papers.

William Howard Taft as a presidential candidate in 1908.

Among these items was evidence that Weeks had illegally sold lottery tickets. In addition to the federal agents, the local police also searched Weeks's home and seized other items. The seized items were used in his trial, despite Weeks's pleas that his Fourth Amendment rights were being violated.

The Supreme Court, in a decision written by Justice William Rufus Day, said that the federal agents who had entered his home had indeed violated his rights, but what was seized by the local police was not covered under the Fourth Amendment: "As to the papers and property seized by the policemen, it does not appear that they acted under any claim of federal authority such as would make the amendment applicable to such unauthorized seizures."

The right against search and seizure by federal employees had been affirmed, but it would be 50 years before protection against searches by local police was ensured.

Mapp v. Ohio (1961)

When the police knocked on the door of Dollree Mapp's Cleveland, Ohio, home on May 23, 1957, they were looking for a bombing suspect that they believed was lodged in Mapp's home. Before she did anything else, she called her lawyer, and on his advice she did not let the officers inside. There was a tense standoff for a few hours, and then additional police officers arrived. The police forcibly entered her house and produced what they claimed was a warrant. Mapp took it from them and looked at it before they wrested it back from her. Mapp was not cooperative, and the po-

lice handcuffed her. Upon searching her home, the police found the suspect they were looking for. While searching, they opened drawers, closets, and other storage areas and found books that they claimed were obscene and illegal according to an Ohio law.

Mapp was arrested and brought to trial. The police could not produce the warrant they had allegedly showed Mapp, but she was convicted anyway and sentenced to serve one to seven years in prison. She and her lawyers appealed the case to the Ohio State Supreme Court, claiming her Fourth Amendment rights had been violated. The State Court said that the material was admissible because it was not forcibly seized from Mapp's person. The next stop was the U.S. Supreme Court in 1960, where the Justices examined the legal precedents for the case, which was called *Mapp v. Ohio.*

In an earlier case, *Weeks v. United States* (1914), the Court had ruled that federal cases could not be advanced based on unreasonable searches and seizures. In a later case, *Wolf v. Colorado* (1949), the Court had ruled that a state conviction could take place based on whatever rules the state decided to apply. By 1961, many states had applied the *Weeks* standards to their own legal systems, but there was no rule forcing all the states to abide by the unreasonable search and seizure rules.

In the *Mapp* ruling, Justice Tom Campbell Clark wrote:

Presently, a federal prosecutor may make no use of evidence illegally seized, but a State's attorney across the street may, although he supposedly is operating under

Police arrest a man during a protest in 1945.

the enforceable prohibitions of the same Amendment. Thus the State, by admitting evidence unlawfully seized, serves to encourage disobedience to the Federal Constitution which it is bound to uphold.

Justice Clark went on to say that a different set of standards between federal and state courts did cause a conflict in another case, *Wilson v. Schnettler* (1961), where a federal officer was allowed to testify in a state court about evidence he had unconstitutionally seized. As a federal officer, he should have been bound by federal rules based on the *Weeks* decision, but because he was in a state court, his evidence was admissible, because states were not bound by the *Weeks* decision.

In closing, Justice Clark wrote: "Our decision, founded on reason and truth, gives to the individual no more than that which the Constitution guarantees him, to the police officer no less than that to which honest law enforcement is entitled, and, to the courts, that judicial integrity so necessary in the true administration of justice."

In his dissent, Justice John Marshall Harlan claimed that the Court had overreached in its decision to overturn *Wolf.* The more direct issue at hand in the case, he argued, dealt with the Ohio law regarding the "mere knowing possession or control of obscene material," and whether or not it violated the Fourteenth Amendment. He also argued that the fact that half the states used the exclusionary rule while half did not just showed how debatable the whole issue is and how unfair it is to impose the federal standard upon the states.

SEARCH AND SEIZE

IN *Mapp v. Ohio* (1961), the Supreme Court decided that states must abide by the Fourth Amendment search and seizure rules. Knowing your rights where search and seizure is concerned is important, as is keeping track of exactly what occurs during such a search.

YOU'LL NEED

✔ 2 friends
✔ A "warrant" (a piece of 8½" × 11" paper that says "Warrant to search Smith's house and property for a stolen dog named Sam")
✔ Notebook
✔ Pencil
✔ Desk with drawers (preferably your own)
✔ 1 quarter

Place a quarter in one of the drawers, out of plain sight. Have your friends carry the warrant.

Instructions for you: You are Smith, the homeowner. The police suspect that a stolen dog is in your possession. When they come to you, tell them you have no dogs. Use your notebook to keep track of what places the "police" search in your home.

Instructions for your friends: You will play the police. You have come to this house with a search warrant to look for a stolen dog that was reported to be in the homeowner's possession. Knock on the door and show the warrant. Walk around the house, calling the dog's name. Go to the desk and search it until you the find the coin. Tell the homeowner that the coin was very rare and was the same as one that had been reported stolen from the local coin shop the week before. Place the homeowner under arrest.

Smith: What argument can you make against their seizure of the stolen coin? HINT: *What places should the police look if they want to find a missing dog?*

Police: What argument can you make for the seizure of the stolen coin? HINT: *Besides the dog itself, what other evidence could you be looking for relating to the stolen dog?*

There are some people who feel that the exclusionary rule allows criminals to go free. Justice Benjamin Nathan Cardozo once said that the criminal could go free just because the police made a procedural mistake.

The effects of *Mapp v. Ohio* have been far reaching. Search and seizure must be conducted lawfully. The right to privacy is a fundamental right that cannot be invaded without due cause.

Dollree Mapp (*Mapp v. Ohio*, 1961)

In 1957, Dollree Mapp's life took an unexpected turn when she was arrested. Police had searched her house without a proper warrant and found what they claimed were illegal materials. Her case became a landmark when the ruling was issued in June 1961.

Q: *Is that day in 1957 still clear in your mind? It must have been frightening.*

Mapp: Of course. How could I forget it? It wasn't frightening until it was all over. It wasn't a shock, but it was a surprise that they would take the steps that they took. They felt that they were right in what they were doing.

Q: *What did police show you when they finally entered your house?*

Mapp: It was not a warrant. It was a piece of paper with my name on it. I grabbed it and put it in my bosom.

Q: *How were you able to think clearly enough to call your lawyer?*

Mapp: Because I knew that they were wrong, and I just stopped and called him. I called Mr. Kearns [Mapp's lawyer] and I knew that they were wrong. There were about four of them; I knew that I was outnumbered. It was an experience that I don't wish on any person. I imagine to some women, it would be a very upsetting sight. I wasn't excited, I was just angry, I guess, because I thought it was an intrusion. And it was.

Q: *Was it your idea to appeal and keep appealing until you got the Supreme Court?*

Mapp: It was everybody's idea. I said let's go as far as we can go. I didn't know anything about the courts. I kept saying, let's go to the next one. How many? Let's go! It was my idea and they agreed.

Q: *Do you remember when the decision was announced? What did you feel when you heard?*

Mapp: I felt relieved. As a matter of fact, he [the lawyer Walter Greene] called me from his office . . . I was greatly relieved. I was happy. Then the reporters started coming, and I didn't want anything to do with them . . . I just relaxed. I didn't want to go to prison. I was out on bail. When I realized it was over, it was a tremendous relief.

You Have the Right to an Attorney
Gideon v. Wainwright (1963)

Imagine being arrested and trying to defend yourself in court. The judge and the lawyers for the prosecution are all legal experts who went to law school and have been in court many times before. They know all the terms and procedures, all the loopholes and tricks of the trade. When it comes time to defend yourself, how can you compete with these professionals? Yet if you don't, you could wind up in prison.

If it sounds frightening, just think that at one time only people who were accused of murder would be provided a lawyer if they could not afford one; other alleged criminals were not given that privilege. In *Betts v. Brady* (1942), the Court had decided that the right to a lawyer did not apply to state courts. The case came about when a man named Smith Betts was arrested for robbery. When he asked in court to be appointed a lawyer free of charge, his request was denied. He went ahead and represented himself at the trial and was convicted. He appealed the decision, claiming it was a violation of his Fourteenth Amendment right to due process. The Supreme Court refused to overturn his conviction, concluding that the right to counsel was not essential.

For 20 years the decision stood, and poor people around the country were denied the right to a lawyer if they could not afford one. Then 50-year-old Clarence Gideon was arrested for breaking into a pool hall in Florida and brought to trial in 1962. Gideon was poor and could not afford a lawyer. He asked the court to appoint him one. In response to his request, Judge Robert McCrary told him:

"Mr. Gideon, I am sorry, but I cannot appoint Counsel to represent you in this case. Under the laws of the State of Florida, the only time the Court can appoint Counsel to represent a Defendant is when that person is charged with a capital offense. I am sorry, but I will have to deny your request to appoint Counsel to defend you in this case."

Denied the right to an attorney, Gideon had no choice. He proceeded to defend himself at his trial. He seemed to do an OK job for someone with no experience, but when it was all over, he was indeed found guilty and sentenced to five years in prison. After he got to prison, he had time to think about his situation. He decided to write a letter to the U.S. Supreme Court explaining his predicament. Because he had studied the law while in prison, Gideon actually filed the correct paperwork for his case to be heard. The Justices agreed that the time was right to revisit the *Betts* decision.

The Justices looked back to previous cases and found that the Court had actually gone backward with the *Betts* ruling. In a case called *Powell v. Alabama* (1936), the decision had clearly stated the dangers of self-representation. The *Powell* decision was cited by the *Gideon* Justices in their own ruling:

Even the intelligent and educated layman has small and sometimes no skill in the science of law . . . He is unfamiliar with the rules of evidence. Left without the aid of counsel he may be put on trial without a

Justice Hugo Lafayette Black.

proper charge, and convicted upon incompetent evidence, or evidence irrelevant to the issue or otherwise inadmissible. He lacks both the skill and knowledge adequately to prepare his defense, even though he have a perfect one. He requires the guiding hand of counsel at every step in the proceedings against him. Without it, though he be not guilty, he faces the danger of conviction because he does not know how to establish his innocence.

In their review of the *Gideon* case, the Justices also noted that numerous states had taken the time to file *amicus* briefs to say that they agreed that *Betts* should be overturned and Gideon should go free. The decision by the Court was unanimous. Gideon should be released and *Betts* should be reversed.

In his concluding remarks, Justice Hugo Lafayette Black described how the prosecution valued lawyers as a way to show the need for defendants to have lawyers as well:

Governments . . . quite properly spend vast sums of money to establish machinery to try defendants accused of crime. Lawyers to prosecute are everywhere deemed essential to protect the public's interest in an orderly society. Similarly, there are few defendants charged with crime, few indeed, who fail to hire the best lawyers they can get to prepare and present their defenses . . . lawyers in criminal courts are necessities, not luxuries.

INTERVIEW | **Walter Mondale**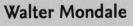

Walter F. Mondale became the Attorney General of Minnesota in 1960. In that position, he filed an *amicus* brief for Minnesota in *Gideon v. Wainwright* (1963). Mondale was appointed in 1964 to a vacant U.S. Senate seat. He was elected in 1966 and reelected in 1972. In 1976, he was elected Vice President of the United States. He was the Democratic nominee for President of the United States in 1984, losing to Ronald Reagan.

Q: How did you get involved with organizing the amicus brief for Gideon v. Wainwright?

Mondale: I was a young, new Attorney General of Minnesota. I got a call from the Massachusetts Attorney General Eddie McCormack and almost at the same time a call from a friend of mine who was a professor of law, asking if I would help prepare and join in an *amicus* brief to take Gideon's side in the case involving the right of an indigent person to an attorney. I agreed with that. Minnesota had a law for many years providing that. Twenty-three states joined in the brief. I was told the Supreme Court was very impressed by that.

Q: *Does a good* amicus *brief have a real effect on the Court's decision?*

Mondale: It can. It is not the same as a direct brief by the litigants. If it's a strong brief, that helps. In this case, the Supreme Court would have to ask themselves, is this an impediment? Here comes along 23 states on the front lines telling the Court this [providing a lawyer to those who cannot afford one] not only works, but it's the right thing to do.

Q: *Even today you are still interested in this issue, serving as Honorary Chair of the National Committee on the Right to Counsel. Is this still a persistent problem in our criminal justice system today?*

Mondale: It is. I'm told there are a lot of questions about quality of counsel. A lot of times lawyers are incompetent, or just asleep. I'm not saying this happens all the time, but it happens. Question of competency becomes a key question. I'm glad to see the President [George W. Bush] support more DNA testing, new evidence that wasn't around before. It can prove that someone who is in the slammer shouldn't be there. A lot of legal defense funds are out of money.

Q: *Is the Supreme Court today more or less protective of citizens' rights than it was in the days of* Gideon?

Mondale: My guess is that the current Court, by a slim margin, would strongly support the principles of the *Gideon* case. But maybe all the Justices would vote for it. I think that the Court in *Gideon*, with Earl Warren and Thurgood Marshall, had a lot of great progressive judges. The case was a unique high point in American history.

Q: *What are some of the challenges the Supreme Court will face in the future?*

Mondale: Cultural issues such as the treatment of gays and political issues such as the congressional redistricting effort. Some states are harshly redistricting. The Court might get their hands on that. I hope they do. There are also some issues about voter access, such as Ohio [in the 2004 presidential election]. When you have voter lines that go 10 hours long, something is wrong. We always ought to be updating our alert list. We should be looking at states that purge voting lists and will not allow a felon who has paid his debt to society to vote. Privacy issues will also be important in the 21st century.

The Issue of Handwriting

Say you are accused of writing a false document, and you claim you did not write it. Can a piece of paper with your handwriting on it be seized from your home and used against you as evidence? One argument goes that handwriting is private property and that, under the Fourth Amendment, it cannot be unlawfully "seized." But in *United States v. Mara* (1973) and *United States v. Dionisio* (1973), the Supreme Court rejected that argument, ruling that handwriting is no more private than your face or voice. There is no question of illegal search and seizure when something is in plain sight. Your voice may be used against you if identified by a victim who heard you talking. You cannot refuse to speak because you consider your voice to be private. Similarly, your face might be recognized in a lineup of suspects. Police do not need a warrant to see your face. You cannot wear a mask. Your voice and face are not private; they are normally within the public view. The Court ruling said handwriting is no different and that it is not protected by the Fourth Amendment and can be used against you.

Another argument against asking for a handwriting sample relates to the Fifth Amendment, which protects people against self-incrimination. The Amendment states that "No person shall be compelled . . . in any criminal case to be a witness against himself." But in *Gilbert v. California* (1967), the Court said that handwriting was a public behavior—not something forced upon one—and not protected by the Constitution. You cannot refuse to speak because your voice might incriminate you, for example. You cannot refuse to appear in a police lineup because a tattoo on your face might incriminate you. The police would not be allowed to force you to write an incriminating statement, but they could get a simple handwriting sample.

You Have the Right to Remain Silent
Miranda v. Arizona (1966)

Once a suspect's right to have a lawyer was established in the *Gideon* case, there remained another important right for the legal system to recognize. What if suspects did not *know* they could have a lawyer? What if they did not know they could be silent when interrogated? The Fifth Amendment guarantees that nobody shall be "compelled in any criminal case to be a witness against himself." That means if people want to confess and waive their rights, they can, but otherwise can refuse to answer questions.

In March 1963, Ernesto Miranda was arrested at his home on kidnapping and rape charges. He was taken to the police station, identified by a witness, and then brought to an interrogation room. After two hours, the interrogating officers emerged from the room with a signed confession from Miranda. The confession paper included a typed statement at the top of the sheet that said the confession was made voluntarily and with "full knowledge of my legal rights, understanding any statement I make may be used against me." In fact, Miranda was never actually advised that he did not have to speak or answer questions, and that he was entitled to a lawyer.

The Arizona State Supreme Court did not believe that Miranda's constitutional rights had been violated and upheld the lower court's ruling. They also noted that Miranda had not specifically asked for counsel.

The case went to the U.S. Supreme Court, where it was combined with other similar cases as *Miranda v. Arizona.* The Court ruled in favor of Miranda. Chief Justice Earl Warren wrote in the Court's deci-sion: "In each instance, we have concluded that state-ments were obtained from the defendant under circumstances that did not meet constitutional stan-dards for protection of the [Fifth Amendment] privilege."

The Court's landmark decision helped ensure that accused criminals understood their rights. It gave law enforcement officials more reason to take extreme care when arresting a suspect. Even today, *Miranda*-related cases still arise. The familiar "You have the right to remain silent . . ." may be a cliché, but it is one cliché that we should never take for granted.

Earl Warren wrote the *Miranda* opin-ion. He is seen here in his earlier career as Governor of California.

INTERVIEW   ## Seth Waxman (part 2)

Seth Waxman was the Solicitor General of the United States under President Bill Clinton.

Q: *Were there ever times as Solicitor General (SG) when you had to argue a case you were not 100 percent behind or personally didn't feel enthusiastic about?*

Waxman: I suppose if I had allowed myself the luxury to think about that, the answer would have been yes. The So-licitor General ordinarily has a duty to defend Acts of Con-gress, and it's not really relevant whether the Solicitor General happens to think that it's a good law, or whether as a Justice he would vote to uphold it. It's quite unusual for the government to refuse to defend a law that Con-gress enacts. One such unusual occasion occurred during my tenure as SG when the United States refused to de-fend a law purporting to overrule the Supreme Court's fa-mous *Miranda* decision. That was a politically controver-sial decision at the time, but the Supreme Court agreed with me, in an opinion written by the Chief Justice for seven members of the Court *(Dickerson v. United States).*

Q: *What is one example of a decision that is controversial?*

Waxman: Just yesterday [March 1, 2005] the Court just decided a case that I argued in October [2004], *Roper v. Simmons* [2005], that is on the front page of every news-paper in the world today. The case asks whether it is con-sistent with the Eighth Amendment proscription of cruel and unusual punishment to execute defendants who are under the age of 18 when they commit first-degree murder. I was representing the convicted juvenile, and the Court agreed with me, by a 5–4 vote, that the Constitution prohibits the execution of juvenile offenders.

Q: And Justice Anthony M. Kennedy did bring up what other countries are doing in the decision?

Waxman: Yes, and that's controversial. Justice Antonin Scalia's dissent argues that it's inappropriate for the Court to take account of what other countries think, as a means of interpreting our own Constitution. Other Justices strongly disagree. This issue—the proper role of foreign law in interpreting our own laws and Constitution—is a major issue for the Supreme Court this decade.

THE RIGHTS OF THE ACCUSED TODAY

The Supreme Court continues to see cases that deal with the constitutional rights of the accused. Different variations on Fourth and Fifth Amendment issues arise, dealing with the timing and extenuating circumstances of search warrants and the reading of *Miranda* rights. A case called *Dickerson v. United States* (2000) involved a man indicted for bank robbery. Charles Dickerson wanted to strike from the record a statement he made to the FBI because he had not received his *Miranda* warning. However, Congress had enacted a law that said if a statement was voluntary, the *Miranda* warning did not matter. Dickerson filed a motion to suppress his statement, and the District Court granted the motion. The Court of Appeals reversed the ruling, declaring that his statement could be used.

The case was appealed to the Supreme Court, which was unwilling to overturn *Miranda v. Arizona*.

Chief Justice William H. Rehnquist wrote for the majority: "We hold that *Miranda,* being a constitutional decision of this Court, may not be in effect overruled by an Act of Congress, and we decline to overrule *Miranda* ourselves." Rehnquist added: "*Miranda* has become embedded in routine police practice to the point where the warnings have become part of our national culture."

VICTIM IMPACT TESTIMONY

In two cases, the Court decided that it was a violation of the defendant's Eighth Amendment rights to have a jury hear "victim impact testimony"—testimony about the emotional impact of a crime on the victim's loved ones—during the penalty phase of a trial. In *Booth v. Maryland* (1987), a man was found guilty of murdering an elderly couple. During the sentencing, the jury heard about the emotional impact of the crime on the family and about the personalities of the

ACT OUT AN ARREST

 IN THIS ACTIVITY, four kids will act out the following play script. The rest of the class (or the four kids themselves if there is no class) will follow along on their copy of the script and make notes in the margin every time the suspect's constitutional rights were violated during the course of the play (based upon what you have read in this chapter). Also make note of statements the officers make or procedures they follow that are actually correct or true.

YOU'LL NEED
✔ 4 friends
✔ Classroom of kids (optional)
✔ Chair and table
✔ Photocopies of this play script for each participant and any classmates
✔ Pen

Officer Jones: You are under arrest for the robbery of the First National Bank. Anything you do may be used against you in a court of law. (Leads Mr. Doe to the chair at the table.)

Officer Smith: Have a seat. Tell us why you robbed that bank.

Mr. Doe: I want a lawyer.

Officer Jones: He wants a lawyer.

Officer Smith: Go ahead, call your lawyer.

Mr. Doe: Hello, is Mr. Davis in? I've been arrested, and I need him to come down to the police station right away. OK. Thanks.

Officer Smith: Well?

Mr. Doe: He's on his way down here.

Officer Jones: Good. Now that you have a lawyer, you can talk to us.

Mr. Doe: I should really wait until my lawyer gets here.

Officer Smith: It's OK. You have a lawyer. Whether he's here or not, you have retained him. So you have a lawyer. Now you can talk to us.

Mr. Doe: I don't know…

Officer Jones: Just tell us why you robbed the bank. Did someone else put you up to it?

Officer Smith: You know what? We don't need his confession. We have the note that the bank robber gave the teller. (Puts a pad of paper and a pen in front of the suspect.) Here, write your name and the words "money" and "don't call police."

Officer Jones: This is what we call a handwriting sample.

Mr. Doe: It will never stand up in court. (Picks up pen and writes.)

Officer Jones: We'll see about that. (Enter lawyer.)

Lawyer: Smith, I got here as soon as I could. Now, before we get started, I need to go over my fees with you. I need $500 up front and the rest I can bill you for later.

Mr. Doe: I'm sorry, Mr. Davis. I am kind of strapped right now. I only have $100.

Lawyer: Then I'm afraid I can't help you. Sorry, but I can't give discounts. (He leaves.)

Mr. Doe: I want a court-appointed lawyer.

Officer Smith: Look, if you can't afford a lawyer, then too bad. I'm sorry for you.

Mr. Doe: There's nothing you can do for me?

Officer Jones: Listen, it's time to confess. As we speak, five officers are going through your house, looking for evidence.

Mr. Doe: But how could you have had time to get a warrant? You just arrested me 15 minutes ago.

Officer Jones: We'll have a warrant, don't worry. We should have it in our hands in an hour or so, so don't worry.

Officer Smith: Yeah, you should be worried about what kind of sentence you'll get if you cooperate versus if you don't cooperate.

Mr. Doe: What about my court-appointed lawyer?

Officer Smith: You'll have to wait until you get to trial for that, I'm afraid.

Officer Jones: Now we are going to put you in a lineup to see if a witness identifies you.

Mr. Doe: You can't do that if I object.

Officer Smith: Why not?

Mr. Doe: That invades my right to privacy. My face is private. I cannot be forced to show it and potentially incriminate myself.

Officer Jones: Enough with the smart talk, let's go. The witness is waiting.

victims. The jury opted for the death penalty. Upon appeal, the case eventually reached the Supreme Court, which voted 5–4 to overturn the death sentence. Another case, *South Carolina v. Gathers* (1989), had a similar situation and similar outcome.

Then came a case called *Payne v. Tennessee* (1991). Pervis Payne had murdered a woman and her young child and left a second child badly injured. During sentencing, the jury heard supportive testimony from Payne's family, but also heard from the surviving child's grandmother, who stated that the child missed the victims, his mother and sister. The jury voted to put Payne on death row. Payne appealed and the Tennessee Supreme Court upheld the decision. Upon appeal to the U.S. Supreme Court, 21 states filed briefs of *amicus curiae* in support of the conviction.

Payne's lawyers argued that it was unfair for defendants to be punished more severely if their victims were well loved than if they were not, and that a defendant should not be punished for something he or she could not have known when the crime was committed. The defendant also argued that the Court should adhere to the policy it set in the recent cases of *Booth* and *Gathers.* This principle of keeping to the legal precedent set in similar cases is known as **stare decisis.** This time, however, the Court decided it had previously been wrong about the issue and voted 6–3 in favor of upholding the death sentence. In the Court's opinion, Payne's Eighth Amendment rights had not been violated.

The Court considered one important factor. It was certainly not unfair for the jury to hear testimony about the impact of the crime on the victim's family and community if the jury was allowed to hear positive testimony about the character of the defendant. In the *Payne* case, Payne's parents and girlfriend testified that Payne was a good man.

THE DEATH PENALTY

The death penalty is highly controversial and is legal in some states but not in others. Only those offenders who commit the most heinous crimes are eligible, usually murder in the first degree, meaning that the murder was premeditated (planned). The way in which a person is executed must be put to the test of "cruel and unusual punishment" that is mentioned in the Eighth Amendment.

In one of the early death penalty cases, *Wilkerson v. Utah* (1878), the Supreme Court decided that execution by shooting was not cruel and unusual punishment for first-degree murder.

At any given time, there are about 3,500 inmates on death row across the country. Some of these inmates may wait many years before their execution. Appeals of their cases are among the reasons for this delay. The number of executions per year reached a peak during the 1930s.

In the case called *Furman v. Georgia* (1972), three separate death penalty cases were appealed—one for murder and two for rape. William Henry Furman was attempting to break into a house when the occupants discovered him. His gun went off and killed one of them.

In a 5–4 decision, the Court found that Georgia's standards for applying the death penalty were too arbitrary because the jury had too much discretion in sentencing, and that this was a violation of the "cruel and unusual" clause in the Eighth Amendment. In its ruling, the Court did not go so far as to say that the death penalty itself was cruel and unusual, only that the way it had been applied was unconstitutional. A one-page *per curiam* opinion was followed by 200 pages of opinions, but the majority opinion was summarized by Justice William Orville Douglas:

We deal with a system of law and of justice that leaves to the uncontrolled discretion of judges or juries the determination whether defendants committing these crimes should die or be imprisoned. Under these laws no standards govern the selection of the penalty. People live or die, dependent on the whim of one man or of 12.

As a result of the ruling, the death penalty in America was essentially put on hold, as 40 death penalty statutes across the country were rendered illegal. States had to rework their laws to provide detailed sentencing guidelines for judges and juries to follow before the death penalty would be reinstated, in the mid-1970s.

DEATH PENALTY FOR MINORS?

Though a person of practically any age can commit murder, the psychological differences between juveniles and adults are great. Minors under the age of 18 are not as emotionally mature as adults are, and they are much more vulnerable to peer pressure from their friends. To what degree should juveniles be held accountable for their actions? When it comes to applying the death penalty, there are many more questions, since the punishment is permanent and leaves no chance at reform. Should a child be punished in the same way as an adult, if a premeditated murder for a juvenile is not the same as premeditated murder for an adult? Besides that, a child might not fear or understand death the same way as an adult, so the death penalty for juveniles does not serve the same deterrent purpose that is supposed to be a part of its function for adults.

In 1989, the Court heard a case called *Stanford v. Kentucky*. This combined two cases, one in which a 17-year-old from Kentucky had been convicted of murder and sentenced to death, and another in which a 16-year-old from Missouri had been sentenced to death. In both cases, the State Supreme Courts rejected the defendants' appeals. Upon reflection, the U.S. Supreme Court found in a close 5–4 decision that the execution of those who committed capital crimes while under the age of 18 was in fact constitutional. The Attorneys General of 16 states filed *amicus* briefs in support of the juvenile death penalty. At the time of the decision, there were 37 states that allowed the death penalty. Of those states, 25 allowed the death penalty for defendants aged 17, and 22 allowed it for those as young as 16.

In the *Stanford* case, the Supreme Court rejected the argument that if someone could not yet legally drink or vote, they should not be eligible for the death penalty. The Court felt that it was basic to understand that killing was wrong, as opposed to understanding the responsibilities of voting. They also rejected the notion that public opinion should matter: "Public opinion polls, the views of interest groups, and the positions of professional associations are too uncertain a foundation for constitutional law.

"We discern neither a historical nor a modern societal consensus forbidding the imposition of capital punishment on any person who murders at 16 or 17 years of age."

In the fall of 2004, the Court revisited this sensitive issue when it heard a case called *Roper v. Simmons* (2005). The convicted murderer, Christopher Simmons, had been 17 years old when he broke into a woman's home, bound her, drove her to a bridge, and threw her over the side, killing her. Simmons was 18 years old when he was tried and sentenced to death. He appealed, claiming that the killing of juveniles was cruel and unusual punishment. His petitions for revocation of the death sentence were rejected.

Then the Supreme Court decided a case called *Atkins v. Virginia* (2002), in which it ruled that it went against the Eighth Amendment's "cruel and unusual" clause for a state to execute someone who was deemed mentally retarded. Suddenly, several years after his conviction, Simmons had a legal leg to stand on because now a new standard for execution was developing. He appealed to the Missouri Supreme Court, which agreed and set aside his death sentence. Missouri appealed to the Supreme Court. At the time, there were about 75 juvenile inmates awaiting the death penalty.

The Court ruled 5–4 in favor of Simmons, reversing *Stanford* and banning the execution of anyone whose crime was committed before they reached the age of 18. Justice Anthony M. Kennedy wrote for the majority that "evolving standards of decency" had caused the Court to reexamine the issue. He wrote: "Because the death penalty is the most severe punishment, the Eighth Amendment applies to it with special force." He noted how the United States was the only country that still applied the death penalty to juveniles. The Court's majority felt that it did not undermine our Constitution to use other countries' standards.

"When a juvenile commits a heinous crime, the State can [take away] some of the most basic liberties, but the State cannot extinguish his life and his potential to attain a mature understanding of his own humanity."

Justice Antonin Scalia, in his fiery dissent, looked with scorn at the decision of the majority. He frowned upon using other nations' justice systems as a reality check for the United States.

"It [the majority] then finds, on the flimsiest of grounds, that a national consensus which could not be perceived in our people's laws barely 15 years ago now solidly exists."

Scalia accused the Court of looking for any evidence it saw to support its views, while disregarding any other evidence to the contrary. "Today's opinion provides a perfect example of why judges are ill equipped to make the type of legislative judgments the Court insists on making here. To support its opinion . . . the Court looks to scientific and sociological studies, picking and choosing those that support its position."

Rudolph Giuliani was the mayor of New York City from 1994 to 2002. Prior to that he was the Associate District Attorney under President Ronald Reagan and Associate Deputy Attorney General under President Gerald Ford. He has argued one case before the Supreme Court.

Q: *Do you think that the Supreme Court is moving away from the rights of the accused that it granted during the 1960s, with* Miranda *and other cases?*

Giuliani: The core of those decisions have remained. They all remain today. *Miranda* still exists and the exclusionary rule still exists, even though there was a lot of debate about whether there should be such decisions, and there continues to be, particularly over the exclusionary rule, quite a bit of debate. At most what the Court has done in subsequent years is to refine them somewhat, but it hasn't changed them. The exclusionary rule is one that I always questioned more than *Miranda*. I never saw the wisdom of punishing society by letting a criminal go free for the mistakes of a police officer. If a police officer makes a mistake, I don't see the point in endangering society as a result of that, as somehow deterring future mistakes. People disagree about that, obviously that's the core of the theory, but I never was comfortable with that theory. And the Court has refined it a little with good faith exceptions and removed some of the more exaggerated interpretations. I'd say that's more what has happened since the '60s. *Gideon v. Wainwright* and *Miranda* are still the law. You still have to give counsel to the indigent, as you should, and you have to give warnings to people before a

confession, and the penalty of the exclusionary rule for the violation of the Fourth Amendment, but those decisions at some point stop being expanded and have been refined a bit. But they haven't been changed.

Q: *What traits would you look for in selecting a Supreme Court Justice?*

Giuliani: I'll tell you what I looked for in judges I appointed to a different court, to the criminal court in New York and some of the civil openings. I appointed and reappointed over 100 judges. I used to interview them, after several committees would interview them first, particularly the ones that I was appointing. The ones that I was reappointing would also go through a review. But the ones you were appointing for the first time went through a very, very intensive review. The ones I was appointing for the first time I would meet with, and I'd interview them myself. And what I was looking for was the best lawyers that I could find. People of integrity, people who had enthusiasm for wanting to be a judge, which is a difficult job, and people who would be fair and would strive to do the best that they could to decide a case based on the law. I think those are the criteria that you use in selecting a judge.

7

REGULATION OF BUSINESS

Business enterprise has long been one of the trademarks of American life. Over the years, businesses have taken an active interest in politics. They have paid close attention to who is running for election and what the candidate's record is on business-related issues such as tax breaks, labor laws, and regulation of factory emissions. They have contributed money to political fundraisers to bolster favored candidates into office. Businesses can also lobby Congress to get influential Representatives and Senators on Capitol Hill to listen to their causes and pass legislation in their favor.

In turn, the government keeps a close eye on business. When a company gets too large and buys out all the competition, it becomes a **monopoly** and is subject to government intervention. The federal government was given authority by the Commerce Clause of the Constitution to regulate interstate commerce and commerce with other countries. State and city governments also regulate business as part of their "police power" to ensure health and safety.

When business-related disputes wind up in litigation, they sometimes end up at the nation's highest court. The earliest business-related cases heard by the Supreme Court involved taxes, **patents**, and insurance. In the early 1800s, there were no huge corporations. There were prosperous merchants and large shipping firms, but nothing to the scale that we have today.

One example of a typical 19th-century business case was *Isaac R. Smith v. The State of Maryland* (1855), in which a ship owner filed suit when the State of Maryland seized his boat because he had not followed the laws regarding oyster fishing. The state law said that a ship could not use a scoop to gather oysters from the seafloor because that would prevent the growth of oysters. Only a rake was to be used for that purpose. The penalty for anyone found gathering oysters in this illegal way was the seizure of their boat. The owner of the sloop *Valant* argued that the law was unconstitutional.

Justice Benjamin Robbins Curtis delivered the ruling, in favor of Maryland. He said that the law was not intended to prevent oyster fishermen from doing their business, but to protect the oysters' habitat so that all might enjoy them.

CONTRACT INTERFERENCE
Dartmouth College v. Woodward (1819)

Among these more mundane business cases were several landmark cases, beginning with *Dartmouth College v. Woodward.* As time passed and the economy grew with the country, the business implications of Supreme Court decisions became more far-reaching.

Dartmouth College was founded in Lebanon, Connecticut, by the Reverend Eleazar Wheelock. When he received funding from generous English donors, he decided to relocate to Hanover, New Hampshire, where large tracts of land were donated for the college's expansion.

The English donors were made trustees of the school. This meant they would have some say in how their money was spent and how the school was run. The original contract or charter of the school was made between the trustees and the British royal government in 1769.

After the American Revolution, the State of New Hampshire became the contracting authority with the trustees. John Wheelock, son of the founder Eleazer, became the president of the college. There was some animosity between Wheelock and the trustees. Wheelock accused them of using college funds improperly. The trustees dismissed Wheelock and replaced him with someone else. Wheelock went to the state legislature to complain about the state of affairs at the college. Investigators were sent to examine the allegations.

Suddenly, on June 27, 1816, the state legislature of New Hampshire decided that it wanted to appoint new trustees to the college. It also decided that there should be a 25-person Board of Overseers to watch over the trustees (21 of whom were to be appointed by the Governor). The changes would basically transform the private college into a state-run university.

The extreme nature of the conversion was evident in the section of the act that said, "The president and professors of the university, before entering upon the duties of their offices, shall take the oath to support the Constitution of the United States and of this state."

On August 28, the trustees met and decided they would not accept the new rules. The state government was not happy. It went so far as to order the president, trustees, and professors of the college to comply, or face a $500 fine each.

The New Hampshire Superior Court took the case, but refused to invalidate the state legislature's act. In their view, a charter could be granted or revoked in an instant. The school did not belong to the trustees. Meanwhile, Dartmouth was in a state of chaos. The state-appointed overseers named Wheelock as president of the university, while the ousted administration and faculty of the college met secretly and held classes in homes.

Thomas Jefferson, who sided with the state of New Hampshire, wrote about the controversy in an 1816 letter:

The idea that institutions established for the use of the nation, cannot be touched nor modified . . . is most absurd . . . we . . . can make laws, and impose burdens on future generations, which they will have no right to alter; in fine that the earth belongs to the dead, and not the living.

Daniel Webster took the case for the trustees of the college, and it wound up in the U.S. Supreme Court in March 1818. Webster tried to convince the Justices that Dartmouth was a corporation, and the charter was a contract. Just because the college was useful and beneficial to the general public did not mean it should become an instrument of the state.

Also, Webster argued, according to the Constitution, "No state shall pass any . . . law impairing the obligation of contracts."

Chief Justice John Marshall wrote: "The opinion of the Court, after mature deliberation, is that this is a contract, the obligation of which cannot be impaired without violating the Constitution of the United States." The Court said that indeed the Con-

Dartmouth College, early 19th century.

stitution meant to protect certain contracts involving property.

The original charter had been reorganized to convert a private college molded by the "will of its founders" into one that was subject to the will of the government instead. The Court said that while this change may work out to the advantage of the college, it was not relevant. A change to government control was not the will of the founders and was not part of the original contract of 1769. The original contract created a system of privately selected trustees to oversee the college. This system could not constitutionally be replaced with a new system that gave the state government control. The state could not simply take control of a private entity.

The *Dartmouth* decision was very important because it set a precedent for the way the government must not interfere with certain aspects of private business. In closing, the decision noted another important feature about the Supreme Court—objectivity: "It is not for judges to listen to the voice of persuasive eloquence, or popular appeal."

No One Else Can Sail These Waters
Gibbons v. Ogden (1824)

The interpretation of the Commerce Clause has been debated in the Supreme Court over the course of several key cases during the past 200 years. The clause says that Congress regulates commerce among the states and not within the states. Several Supreme Court cases have examined the boundaries between the two.

The first major case dealing with interstate commerce was set on the waters of New York harbor in the early 19th century. Robert Fulton (an inventor) and Robert Livingston (his wealthy backer) launched the first steamship, the *Clermont,* in 1807. Sailing in the waters of New York's Hudson River, the ship made a 32-hour trip up the river to Albany to a cheering crowd.

In 1808, the State of New York granted a 30-year monopoly to Fulton and Livingston to run steamships in New York's waters. This decision was especially unpopular with others who wished to run their own version of the steamboats. If Fulton and Livingston had been granted a patent, their exclusive rights would have lasted only 14 years, and others would have been allowed to develop steamships (as long as they were not too similar to the *Clermont*). Instead, the other entrepreneurs and inventors were banned from using steamships without license or permission from Fulton and Livingston.

Colonel Aaron Ogden of New Jersey felt the monopoly was unfair and worked to get his own steamship built. The ship, called the *Sea Horse,* was run exclusively in New Jersey waters while Ogden tried to get the New York State Legislature to overturn the *Clermont* monopoly. All his best efforts were unsuccessful. Within a few years, Ogden gave in and bought a 10-year license from Fulton and Livingston to run a steamship from Elizabethtown, New Jersey, to New York City.

Then, in 1818, a man named Thomas Gibbons wanted to navigate the lower part of the Hudson River in New York State with his two steamboats, called the *Stoudinger* and the *Bellona*. Gibbons, a citizen of New Jersey, also wanted to sail between New York City and Elizabethtown, New Jersey. With the tables turned, Colonel Ogden now wanted to protect the monopoly he had paid to become a part of. Ogden got an injunction in court that ordered Gibbons to immediately stop sailing in those waters.

Gibbons felt that he had every right to operate his ships in the port. He had registered his ships as per an Act of Congress from 1793 that allowed properly licensed ships to go about the "coasting trade" and sail into ports along the coast of the United States to do their business.

The Supreme Court had to ponder several questions in *Gibbons v. Ogden.* Could a state grant a monopoly of trade? Could New York close her ports to everyone except her own citizens? Could New York refuse admission to ships of particular nations? If New York could regulate its harbor, couldn't Virginia regulate the Chesapeake Bay? Wouldn't a monopoly of navigation be equal to a monopoly of trade?

Daniel Webster (who had won the *Dartmouth* case), arguing for Gibbons, said that if the New York grant of exclusive rights was inconsistent with any constitutional power of Congress, then the grant was void because the laws of Congress were supreme to the laws of a state. But the Court noted that the power to regulate commerce was a "concurrent power." That meant both the federal government and the state government could exercise it. One example of this idea of concurrent power is taxes—both federal and state governments can tax the citizens.

Chief Justice John Marshall felt that in this case, the concurrent powers were in conflict. He maintained that, therefore, the federal power had to take precedence over the state power. The Supreme Court decided that the Congress did in fact have the exclusive power to regulate commerce on waterways throughout the United States, and that no monopoly could be given to any one person or group by states. The grant of New York State to Fulton and Livingston was in opposition to the Act of Congress that authorized vessels for coastal trade, and therefore the

Robert Fulton's *Clermont,* still seaworthy in the late 19th century.

New York grant was illegal. Aaron Ogden had been right in the first place, but now found himself on the losing side of the argument.

The waters were thus opened up, and the steamboat industry exploded in ports and along rivers from the East Coast all the way to the Mississippi River.

Community Rights

Charles River Bridge v. Warren Bridge (1837)

Harvard, one of North America's first colleges, had been granted the right to operate a ferry from Charlestown to Boston, Massachusetts, in 1650. The ferry operated successfully for many years. But by the late 18th century, many people felt that a bridge would be a more efficient means of crossing the river. In 1785, the Massachusetts legislature incorporated a company, called the Charles River Bridge Company, specifically to build a bridge over the Charles River. The company was allowed to collect tolls on the bridge for 70 years, each year paying a sum of money to Harvard College. After 70 years, the bridge would become the property of Massachusetts. The bridge was built in 1786, and everything went smoothly until 1828, when the Massachusetts legislature decided to add another bridge across the river.

The newly created Warren Bridge Company would be allowed to collect tolls for no more than six years, after which passage over the bridge would become free. The owners of the Charles River Bridge Company knew all their paying customers would be lost at that point. The value of the franchise granted to the Charles River Bridge Company that was supposed to last until 1855 vanished.

The Charles River Bridge Company filed suit in the Massachusetts Supreme Court to prevent the state from building the new bridge. When that did not work, the owners filed for monetary damages. They believed that the obligations of their contract had been violated. The Massachusetts Supreme Court dismissed their claim, and the suit wound up in the U.S. Supreme Court.

The great orator Daniel Webster argued for the Charles River Bridge Company. Chief Justice Roger B. Taney, who had recently succeeded Chief Justice John Marshall, wrote the decision for the majority. He pointed out that though there may have been exclusive rights for Harvard to operate a ferry, there was no longer any ferry. Those rights had vanished when the bridge was constructed. "The exclusive privileges, if they had such, must follow the fate of the ferry, and can have no legal existence without it," he wrote.

Taney explained that the ferry and the bridge were each established by separate grants. There was no connection between the privileges of one and the privileges of the other. The bridge charter had to be interpreted on its own merit, without any consideration of the 1650 charter.

The state could not be restricted in its ability to promote the health and happiness of its citizens for 70 years. The United States was "free, active and enterprising, continually advancing in numbers and wealth," and in such a situation "new channels of communication are daily found necessary, both for

Daniel Webster was one of the greatest attorneys of the 19th century.

Chief Justice Roger B. Taney's first major case was *Charles River Bridge v. Warren Bridge* (1837).

travel and trade, and are essential to the comfort, convenience and prosperity of the people."

Under these circumstances, the government would be shirking its duties to assign control of a river crossing to one company for a period of 70 years. "While the rights of private property are sacredly guarded, we must not forget that the community also have rights, and that the happiness and wellbeing of every citizen depends on their faithful preservation."

There were no exclusive privileges granted with the 1785 charter, only to build and operate one bridge for a 70-year period. Whatever else happened around the bridge, however else the city changed, was immaterial to the charter. Turnpike roads had been built and rebuilt, and railroads replaced turnpike roads. In none of those circumstances should any company have thought it had exclusive rights or was entitled to damages because improvements were being made.

Taney worried that if the Court decided in favor of the Charles River Bridge Company, it would take the country back to the technology of the 18th century. All the old and defunct turnpike companies would rise from the dead and bring their claims to court.

Not all the Justices were in agreement. Three dissented, including Justice Joseph Story, who wrote to his wife: "Mr. Greenleaf [the Warren Bridge lawyer] has gained the cause, and I am sorry for it. A case of grosser injustice, more oppressive legislation, never existed. I feel humiliated, as I think everyone here is, by the Act which has now been confirmed." In a letter to Justice John McLean written in May 1837, Story wrote that given the way the Court's views had shifted of late, he feared that no federal or state laws would ever be declared unconstitutional. He was so disgusted he wanted to resign from the Supreme Court, but his friends intervened to prevent him from doing so.

STATE-SPONSORED BUSINESS
Slaughterhouse Cases (1873)

Where business interests and public health and safety collide, the state may have to use its "police powers." On March 8, 1869, the Louisiana Legislature passed a law that stated that starting June 1, 1869, it would be illegal to keep or slaughter any livestock or to have stockyards or slaughterhouses anywhere in the city of New Orleans or its immediate vicinity. There was one seemingly unfair exception to that rule—the Crescent City Stock Landing and Slaughter-House Company was allowed to establish itself anywhere in New Orleans and surrounding areas for a period of 25 years. Anyone else who tried to keep or slaughter animals within New Orleans would be fined $250 for each violation.

Since the area covered by the Act was more than 1,000 square miles, hundreds of people would be affected by the new rules. The Butchers' Benevolent Association of New Orleans filed a lawsuit against the Crescent City monopoly. Their livelihood had been destroyed by the Louisiana Legislature. The butchers found two new legal legs to stand on—the Thirteenth and Fourteenth Amendments, which had been ratified just a few years earlier.

The Association claimed that they were not receiving the "equal protection under the law" that the Fourteenth Amendment promised to all citizens. The lawyers for the butchers made a strong case. They explained that the colonists sought free competition in business when they came to America, and they sought to escape the monopolies that were common in England. If 1,000 people can suddenly no longer use their land to make a living as they wished, the lawyers argued, that abridged their "privileges and immunities" mentioned in the Fourteenth Amendment.

They also cleverly argued that being bound to use only Crescent City Slaughter-House was in essence placing the butchers of the 1,100 square mile area in "involuntary servitude," something which was outlawed by the Thirteenth Amendment.

Yet the Supreme Court was not swayed by these arguments, saying, "a critical examination of the act hardly justifies these assertions." After all, butchers could still slaughter their own animals, but for health reasons they had to go to the prescribed slaughterhouse and do it there, for a fee.

What if Louisiana had decided to assign all the slaughterhouse duties to the City of New Orleans? Then it is unlikely anyone would have questioned the constitutionality of the Act. Why should assigning these rights to a corporation be any different? Justice Miller compared the right of a state to establish a corporation for the purpose of running a certain business to the right of the United States to form a bank to help run its fiscal operations (see *McCulloch v. Maryland*).

The Court declared that the Thirteenth and Fourteenth Amendments really were meant to apply to the former slaves, and that it was a great stretch to try to apply it to the particulars of the slaughterhouse case. It said, "It is necessary to look to the purpose which we have said was the pervading spirit of them all [the Amendments], the evil which they were designed to remedy . . ."

REGULATION OF PUBLIC SERVICES
Munn v. Illinois (1877)

It had been a long-established tradition that certain professions offering services to the general public could be regulated. Innkeepers, carriage drivers, and ferry operators were held to maximum rates they could charge for their services. A particular ferry company might offer the only river crossing for miles or an inn might be the only place to stay for miles in any direction. It was in the public interest to establish a ceiling price that could be charged for these particular services.

Private property devoted to a public use, such as the storage of grain, could also be regulated by the state government. On the other hand, in strictly private contracts, where the general public had no interest, the government had no right to interfere.

In *Munn v. Illinois*, the owner of a grain warehouse protested against certain regulations enacted by the State of Illinois to determine the maximum rates charged for storage of grain. The owner, Munn, said that his rights were being violated in several ways. First, the Commerce Clause of the Constitution said that only Congress could regulate commerce between the states. He also claimed that the State of Illinois, in violation of the Fourteenth Amendment, was depriving him of life, liberty, and property.

The Supreme Court disagreed. Justice Morrison Remick Waite said that regulation of private property was an accepted practice, and that did not mean Fourteenth Amendment rights were being violated. "When one becomes a member of society, he necessarily parts with some rights or privileges which, as an individual . . . he might retain."

The bottom line was that when private property is devoted to a public use, it is subject to public regulation. Though sometimes these rules may not be fair, there was a way to remedy them: "For protection against abuses by legislatures, the people must resort to the polls, not to the courts." Though the grain warehouses did comprise an element of interstate commerce, it was an area upon which Congress had not yet ruled, so it was an acceptable use of the state's regulatory powers.

The principles of this case were soon further redefined in a case called *Wabash, St. Louis & Pacific Railroad Company v. Illinois* (1886). In that case, the Supreme Court struck down state regulations that attempted to regulate shipment rates for interstate railroads. The decision led to the creation of the Interstate Commerce Commission in 1887 to avoid future conflicts.

Michael Dukakis

Michael Dukakis served eight years in the Massachusetts Legislature beginning in 1962. He was a popular three-term Governor of Massachusetts, serving from 1975 to 1979, and again from 1983 to 1991. Dukakis rose to national prominence as the Democratic candidate for President in 1988. Dukakis has done extensive research on health-care reform, an issue about which he is passionate.

Q: *In Pharmaceutical Research v. Walsh [2003], the Court ruled that it did not violate the Commerce Clause if Maine made deals with drug companies to reduce their prices for state-sponsored programs. Was this a solid victory for the consumer, or will this issue come up again in the future?*

Dukakis: The Maine case is a consumer victory, but it underlines the absurdity of a situation where we refuse to regulate drug prices or, at least, give the government the right to bargain for the lowest possible price while our friends in Canada regulate, and at least some states and cities try to take advantage of their lower prices for the same drugs. We ought to make up our minds, not leave it to Canada to do the regulating.

Q: If truly major health-care reforms are passed by Congress, are they likely to be contested? Do you see the Supreme Court eventually being forced to rule on the legality of the legislation?

Dukakis: I don't see how universal health care could be challenged in the courts. We already have Medicare, which is universal coverage for those of us 65 and older. We have an extensive Veterans Administration system, which not only works well these days but is our version of the British national health service. We require employers and employees to contribute to social security, and we require employers to contribute to unemployment compensation, so there isn't much doubt about the constitutionality of a national employer mandate on health care. Whether or not we have the political will finally to guarantee working people and their families' comprehensive health insurance is another matter. I don't think there is much doubt that legislation to do it would pass constitutional muster.

CROSSING STATE LINES
Leisy v. Hardin (1890)

During the middle and late 19th century, there was a growing "temperance movement" to reduce the use of alcohol. The movement had blossomed during the 1830s, when more than one million people were members of temperance societies. In the years that followed, some states tried to ban alcohol altogether.

The State of Iowa enacted a code in 1873, and then a law in 1886, that said "no person shall manufacture for sale, sell, keep for sale, give away, exchange, barter, or dispense any intoxicating liquor." The only exceptions were for medical use and for use during church rites.

The original code of 1873 had allowed Iowans to import alcoholic beverages into the state and then sell them. However, in 1886, it became illegal for anyone to bring alcohol into Iowa without a special certificate proving the alcohol was going to a pharmacist.

A beer manufacturer from Illinois had transported 122 one-quarter barrels of beer, 171 one-eighth barrels of beer, and 11 sealed cases of beer into Iowa. These were seized by the marshal of Keokuk, Iowa, as being in violation of state law. Christiana, Edward, Lena, and Albert Leisy sued to get their beer back. The case, called *Leisy v. Hardin,* was nicknamed "The Original Package Case" (*package* being a term for alcoholic beverages).

The Supreme Court had already ruled in an earlier case that it was OK for a state to ban the production of alcoholic beverages within that state. It was up to the states to decide what was good for the public health and what was a nuisance. That was

The temperance movement was begun by women, many of whom were wives of men who came home drunk.

an article of commerce. The State of Iowa should not have seized the beer from Leisy.

The dissenting Justices (Horace Gray, John Marshall Harlan, and David Josiah Brewer) felt strongly that it was well within the rights of a state's police powers to regulate. For example, they wrote, a city could ban gunpowder because of its dangerous nature, even though it was an item of commerce and should be protected by the Commerce Clause of the Constitution. These dissenting Justices felt that self-preservation and public health were exceptions that could override Congress' authority to regulate commerce between the states. They cited a case called *Sherlock v. Alling* (1876) in which the decision said that regulating commerce "was never intended to cut the states off from legislating on all subjects relating to the health, life, and safety of their citizens . . ."

They felt that the liquor laws of 1886 had nothing to do with movement of goods from one state to another, and were only concerned with protecting the citizens of the state "against the evils, physical, moral, and social" from the use of alcoholic beverages.

within the states' so-called police powers. However, once a state border was crossed, the Court asserted, it became a matter for the federal government to regulate. Thus the Court decided in favor of the Leisys. Chief Justice Melville Weston Fuller spoke for the majority: "Whenever the law of the state amounts essentially to a regulation of commerce with foreign nations or among the states . . . it . . . is therefore void."

It did not matter how the Justices felt about the dangers of alcohol if Congress recognized alcohol as

As it turned out, the manufacturing and sale of liquor was totally banned within the United States in 1919, with the ratification of the Eighteenth Amendment. Prohibition was repealed in 1933, when the twenty-first Amendment was passed.

Regulation of Working Hours

Lochner v. New York (1905)

Workplace conditions during the late 19th and early 20th centuries were abysmal. Long working hours, low pay, dangerous conditions, and underage employees were all common throughout the United States. Finally, local governments began to pass laws to correct some of these problems. In New York State, one 1897 law regulated the working hours in bakeries and confectionary establishments. It said bakery employees could not work more than 60 hours per week or 10 hours per day.

Though the New York law seems beneficial on the surface, imagine for a moment that you are a bakery owner. At first you struggle to make ends meet. A few years pass and business slowly builds up. Finally, people come from miles around to sample your bread and cakes. You can no longer do all the baking yourself, so you hire staff. At first just a couple of bakers, but soon you need more people.

On weekends and especially holidays, things get even busier than normal. Your bakers have to work 10-hour and longer days, six days a week, just to keep up with the demand. A local judge says it is against the law to make your employees work so many hours and fines you one day. Sure enough, you see that the state has passed a law restricting work hours.

This was the situation for Joseph Lochner, a real-life bakery owner. He argued that it was his right to set the hours he needed. The government could not interfere with his possessions and his right to life, liberty, or property. The bakery was his livelihood and he needed to have his employees work long hours for his business to stay afloat. For the government to get involved in his private business and tell him what to do with his employees was unconstitutional, he argued. He took his argument to court.

The State Supreme Court ruled 3–2 in favor of the act regulating working hours. The ruling was appealed by the bakery owner, and the Court of Appeals ruled 4–3, again in favor of upholding the regulations. The case then went to the Supreme Court.

In *Lochner v. New York,* the U.S. Supreme Court examined whether the state could regulate the working hours of a business, which is a private contract between employer and employee. The Justices recognized that the states had "police power" to control the health and welfare of their citizens. In a case called *Jacobson v. Massachusetts* (1905), the Court ruled that a mandatory vaccination against a contagious disease was one example of a legal use of a state's police power. The Court had also ruled in the *Slaughterhouse Cases* that a state could create a monopoly of business under the pretext of ensuring public health and safety. On the other hand, a law attempting to regulate the trade of people who made horseshoes was ruled as invalid by a state court in 1904 because it interfered with the right of a business to contract with an individual.

Was the public health affected by the working hours of a baker? The state argued that workers who toiled longer hours were more likely to be dirty with sweat and grime, and therefore their work product—

bread—was also likely to suffer. The majority thought this was not necessarily true: "Clean and wholesome bread does not depend upon whether the baker works but ten hours per day or only sixty hours a week."

Was baking itself unhealthy? It was not among the healthiest of trades, but there were also occupations that were far worse. Did that mean that locksmiths, bankers, carpenters, and clerks should be regulated by the state as well? Many office workers sit at their desks all day and receive little sunlight. Was this unhealthy? Wasn't the 10-hour mark arbitrary? A 10-hour work day was OK, but a 10-and-a-half or 11-hour day was unhealthy and therefore not OK?

Finding for the bakery owner, the Court declared that "limiting the hours in which grown and intelligent men may labor to earn their living, are mere meddlesome interferences with the rights of the individual." In the majority opinion, Justice Rufus Wheeler Peckham wrote:

[T]he limitation of the hours of labor . . . has no such direct relation to, and no such substantial effect upon, the health of the employee . . . It seems to us that the real object and purpose were simply to regulate the hours of labor between the master and his employees . . . Under such circumstances, the freedom of master and employee to contract with each other in relation to their employment . . . cannot be prohibited or interfered with without violating the Federal Constitution.

It was not, after all, the same as a state regulating the working hours of coal miners, whose profession was more dangerous.

The Court let stand the other portions of the laws regulating bakeries. It was OK if the state sent inspectors to the bakery, and it was OK for the state to tell bakery owners the height of the ceiling and the materials the floors should be made from. It was also OK for the state to regulate the storage of flour, the existence of washrooms, and the presence of pets within

Bakers and a big loaf of bread on parade, 1909.

the bakery. But it was not acceptable to limit working hours.

The ruling was a victory for business and a defeat for the rights of the worker.

It was a close call, with four of the nine Justices dissenting from the majority. Justice John Marshall Harlan felt that the Court was being too strict in its interpretation of police powers of the state and the public health. He felt that the liberty given to citizens in the Constitution was not complete freedom; it necessarily came with some restraints. Justice Harlan quoted the report of an expert on workplace health, who said bakery work "is hard, very hard work, not only because it requires a great deal of physical exertion in an overheated workshop."

He went on to explain that "neither the [Fourteenth] Amendment—broad and comprehensive as it is—nor any other Amendment was designed to interfere with the power of the State, sometimes termed its police power, to prescribe regulations to promote the health, peace, morals, education, and good order of the people."

The Court took the workers' side in a couple of other cases involving regulation of working hours, *Muller v. Oregon* (1908) and *Bunting v. Oregon* (1917), but the record of the Supreme Court in regulating labor was still very much in flux.

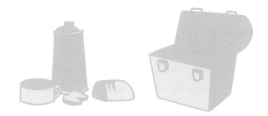

STAGE A BAKERY PROTEST

IN *Lochner v. New York* (1905), the Court decided that it was legal for a bakery owner to let his workers toil more than 60 hours per week, and that a state law restricting work hours should be thrown out. In this activity, bakery workers and bakery owners will protest as the classroom Supreme Court hears arguments on the issue of regulation of work hours.

YOU'LL NEED

✔ 6 wooden dowels, between 24″ and 36″ long
✔ 6 pieces of white poster board or thick paper, at least 11″ x 17″ (preferably 20″ x 30″)
✔ Thick markers or poster paints and paintbrushes
✔ Roll of clear packing tape
✔ 3 loaves of Italian bread, dirty from being rubbed on the floor
✔ Classroom Supreme Court

Select six classmates to be the protesters. Three people should be bakery workers who are in favor of government-regulated work hours, and three people should be bakery owners who are against them. Decide on six different slogans that can be written or painted on the posters. They should be short, catchy, and easy to read. Examples for each side:

Forced Labor = Unconstitutional

Stay Out of Our Business!

Use the poster board and paints or markers to create your posters. Mount boards to the dowels by firmly taping the dowel to the center of the reverse of each poster, starting about 10 inches from the top of the poster (leaving enough dowel at the bottom so that you can hold the sign up).

Now select two classmates to argue each side of the case before the classroom Supreme Court, as the protesters circle "outside" with their signs at the back of the classroom. The bakery workers each hold a loaf of bread in their free hands, waving them in the air. The workers' lawyer should try to sway the Court to rule differently from how it actually ruled in 1905. How can you convince the Court that working long hours is unhealthy and unsafe? (HINT: *can you draw the Court's attention to the protesters who are holding bread made by people working 12 hours straight?*) The business owners' lawyer should try to convince the Court that working hours are strictly for businesses to regulate and that the government should not interfere. (HINT: *Can you find a phrase or phrases from the Constitution that might help your cause?*) The Justices of the Court should discuss, and then write a three- or four-paragraph decision, to be read aloud by the Chief Justice.

William Barr was Attorney General of the United States, serving from 1991 to 1993 under President George Bush. Barr argued three cases before the Supreme Court and currently serves as counsel for Verizon.

Q: How much involvement should the government have in the control of business?

Barr: I think in general, the government should let the market work as far as possible. There are certainly areas where the market may not work or where there are other values that have to be protected by government intrusion into the marketplace. The market can't be relied on for everything. But there should be a general bias in favor of allowing the market to work. I think the real culprit here isn't so much the courts. The initial culprit isn't so much the courts as the legislative bodies.

But I'll just tell you my fundamental critique . . . the framers were wrong that the judiciary is the least dangerous branch. I think it's proving that over 200 years of history that it's a very dangerous branch, and that the tendency to act like philosopher kings and impose one's own view of how things should be rather than follow the fundamental precepts set forth in a statute or in the Constitution itself and adhere to them. There is an increasing tendency to make the law rather than interpret the law.

Q: Is Hamdi v. Rumsfeld [2004] [a case in which the Court held that the United States could not detain indefinitely an American citizen who was arrested in Afghanistan and accused of working with the Taliban,

then transferred to a military prison in the United States] one of the cases to which you are referring?

Barr: Well, that was one of the cases, although Hamdi was an American citizen, so that brings the issue about how American citizens should be treated. But actually, they also ruled that they would have exercised jurisdiction over non-Americans in Guantanamo. Just to give you historical perspective, there were over 300,000 Axis prisoners here in the United States [during World War II], several of whom were American citizens. Be that as it may, there were Germans and Italians who were being held in prison camps. The idea that the Court could then get into their claims would have just been a joke in 1944, 1945. Now you have courts asserting that they can get into that stuff. It's just nonsense.

That's just one example. But there are very few institutions left in the United States which courts have not decided they can make these kinds of judgments about. I think one of the things we have to think about is, why do we care what judges say? When someone stands up there in a black robe and pontificates about something, about how our society should be, why does what they say make a difference or should make a difference? Why do we give deference to them? There is a tendency in society to get a judge involved. Let's get a judge to make the decision.

I think we lose sight of the fact that the only reason anything a judge says should make a difference is because in theory, all the judge is saying is what the people have said. The people have either said it by passing a law, therefore the authority of that law comes from the people, not from the judge. All the judge is doing is saying this is what the people have said, therefore it has authority. Or the people have said it through adopting the fundamental rules and statements of the Constitution, in which case all the Court is doing is what the people have said. The judge is simply supposed to be the articulator of things that the people themselves have said, either through Constitution or statute. The reason that a judge's statements should be given any deference or have any importance is that they're supposed to be the statements of the people. I think there's a growing tendency in society to think that judges are some sort of philosopher kings that have special wisdom. And they don't.

BREAKING UP MONOPOLIES

John D. Rockefeller was one of the richest men in America by the end of the 19th century. Born in 1839, he began to invest in the relatively new oil business in 1863, and by 1870, his Standard Oil Company was a thriving and profitable enterprise. He was not content to operate a successful local business; he wanted more. He soon owned more than 50 refineries. He got around business laws preventing corporations from having an interest in other corporations by creating a holding company, known as a "trust," which held the stock of different businesses.

The trust was run by nine trustees (including Rockefeller), who effectively made decisions that ran all the corporations. By 1882, John D. Rockefeller and his Standard Oil Trust controlled 90 percent of the oil business in the United States.

Before long, other industries, including sugar and rubber, were also largely controlled by trusts. These trusts created something called a monopoly, which meant nearly all competition had been eliminated, and the corporations held by the trust could control the release of the product and set prices to any level desired.

There was a growing recognition in the country that something had to be done about the monopolies that were becoming rampant. In 1890, Congress passed the Sherman Anti-Trust Act. This law stated that any trust, monopoly, or conspiracy, in restraint of trade or commerce among the states, or with foreign nations, was illegal.

The Sherman Anti-Trust Act did not set its sights on innocent businesses. What if you owned an iron forgery, and your business grew until it forged most of the iron in a five-state radius? As long as you were not preventing others from starting their own forgeries, or buying out all the other forgeries in sight, you

John D. Rockefeller (left, with his son John D. Rockefeller Jr.) was one of the richest men in the country and the father of the Standard Oil Trust.

the refining business in the United States, but the Court nonetheless found that the Anti-Trust Act did not apply to manufacturing. Subsequent businesses challenged by the government were not so lucky.

One of the many areas of commerce that was threatened by monopolies was the nation's railways. The large and powerful Great Northern Railway and Northern Pacific Railway companies conspired in 1901 to combine into one super railway line by creating a holding corporation based in New Jersey. The holding company essentially controlled both the railways and made them one and the same. Creation of the holding company, called the Northern Securities Company, eliminated competition and thus the railway could charge whatever price it wished to manufacturers who wanted to ship their goods across the country. The railways ran trains from the Great Lakes all the way to the Pacific Ocean.

In *Northern Securities Co. v. United States* (1904), the Supreme Court, in a decision authored by Justice John Marshall Harlan, said that the constitutional guarantee of freedom of contract did not prevent Congress from prescribing how to ensure free competition between businesses dealing in interstate commerce. Just because the holding corporation did not actually run any trains itself, and was headquartered within New Jersey, did not exempt it from the interstate commerce rule. The Court cited its ruling in *Gibbons v. Ogden* and explained that there were no limitations to regulating interstate commerce besides what may be written in the Constitution itself.

Soon after the *Northern Securities* case came another important monopoly case. This time, it was

were not in violation of the Anti-Trust Act. It was the scheming and maneuvering of huge businesses to dominate the market that the government aimed to regulate.

But John D. Rockefeller's business was not the first one taken to the Supreme Court for allegedly violating the Anti-Trust Act. That distinction belonged to the E.C. Knight Co., a sugar refinery that was challenged in 1895. The company controlled 98 percent of

John D. Rockefeller who was in trouble with the law. Rockefeller's Standard Oil Company insisted that it had used legal, competitive methods to become so large and had been guided by economic genius, with a sharp insight into commerce. In 1909, a Circuit Court decided against Standard Oil and in favor of the United States. The case then went to the Supreme Court, as *Standard Oil Co. of N.J. v. United States* (1911).

One of Standard Oil's arguments was that they did not control the production of crude oil, so they did not have a monopoly of the oil business. They only dealt in refining the oil. However, the Supreme Court saw through this excuse, and upheld the lower court's decision. By controlling the vast majority of the coun-try's oil refineries, Standard Oil did in effect control crude oil. For where else did the crude oil have to go except to a refinery owned by Standard Oil?

The same year as the Standard Oil decision, the Supreme Court ordered the breakup of a cigarette trust. The American Tobacco Company controlled the production of 95 percent of the domestic ciga-rettes and was ordered to dissolve within six to eight months. The days of the huge monopolies and trusts were finally over.

But while the Supreme Court was willing to break up monopolies and trusts, it was not so eager to inter-fere in other areas of commerce that it perceived to be the domain of the states. Child labor was one of these areas.

Headlines proclaim government victory in breaking up a tobacco trust, 1911.

Regulating Child Labor

During the late 19th and early 20th centuries, working conditions were often poor, and child labor was common. In 1916, Congress passed the Keating–Owen Child Labor Act. This law forbade the interstate trade of goods produced in factories by children under the age of 14, or by children between the ages of 14 and 16 who have worked more than eight hours per day.

Hammer v. Dagenhart (1918)

In *Hammer v. Dagenhart,* a North Carolina father filed suit because under the new Keating–Owen Child Labor Act, his two sons could not work in a textile mill. The Act regulated only interstate commerce, but that meant North Carolina textile mills employing minors could sell their products only within North Carolina and not to other states. There was not a strong enough market in North Carolina alone to keep the mills in business, so they had no choice but to refuse employment to anyone under the age of 14.

The case, *Hammer v. Dagenhart,* reached the Supreme Court, which struck down the new Child Labor Act. According to the majority opinion by Justice William Rufus Day, federal authority had no business getting involved in a matter that was "purely local," and therefore the law was invalid.

Many states had laws to regulate when children could legally be allowed to work. In North Carolina, there was a law that stated a child had to be at least 12 years old to work in a factory. The Supreme Court majority felt that this was strictly something for the states to regulate.

Justice Day said: "The grant of power of Congress over the subject of interstate commerce was to enable it to regulate such commerce, and not to give it authority to control the states in their exercise of the police power over local trade and manufacture."

Bailey v. Drexel Furniture Co. (1922)

Bailey v. Drexel Furniture Co. was similar to the *Hammer* case. The Drexel Furniture Company of North Carolina received a tax notice in 1921 from J. W. Bailey, who was the U.S. collector of taxes for the district. Because the company employed a boy who was under the age of 14, it was taxed at a rate of 10 percent of its net profits. The Child Labor Tax Law of 1919 ordered the 10 percent tax on any factories, canneries, or mills employing children under 14, and on any mines or quarries employing children under 16.

The Court ruled in favor of the Drexel Furniture Company. Chief Justice William Howard Taft, writing for the majority, noted that the tax seemed unfair. A company would be fined a total of 10 percent of its profit whether it employed one child or 500 children under 14 years of age. He acknowledged that the tax law was "designed to promote the highest good." But he explained that the good intentions of unconstitutional laws like the tax law were an "insidious feature" because they gained support and led citizens to believe in something that was actually breaking away from the prescribed powers of the federal government.

Taft said, "The case before us cannot be distinguished from that of *Hammer v. Dagenhart.*" He explained, "Here the so-called tax is a penalty to coerce people of a state to act as Congress wishes them to act in respect of a matter completely the business of the state government under the federal Constitution." Accordingly, the Court struck down the Child Labor Tax Law of 1919. Business had won again.

In 1941, the Court overturned *Hammer* in *United States v. Darby Lumber Company.* The Fair Labor Standards Act had been passed in 1938, and it regulated wages and working hours for goods that were to be shipped interstate. Only some of the Darby goods were shipped interstate, but the Supreme Court held that it did not matter; all of the labor fell under the control of the Fair Labor Standards Act.

Child working in a mill.

ROOSEVELT'S NEW DEAL ATTACKED

The hands-off approach of the Supreme Court with regard to business continued into the 1930s. When President Franklin D. Roosevelt took office in March 1933, the country was in the midst of a deep economic depression. With soaring unemployment and failed banks, Roosevelt wasted no time. He enacted a series of bills that were designed to jumpstart the economy and boost morale. Because of the severe nature of the country's economic woes, the President's measures were very comprehensive, and many of them sought to give the government broad new powers over business.

Part of the problem, he felt, was the unfair wages paid by some employers. "It seems to me to be equally plain that no business which depends for existence on paying less than living wages to its workers has any right to continue in this country," President Roosevelt told the country about the newly created National Industrial Recovery Act (NIRA) in 1933.

Much to Roosevelt's dismay, some of his "New Deal" legislation was challenged in the Supreme Court. The administration was also challenged in the case known as *A.L.A. Schechter Poultry Corporation v. United States* (1935).

This case involved a poultry slaughterhouse operated by Joseph Schechter in New York City. The business was subjected to new rules that were part of the NIRA. The Live Poultry Code provided that no employee was allowed to work more than 40 hours in any one week, and that no employees would be paid less than 50 cents per hour. The defendant was indicted on 18 counts of violating various parts of the code.

The Court ruled for the defendant, with Chief Justice Charles Evans Hughes writing in the decision: "We are of the opinion that the attempt through the provisions of the code to fix the hours and wages of employees of defendants in their intrastate business was not a valid exercise of federal power." The Court also claimed it did not matter whether the measure was good for the economy: "It is not the province of the Court to consider the economic advantages or disadvantages of such a centralized system. It is sufficient to say that the Federal Constitution does not provide for it."

Soon after, the President received another blow to his well-intentioned policies. Besides NIRA, the President's measures included the Agricultural Adjustment Act (AAA). The AAA provided that in order to stabilize the economy, the government could regulate how much of a crop farmers could produce and could levy taxes on them depending on their output. In a case called *United States v. Butler* (1936), the Court struck down the AAA as being unconstitutional.

Justice Owen Josephus Roberts delivered the opinion of the Court: "The act invades the reserved rights of the states. It is a statutory plan to regulate and control agricultural production, a matter beyond the powers delegated to the federal government." Once again, though, the Court tried to be diplomatic: "This court neither approves nor condemns any legislative policy . . . The question is not what power the federal government ought to have, but what powers in fact have been given by the people." The Court maintained that the federal government could not exert such close control over agriculture in the individual states and said the federal government's regulations were too restrictive.

An angry President Roosevelt said of these attacks on his programs that "[t]he Court has been acting not as a judicial body, but as a policy-making body." His attempt to reorganize the Supreme Court to his advantage was unsuccessful, but it did seem to lead the Court to back off from attacking his New Deal policies, and the rest of his presidency did not see any more major challenges to his recovery laws.

LABOR RIGHTS
West Coast Hotel Co. v. Parrish (1937)

The late 1930s were a turning point for labor rights and the regulation of business. One of the first such cases involved a female employee fighting for her rights. Elsie Parrish worked as a maid in a Washington State hotel for 25 cents per hour, instead of the 35 cents per hour that the State of Washington set as the

Robert Reich

Robert Reich was the 22nd Secretary of Labor of the United States, from 1993 to 1997, serving under President Bill Clinton. Prior to that position he taught at Harvard, worked for the Federal Trade Commission under President Jimmy Carter, and was an assistant to the Solicitor General under President Gerald Ford.

Q: In the early 20th century, several federal acts regulating labor (including work ages and hours) were struck down by the Supreme Court. Why has the federal government fared better regulating labor in recent years?

Reich: Before the 1930s, the Supreme Court was opposed to federal regulation of wages, hours, and other aspects of work. The Justices felt that the states, rather than the federal government, had the constitutional authority to deal with these matters. But sometimes the Court even struck down state regulations, arguing that government had no business telling workers and employers how to deal with one another. President Franklin D. Roosevelt, who came to office at the height of the Great Depression, felt strongly that America needed national labor laws to protect workers across the land. He threatened to enact legislation that would expand the number of Supreme Court Justices, and

put his own nominees on the Court, unless the Court recognized the urgency of the times and changed its old-fashioned notions. The Court got the message.

Q: The Family Medical Leave Act (FMLA), which you helped implement, is one of the most important labor-related laws in recent history. Do you think it will stand up to any future court challenges?

Reich: The Family and Medical Leave Act has been enormously important to working parents. It allows them to leave work for a time to take care of a sick child or parent, knowing that they can get their old job back again. I'm sure it will withstand any future court challenge. It doesn't violate any provision of the U.S. Constitution, and I can't imagine that a court would interpret the law differently than it's been applied.

minimum wage for women. The Washington State law enacted in 1913 said women could not be employed under labor conditions detrimental to their health or morals or at wages that were not adequate.

When Parrish was laid off from her job in 1935, she decided the hotel owed her a large sum of money. She requested that her employer pay her the $216 that was the difference between her wages and what the state said was the minimum. The hotel's lawyers looked to a previous case, *Adkins v. Children's Hospital* (1923), in which the Supreme Court had struck down the constitutionality of a minimum wage for women.

Parrish claimed the hotel's refusal to follow the state's law was a violation of her freedom of contract and Fourteenth Amendment rights to due process. The case appeared before the Supreme Court at the height of the Great Depression. Millions were unemployed, and companies that had not failed right away struggled to stay in business.

The Washington Supreme Court upheld the labor law, overturning the decision of the trial court. The hotel appealed, and the case went to the U.S. Supreme Court.

In a 5–4 decision, the Court ruled in favor of Parrish, overturning the *Adkins* decision. Chief Justice Charles Evans Hughes felt that women were exploited and that a minimum wage for women was constitutional because being exploited "is not only detrimental to their health and well-being, but casts a direct burden for their support upon the community."

In his dissent, Justice George Sutherland explained that a law fixing maximum wages would never be tolerated, so one setting minimum wages should not be allowed.

REGULATION OF BUSINESS TODAY

The federal government, through Congress, continues to regulate businesses and protect workers and consumers. For example, the Family Medical Leave Act (FMLA) of 1993 was signed into law by President Bill Clinton. This act gave expectant mothers and others with medical reasons 12 weeks leave from work, after which time the employer must allow them to return to work.

The Environmental Protection Agency (EPA), founded in 1970, creates and enforces federal regulations to ensure that factory emissions are reduced and air and water are kept as pollutant-free as possible. The Federal Communications Commission (FCC) controls decency standards and communications over many media, including telephone, radio, and television. The Food and Drug Administration (FDA) reviews new drugs before they are released to consumers and creates standards for food manufacturers and processors. The Occupational Safety and Health Administration (OSHA) regulates workplace safety issues. Many other agencies regulate and supervise a wide spectrum of business activities across the country.

Because they regulate industries worth many billions of dollars, all of these agencies see challenges to their authority from time to time. For example, the EPA was challenged in a case called *Whitman v. American Trucking Associations* (2001). This case arose after EPA Administrator Christine Todd Whitman changed air pollution standards. The question was whether the Clean Air Act unconstitutionally delegated legislative power to the EPA's administrator that should actually belong to Congress. In its decision, the Supreme Court said that there was not a problem with the Clean Air Act's delegation of authority. For the most part, today's Supreme Court is sympathetic to the need for government to regulate commerce, as per the Constitution.

Robert Morgenthau is the District Attorney for Manhattan (New York). He is the son of Henry Morgenthau Jr., who was Treasury Secretary under President Franklin D. Roosevelt. He was appointed as a U.S. Attorney by President John F. Kennedy in 1961 and served in that role until 1970. He was first elected as District Attorney for Manhattan in 1974.

Q: What is the role of U.S. Attorney versus District Attorney?

Morgenthau: The United States Attorney's job is to enforce federal laws, and the District Attorney's job is to enforce state and local laws. There is some concurrent jurisdiction, for instance, bank robberies. But take something like tax fraud, if it's federal taxes it's the United States Attorney's job, if it's state and local taxes, for instance sales tax, it's the District Attorney's job. Most crimes of violence, murders, rapes and robberies, burglaries, they're only subject to the jurisdiction of the District Attorney.

Q: You have dealt with a lot of corporate fraud in your office. Should the government, including the Supreme Court, regulate business more closely?

Morgenthau: I think that the laws have got to be enforced.

The laws are on the books. I think that sometimes they're not as closely enforced as they should be. But it's not a lack of laws. It's a lack of resources, perhaps, and the will to look at those kinds of cases. I think in a democracy you have to rely to a large extent on people complying with law voluntarily, and not rely on the government to enforce the laws.

Q: The United States Justice Department has a separate Anti-Trust Division. Is this still a big problem in this country, even after the big trusts and monopolies were busted a long time ago?

Morgenthau: It's still a problem, but certainly not the problem it was at one time. But we have a state anti-trust law, and if somebody tries to monopolize business in a particular area, we enforce the state anti-trust laws.

8

PROPERTY RIGHTS

NOT FOR SALE
www.IJ.org

Spencer Platt/Getty Images

One of the most fundamental rights that American citizens cherish is the right to own property. There are different types, including physical property (land and possessions) and intellectual property (designs, songs, and writings you create).

Throughout much of recorded history, the great majority of people in the world did not have much property. Immigrants came to America, lured by the dream of owning a large plot of land of their own. Once they arrived and staked a claim, they expected to keep their land. When a challenge to their ownership arose, people were fiercely protective. Many land ownership cases wound up in the courts.

As capitalism prospered in America, people obtained many personal possessions. The Industrial Revolution helped Americans by creating mass-produced, affordable furniture and accessories. As the 19th century progressed, American inventors were prolific, turning out thousands of pieces of machinery and technology such as the sewing machine, telephone, and phonograph. Many of these inventions were highly lucrative. Competition among inventors and manufacturers was fierce. Lawsuits crowded the court system over patents. Who invented what first? Who was entitled to the profits?

New technology also meant new types of property. Authors and songwriters could profit as cheaply printed books became available to the general public and as inventions such as the record player translated into sales of popular songs. As technology is invented to distribute these creations, disputes arise. When has copyright been infringed?

PHYSICAL PROPERTY

Land Ownership

Many cases in the early 19th century involved disputes over land. Complicating factors were the original ownership of colonial land by British subjects and competing claims due to rapid expansion of settlers into the American West. Early surveys and land grants were not always accurate, and there were disputes from people claiming to own the same piece of land.

Some property cases involved complex chains of ownership. The Justices had to not only sort through all the tangled relationships but also figure out what the most appropriate legal solution was.

Though seemingly trivial in nature, these land disputes were important. Their outcomes could make a difference in many people's lives. The plots of land were huge, often several thousand acres, and the Court's opinion on the validity of surveys and the dis-

position of deeds could affect many other landowners in the same situation.

As Chief Justice John Marshall wrote in the decision of one land case in the early 19th century: "Were

An 1844 deed for land in Massachusetts.

the validity of this objection to be administered, it would shake almost every title in Kentucky."

One case, *Matthews v. Zane's Lessee* (1809), dealt with a man named Matthews who purchased land in Ohio in 1804. He bought the land from the Marietta Land Office just after the Zaneville Land District was created. Soon after, the neighboring Zaneville Land Office was opened, and it included the land that Matthews purchased from the Marietta Land District. A man named Zane purchased the land that Matthews claimed to own. The two men went to court to settle the dispute. The Supreme Court ruled in favor of Zane.

In another early land case, the lawyer for the plaintiff argued that the policy for the settlement of the western frontier of the country "has been an object of anxiety at all times from the first organization of the union."

Treaties with other countries sometimes confused the situation. The case known as *Martin v. Hunter's Lessee* (1816) (see page 26) dealt with the ownership of land that had been owned by an Englishman before the American Revolution.

As the expansion of settlement across the country reached its peak in the latter part of the 19th century, most of the available land was claimed from coast to coast. Owner-versus-owner cases over land disputes became less common. By the turn of the 20th century, there were no more questions about ancient English land deeds and questionable survey boundaries.

Another type of land dispute case does remain common, however, and it pits the government against private citizens.

EMINENT DOMAIN

This Land Is My Land

According to the Fifth Amendment to the Constitution, "nor shall private property be taken for public use, without just compensation." This clause, known as the "takings" clause, deals with the right of "eminent domain," where governments can claim the privilege of taking land from private citizens. Over the years, many states and cities have taken thousands of pieces of property from citizens to build highways, schools, railroads, power lines, and other public projects. Often, the goal is to replace slums with new and more sanitary public housing or beautiful parks. The properties to be taken are first assessed, meaning the fair market value is determined, in order to compensate the owner. Though mentioned in the Constitution, eminent domain can be a prickly subject.

Barron v. Mayor and City Council of Baltimore (1833) was the first eminent domain case to be heard. John Craig and John Barron were the owners of a successful wharf on the Baltimore waterfront. The wharf was located on deep water, making it highly valuable. In the process of paving roads, the city of Baltimore diverted streams from their natural courses and changed the slope of certain roads. These improvements changed the conditions during a rainstorm. As a result, excess storm water caused hillside erosion, and sand and dirt wound up in the Baltimore harbor. The once-successful wharf was reduced in importance. Large ships could no longer use the wharf because the water was too shallow.

Barron argued that the city should pay for repairs so that the wharf could be restored to its former glory. It was only through the city's modifications that the damage was done to his private property. Chief Justice John Marshall wrote the decision for the Court. He explained that the Amendments to the Constitution were never intended to apply to the state governments.

"We are of opinion, that the provision in the Fifth Amendment . . . is intended solely as a limitation on the exercise of power by the government of the United States, and is not applicable to the legislation of the states."

When the Fourteenth Amendment was ratified in 1868, it applied the Fifth Amendment to the states. Though it was 35 years too late for Barron, reimbursement for property taken by eminent domain by state and local governments could no longer be disputed.

In a case called *Cherokee Nation v. Southern Kansas Railway* (1890), Congress authorized the Southern Kansas Railway to take land owned by the Cherokee Indians in order to lay railroad tracks and build a telegraph line. The Cherokees rejected the compensation that the railroad offered: $4,051.44 for a 148-mile strip of land to be taken from them. They felt that it was impossible to place a value upon their land. In fact, in their opinion, the land was priceless. They felt they had to agree to the amount before the government could take any land.

But in their decision, the Supreme Court upheld the right of the government to use eminent domain on land owned by Indians. "It would be very strange if the national government . . . could exercise the power of eminent domain in the several states, and could not exercise the same power in a territory occupied by an Indian nation or tribe, the members of which were wards of the United States, and directly subject to its political control."

Eminent domain came up again in Washington, D.C., when the District of Columbia Redevelopment Act of 1945 was challenged. The city wanted to take over an underdeveloped area of Washington, D.C., where 64 percent of the homes were beyond repair, 60 percent had no indoor toilets, and 30 percent lacked electricity. Some of this land would then be given to public agencies and some of it would be sold to private developers. The owner of a department store objected to the land being taken under this Redevelopment Act. His property was not a slum residence; it was a store. He also objected on the grounds that the land would be redeveloped for private use instead of public use.

The Court rejected the department store owner's argument. Justice William Orville Douglas wrote for the majority in the case, known as *Berman v. Parker* (1954): "If those who govern the District of Columbia decide that the Nation's Capital should be beautiful as well as sanitary, there is nothing in the Fifth Amendment that stands in the way."

The Justices noted that sometimes private use of land serves the public interest, and sometimes private developers can accomplish results that would be hard for the government to achieve on its own. The Court also noted that a whole neighborhood might have to be demolished to accomplish the redevelopment. One store could not be spared; it was within the right of the government to do what was best to promote public health.

In 2005, the Supreme Court heard a case called *Kelo v. City of New London.* In this instance, the City of New London, Connecticut, wanted to take and demolish private homes and replace them with office space. The lawyer for the homeowners argued that this was not "public use" as dictated by the Fifth Amendment. The city believed that the plan was legitimate because it would ultimately benefit the city's economy by revitalizing a faded section of town. The Supreme Court ruled in favor of the city.

Zoning Laws

In the old days, people built whatever they wanted on their land. The first regulations about what you could build and where (called "zoning laws") only evolved around the turn of the 20th century, as urban growth blossomed. People in cities and towns did not want to buy a house only to have a polluting factory built next door.

Before official zoning laws, property deeds sometimes contained restrictions upon the use of the land after purchase. A 1907 deed for a Queens, New York, property forbid the construction of "any slaughter house, smith shop, forge, furnace, steam engine, brass foundry, nail or iron factory, or any manufactory of gun-powder, glue, varnish, vitriol, ink or turpentine, or for the tanning, dressing or preparing skins, hides or leather, or any brewery, distillery or other noxious or dangerous trade or business."

In 1922, the village council of Euclid, Ohio, passed an ordinance that created a comprehensive zoning plan for various types and sizes of buildings. The zoning laws divided the village into six different zones. (Zone 1: single family homes, parks, farming, and greenhouses. Zone 2: everything in Zone 1, plus two-family homes. Zone 3: everything in Zone 2, plus apartment houses, hotels, churches, schools, hospitals, playgrounds, and government buildings, and so on through Zone 6.)

The 68-acre tract of Euclid land in question was empty. The owner had held it for years, for the purpose of selling and developing it for industrial uses. He was told that the village's zoning laws prohibited him from doing so. He felt this was unfair and believed that the law forced him to lose money on the land that he owned because he could not build what he wanted. The businessman argued that if the use of his property was limited to residential purposes the value was only $2,500 per acre, not the $10,000 it would be worth otherwise. The lower court had held that the ordinance was indeed unconstitutional and void, preventing its enforcement.

This businessman thought that the town was violating his constitutional right to engage in business, saying that the village ordinance would "deprive him of liberty and property without due process of law." In *Village of Euclid v. Ambler Realty Co.* (1926), the Supreme Court overturned the lower court's ruling and ruled against the businessman 6–3, saying that it was within the town's rights to regulate zoning. They cited the "changing world" as a reason for the wisdom of the zoning laws. The ability to make laws to ensure public health and safety was part of the police power of the local government.

The Court urged citizens to change the laws if they did not like them: "We have nothing to do with the question of the wisdom or good policy of municipal ordinances. If they are not satisfying to a majority of the citizens, their recourse is to the ballot—not the courts."

INTELLECTUAL PROPERTY

Patent Pending

Early intellectual property cases before the Supreme Court concerned patents. In *Evans v. Jordan* (1815), the Court decided that an act that extended the patent on a machine did not authorize general use of machines that were made after the time when the expiration of the patent occurred and when the patent was extended. The 1840s and 1850s saw many patent cases over profitable products such as Morse's telegraph, Goodyear's India-rubber, McCormick's reaper, and Howe's sewing machine.

In the McCormick case (*Seymour v. McCormick,* 1857), the dispute was over the patent for a machine that collects grain from fields. The inventor, Cyrus McCormick, had first patented his machine in 1834, then improved it and patented it again in 1845 and 1847. McCormick sued William Seymour and Layton Morgan, two men who had manufactured and

ARE ZONING LAWS CONSTITUTIONAL?

 In *Village of Euclid* v. Ambler Realty Co. (1926), the Court said that zoning laws may not have been wise, necessary, or valid 100 years earlier. However, they cited the "complex conditions of our day" as a reason for having those laws. Zoning regulations were similar to traffic regulations. Before the streetcar and the automobile, they were unnecessary, but with the new conditions they became absolutely important.

Is your neighborhood zoned? In this activity you'll map out the uses of buildings in your neighborhood and see if a pattern emerges.

YOU'LL NEED

✔ Graph paper

✔ #2 pencil

✔ Colored pencils or markers (red, blue, green, purple, etc.)

With the help of an adult, walk or drive four square blocks in your neighborhood. Make a map of the neighborhood on graph paper, drawing each building on the map. Assign each color to a type of building:

Red = *school/library/hospital/museum/ courthouse/town hall (institutional)*

Blue = *store or restaurant (retail)*

Black = *industrial (factory)*

Orange = *private home (house)*

Yellow = *apartments/condos*

Green = *parks*

Color in a square for each building you see. Can you see a pattern of colors emerge? Are factories next to homes? Are stores clustered together? Are schools next to apartment houses?

Take a trip to your local town hall's buildings department or local library and find your town's zoning map. Does the map you drew match up to the zoning map you found? Should towns be allowed to make zoning laws as they please? Why do you think your town is zoned the way it is? Was the Supreme Court right in ruling against the businessman who was the plaintiff? What changes would you make to your town's zoning laws to make your town a better place?

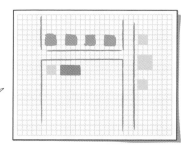

sold machines that were very similar to McCormick's without getting his permission. The Supreme Court ruled in favor of McCormick and said that just because an Encyclopedia of Agriculture published in 1831 (before McCormick got his patent) showed a reaper-like machine, it did not mean the machine actually worked and was successfully operated.

Samuel F.B. Morse invented the telegraph machine, an electromagnetic system of communicating through wires over long distances. He patented

Samuel Morse and his telegraph machine, circa 1850.

his invention in 1840, and again in 1846 and 1848. Another inventor claimed that Morse was not actually the inventor. The Supreme Court rejected these claims: "The Columbian [O'Reilly's] Telegraph does not profess to accomplish a new purpose, or produce a new result . . . The object and purpose of the Telegraph is the same with that of Professor Morse."

In *Blake v. Robertson* (1876), the only difference in two inventors' stone-crushing machines was the power source—one had a revolving shaft through rods and levers, and the other had a revolving shaft powered by falling water. The Court ruled that there had been **infringement** of Blake's patent, but only allowed nominal damages Robertson had only made four machines. Then, in the 1888 "Telephone Cases," Alexander Graham Bell's claims as rightful inventor of the telephone were upheld in the Supreme Court.

Other patent cases dealt with delays in obtaining a patent. In *Woodbridge v. United States* (1923), the Court examined the case of William Woodbridge, who had originally filed for a patent on a weapon he invented in 1852 but wanted the Patent Office to hold on to his patent application in their "secret archives" for the moment. In 1861, when Woodbridge wanted to finalize his patent, he was told that others had in the meantime invented and patented similar weaponry. The Court ruled against Woodbridge, citing *Bates v. Coe* (1878), where the Court said: "Inventors may, if they can, keep their invention secret; and if they do for any length of time, they do not forfeit their right to apply for a patent, unless another in the meantime has made the invention, and secured [it] by patent."

Theodore Olson

Theodore Olson was Assistant Attorney General under President Ronald Reagan from 1981 to 1984. He was Solicitor General of the United States under President George W. Bush from June 2001 until July 2004. He has argued more than 40 cases before the Supreme Court.

Q: *In Eldred v. Ashcroft [2003], you defended the right of Congress to extend copyright protection. At what point is the spirit of the word "limited" in the Constitution exceeded?*

Olson: Congress has got to be given great deference in fleshing out the phrase "limited" in the Copyright Clause, and in this case, was adjusting U.S. law to international conventions. It is impossible to describe a fixed number of years that might be deemed excessive; that would have to reflect the judgment by five of the Justices that some degree of extension was tantamount to "unlimited." A number of factors would probably be involved.

Patent-Worthy?

What can be patented? How unique or different does an invention need to be in order to qualify for patent protection? The Stiffel Company had designed an upright floor lamp called a pole lamp. They obtained a patent and successfully sold the lamp. Around the same time, the national retailer Sears, Roebuck & Co. also introduced a pole lamp. Their version was cheaper than the Stiffel version. The Stiffel Company felt this was unfair and filed a lawsuit. The District Court and Court of Appeals both ruled in favor of Stiffel. They believed that the patent was invalid, because there was no real invention or improvement upon an existing invention. However, they felt that Sears was guilty of unfair competition and ordered Sears to stop selling lamps that might be confused with Stiffel's lamps. Sears appealed the decision and it wound up as *Sears, Roebuck & Co. v. Stiffel Co.* (1964) in the Supreme Court.

The Supreme Court agreed with the lower courts that the patent was not valid. But if that was the case, then the Stiffel Company had no real protection. The lamp was in the public domain, meaning that anyone could copy or sell it legally. There could be no unfair competition if the invention was not protected. Speaking for the majority, Justice Hugo Lafayette Black said that the lower courts "gave Stiffel the equivalent of a patent monopoly on its unpatented lamp. That was error, and Sears is entitled to a judgment in its favor."

Trademarks

While patents are exclusive claims to the design of a machine, process, or substance, **trademarks** are exclusive claims to the use of a name. More specifically, a trademark is a unique name or phrase that is used in association with a business. Common words by themselves could probably not be trademarked. For example, "pizza" or "cookies" could not be trademarked. However, combinations of common words, such as "The Cookie Place" or "Pizza for Everyone" could be trademarked.

The Trademark Act of 1946 provided protection against infringement (illegal usage or copying of a trademark). This meant that another businessperson could not open a store called "The Cookie Place." In addition, he or she could not open "Cookie Place" or "The Cookies Place," which might be confused with the original, trademarked name. In 1995, Congress added more protection for trademark holders with the Federal Trademark Dilution Act (FTDA). It said that any name or phrase that tarnished a trademark in people's minds would not be allowed.

Two made-up examples that the House Judiciary Subcommittee gave of "diluted" brand names were Buick Aspirin or Kodak Pianos. Because Buick was known for making cars and Kodak for film and cameras, associating aspirin and pianos with these two companies would tarnish their reputations. A car company also has something to do with medicine? How good could their cars be? A photographic company is making pianos? Consumers might form a negative opinion. The trademark would be diluted.

Imagine that you visit a chain restaurant called "The Pirate's Place." When you go inside, you see that they have miniature treasure chests on every table, pirate swords on the walls, and a huge aquarium with small sharks. The waiters give all kids gold pirate coins.

You think this is a great idea. But you want to be careful not to be accused of trademark infringement, so when you open up your restaurant you call it "Bluebeard's Ship." Inside, you put a little treasure chest on every table and swords on the walls. You custom order a large fish tank and stock it with scary-looking fish. And of course, you make sure each kid gets a gold pirate coin. According to the law, you may have still been guilty of infringement. You have infringed the "trade dress" of the Pirate's Place. The trade dress is the overall appearance of a store or restaurant.

This case actually happened in 1985, when two Mexican restaurants wound up in the Supreme Court over trade dress. The Taco Cabana sued Two Pesos, claiming that Two Pesos copied its trade dress of festive colors, awnings, and artifacts in the restaurant (*Two Pesos, Inc. v. Taco Cabana, Inc.*, 1985). Two Pesos argued that it did not matter, because the trade dress of Taco Cabana was not so distinctive that the public automatically thought of Taco Cabana when they saw that decoration. In 1992, the Supreme Court agreed with Taco Cabana that its trade dress had indeed been infringed.

In *Wal-Mart Stores, Inc. v. Samara Brothers, Inc.* (2000), the Supreme Court said it is easier to prove infringement of restaurant design than of product design. Products come and go rapidly in stores, too quickly for their colors or designs to be associated with a particular brand. If you buy a penguin-shaped salt shaker, you will not be aware who made it, even if one company is the only one that makes them.

Piano Rolls: Machine or Theft?

Long before digital music was invented, the duplication of popular songs was already a hot issue. Back in the late 1800s, a new technology became available. A pattern of small holes could be punched into long rolls of paper. These rolls could then be loaded into "player pianos." These special pianos used air pressure to "read" the pattern of the holes and convert the pattern into musical notes that would be played. The piano rolls could be used at home to play popular songs without any special talent; the piano did all the work. The player could use the foot pedals to make the music softer or louder as required.

By the year 1902, there were about 75,000 of these special pianos in use in the United States, and more than one million piano rolls were made every year. Manufacturers were purchasing one copy of the sheet music for a popular copyrighted song and converting the notes into perforations. These holes were punched on a template roll of paper dozens of feet in length. This template was used in a perforating machine to make mass copies of the piano roll. The finished rolls, which measured 12 inches long by 1½ inches wide, were capped on either end with metal or hard rubber and placed in labeled cardboard boxes and sold.

PUT A TRADEMARK TO THE TEST

Moseley v. V. Secret Catalogue, Inc. (2003) concerned a businessman named Victor Moseley who had opened a shop in Kentucky called Victor's Secret. The women's undergarment company Victoria's Secret felt it was infringement. The company requested that Moseley not use the name or any variations of it. He then changed the store's name to Victor's Little Secret, but that did not satisfy the large company and they filed suit in Federal District Court.

The Supreme Court ruled in favor of Moseley. The Court felt that there was no real dilution just because people might think of Victoria's Secret when they hear the name Victor's Little Secret: "Mental association will not necessarily reduce the capacity of the famous mark to identify the goods of its owner . . ."

In this activity, you will test the trademark waters.

YOU'LL NEED
✔ Paper
✔ Pens
✔ Pizza Playground lawyer
✔ Parade of Pencils lawyer
✔ Pizza Playground copycat lawyer
✔ Parade of Pencils copycat lawyer
✔ Classroom Supreme Court
✔ Clock or timer

The Pizza Playground and Parade of Pencils (or you can come up with your own names) are two stores that have trademarked names. Break the class up into two groups—one for each trademarked name. Each group should try to come up with several similarly playful names that are close, but not too close to the original. Select one that you think is the best.

Each group should give the selected "copycat" name to the lawyer for the respective trademarked companies. Each trademark-infringed lawyer will then have five minutes to argue why he or she believes the copycat name infringes the trademark. The copycat lawyers will have five minutes each to argue why they feel their names do not infringe or dilute the Pizza Playground or the Parade of Pencils. Remember, Supreme Court Justices can and should ask questions and interrupt if necessary. The Court will then have five minutes to confer and make its decision.

Make a Song Note Shirt

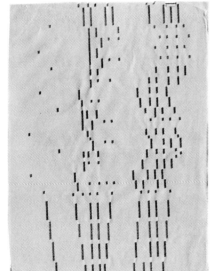

Piano rolls took popular songs and converted them to punched holes on a roll of paper that could be fed into a special piano. The piano roll by itself looked rather alien and could not be read and played as if it were sheet music. The Court ruled it was not within the scope of the copyright laws. What if you took musical notes of part of a song and converted each note to a color, then transcribed the song in those colors?

YOU'LL NEED

✔ Paper
✔ Pencil
✔ Plain white T-shirt
✔ Fabric markers (seven different colors)
✔ Ruler

Look at the bar of music shown below. Assign a different color to each different musical note. Write out the color code for the musical notes on paper (for example, "red, blue, yellow, green, green, green," etc.). Now, use the fabric markers to make dots, bars, squares, or other shapes on the T-shirt. At the bottom of your color notes, you can write the words "Mozart's Eine Kleine Nachtmusik." Mozart's work is in the public domain, but if it weren't, would this use of the music be considered infringement or fair use? In a sense, have you converted musical notes to art? Or is the tune still recognizable? How do you think the Supreme Court would rule?

A composer named Adam Geibel had copyrighted two of his songs, "Little Cotton Dolly" and "Kentucky Babe," in 1897. He noticed that these songs were appearing on player piano rolls, and he was not receiving any money from the company that made the piano rolls. He felt this was in violation of the copyright laws that gave the author of a musical composition the sole right to publish and print the composition. He filed suit against the Apollo Company, which made player pianos and sold piano rolls. The case was called *White–Smith Music Pub. Co. v. Apollo Co.* (1908).

The Court ruled that piano rolls were outside the scope of what the existing copyright laws covered. The piano rolls were not meant to be read like sheet music, but were merely extensions of machines. Speaking for the majority, Justice William Rufus Day explained that it may not be fair for the piano roll manufacturers to profit, but the Court could do nothing until the laws were changed. They hinted that perhaps the copyright laws might be altered to adjust for this new technology. In intellectual property cases, courts have to keep up with rapidly changing technology:

It may be true that the use of these perforated rolls . . . enables the manufacturers to enjoy the use of musical compositions for which they pay no value . . . but . . . as the act of Congress now stands we believe it does not include these records as copies or publications of the copyrighted music involved in these cases.

Recording music onto a master piano roll on a player piano, 1916.

Taping Television Shows

For more than 60 years, movies were only available for viewing in theaters. This changed during the 1970s, when the Betamax video-recording device (an older version of the VHS format) was introduced. Besides creating a market for the home viewing of movies, the video recorder began a revolution in television viewing. When the case was initiated in 1976, the technology was still in its infancy. By the time the case was heard in the Supreme Court, the technology had exploded. Suddenly, people did not have to stay up late to watch their favorite shows.

Universal City Studios and Walt Disney Productions saw a problem with this new technology. They wanted monetary damages from Sony, the maker of the Betamax. They also sought a court order preventing Sony from making any more Betamax machines.

The District Court ruled in favor of Sony, but the Court of Appeals reversed that decision and said that the Betamax and Sony were liable for infringement. The case, known as *Sony Corp. of America v. Universal City Studios, Inc.* (1984), was argued before the Supreme Court in 1983 and decided in early 1984. The Court ruled by a close vote of 5–4 that Sony was not in violation, overturning the decision of the Court of Appeals. In its decision, the Supreme Court stated that much of the public use of home video recording devices was to record shows that were on while they were not home or while they were asleep. The later viewing of these recorded shows (referred to as "time-shifting") increased the shows' audience and did not have a negative effect on the copyright owners.

Sony had explained that much of the time-shifting was for recording sports events, and that representatives from the major televised sports did not object to this practice. Sony also had the testimony of children's television host Fred Rogers ("Mister Rogers"), who said he was perfectly fine with families recording his show for viewing at appropriate times. The Supreme Court noted that only 10 percent of the programs on television were under copyright by Universal and Disney.

Justice John Paul Stevens wrote for the majority:

The copyright holder may not prevail unless the relief that he seeks affects only his programs, or unless he speaks for virtually all copyright holders with an interest in the outcome. In this case, the record makes it perfectly clear that there are many important producers of national and local television programs who find nothing objectionable about the enlargement in the size of the television audience that results from the practice of time-shifting for private home use.

The Court found that the Betamax machine was capable of numerous uses that would not infringe on anyone's copyright. This meant that it was not liable for what a few people did illegally with the technology that Sony created.

The Justices did caution that today's answers would not necessarily be the same as tomorrow's answers. Similar to the piano roll case, the Court noted that under existing laws there was no violation, but Congress could change that.

In conclusion, Justice Stevens wrote: "It may well be that Congress will take a fresh look at this new technology, just as it so often has examined other innovations in the past. But it is not our job to apply laws that have not yet been written."

File Sharing

Music recording and playback technology has evolved a lot since the days of the piano roll. Records were first invented by Thomas Edison and dominated the market for decades. The eight-track tape was popular during the 1970s, and the cassette tape was popular through the 1980s.

It was with the invention of the small audio cassette tape that infringement became easy for the average person. As the cassette tape could be used for both playback and recording, people made cassette copies of records they borrowed from a friend or the library. Some people brought tape recorders to concerts and made and sold "bootleg" (illegal) recordings. The music industry was aware of this but had no real way to determine how much music was being copied.

Next came the compact disc (CD) revolution during the early 1990s. Consumers rushed to replace their old record and tape collections with newly rereleased versions on CD. During the late 1990s and early 2000s, more new technologies became popular. First, CDs, which had once been only for playback, were now also recordable. Prices for these "writable" CDs became very affordable at just cents per disc.

The other technological advance allowed songs and entire albums to be obtained digitally through the computer. Songs could be obtained for free from people who uploaded their song files onto their hard drives or onto the Internet. With the new CD technology, these songs could be "burned," or copied, to CDs. They could also be copied to a pocket-sized device, such as an iPod, that is capable of holding thousands of digital songs.

The situation was ripe for trouble. An Internet file-sharing network called Napster was famously shut down by a Court of Appeals ruling in 2001, despite the arguments of lawyer David Boies that the *Sony* test for noninfringing uses should be applied.

In March 2005, the Supreme Court heard arguments in a case called *Metro Goldwyn Mayer Studios v. Grokster Ltd.* (2005). Grokster made file-sharing software that allowed users to trade files directly from one user to another (instead of using a central computer server). The District Court and the U.S. Court of Appeals both ruled in favor of Grokster. They referred back to the *Sony* decision. They felt Grokster should not be held liable for this possible illegal usage, when Grokster was capable of "substantial noninfringing uses."

In the oral arguments before the Supreme Court, the lawyer for MGM claimed that Grokster was set up for the purpose of sharing copyrighted files, and any "noninfringing" uses were very minor and more coincidental. Justice Stephen G. Breyer asked the lawyer how infringement could be measured and how to apply a test of when some infringement is too much. What if he were the lawyer for the inventor of the copy machine, or the VCR, or even for Gutenberg and his printing press? Justice Antonin Scalia warned the lawyer for Grokster that the Court was not going to rely solely on the *Sony* ruling as the guideline for its decision.

The Grokster lawyer argued that the Grokster software was not alone. There was a "chain" of technology that enabled the software to work, including the computer, the modem, and the Internet service provider. How could any one piece of the chain be singled out for copyright infringement when all the links of the chain were necessary?

The Grokster lawyer also argued that there was no "willful ignorance" of what users were doing with the software, because Grokster had no real way of knowing how the software was being used. Also, many bands allowed consumers to download and share their music for free, to entice them to attend concerts and buy other recordings. The Court rejected these arguments, however, and decided against *Grokster,* holding that the new technology was clearly intended to make copyright infringement possible.

As technology improves, the Supreme Court will face new challenges.

David Boies (part 2)

David Boies was the attorney representing Napster in *RIAA v. Napster* (2001).

Q: *What are the differences between the Napster case that you argued and the Grokster case that went before the Supreme Court in 2005?*

Boies: I think the basic issue is very similar. That basic issue is whether the courts should apply the copyright act to a new technology in ways that Congress did not contemplate when it passed the Act. There is the Home Recording Act that was passed by Congress that was designed to allow people to engage in the noncommercial copying of music. And one issue is whether that law applies to the Internet, which is the modern way of sharing music, the same way it would apply to people simply handing copies to each other. Now there is one difference, and that has to do with the technical way that Grokster and Napster operate in the sense that in Napster, the music was said to reside in Napster equipment for a brief period of time as part of the sharing process. I believe in Grokster, it is said that did not happen.

Q: *Is it difficult to apply the Sony decision as a precedent in cases such as this, because Sony dealt with technology that is now nearly obsolete?*

Boies: I think you can use the Sony case as a precedent. There are obviously some similarities and some differences, but one very important similarity is that you had in *Sony* a technology that while it is old today, was very new then. And what the Court was saying is, we are not going to apply the copyright laws to stifle noncommercial sharing through this new technology. Remember that Sony, like Napster and like Grokster, was often used to copy copyrighted works. Exactly the same arguments were made against the Betamax VCR as are made against Napster and Grokster. What the Court will have to decide is whether the similarities are more important or the differences are more important.

Research Friendly, Copyright Unfriendly

The mid-1990s was the real beginning of the Internet age. What started out as a clumsy system became more user-friendly as years passed. Internet companies started up by the hundreds. Content increased dramatically. Documents of all kinds appeared on the Web. Articles, speeches, and even entire books were uploaded onto the Web. By 2004, the Web site Google indexed many billions of Web pages.

Anyone can create a Web site and upload pictures and text from anywhere. There is no single authority that exists to check the material that is posted on Web sites. Online diaries, blogs, and other personal sites can be updated and changed in an instant. The Internet has changed the way we do research by creating an online library of information. Impatient researchers expect everything to be easily available. "Brick-and-mortar" libraries have digitized important documents, and Web sites offer digitized documents as well.

Today, much research is possible without ever leaving your chair. The ease of Internet research can make students and professional writers careless in attributing proper sources and can create an atmosphere where copyrights are infringed and where plagiarism is common. Some people feel that the Web is theirs to explore and use as they wish.

The 21st century will see new challenges for the Supreme Court as property rights take on new meaning and Web-based content becomes the newest battleground. One case that involved the new technology of the Internet was *New York Times Co. v. Tasini* (2001). The case revolved around several freelance writers, people who contributed articles to various publications but were not employed full-time by those publications.

The *New York Times, Newsday,* and *Time* magazine had a deal with an electronic information provider called LEXIS/NEXIS, whereby LEXIS/NEXIS would have the right to put articles in its online database for paid subscribers to access. The subscribers could enter a search term and find articles that matched the term. The articles would be presented on the screen in isolation, not as part of the newspaper or magazine page on which they were published.

The freelancers noticed that their articles were being included in this database. They complained that their copyrights had been infringed by this unauthorized use of their articles. By law, the publishing companies could reprint the articles in subsequent "revision" editions of the newspapers. The publishers felt it was within their rights to have the articles appear in the database, as this was simply a revision of the original print edition in which the articles appeared.

But the Internet was not the first medium used for reproducing articles in a nonprint format. Two other media had existed for many years: microfiche, small index-card sheets of plastic; and microfilm, which is a roll of plastic film. Special cameras were used to photograph newspapers and the images were captured in miniature on the fiche or film. Several issues of a newspaper could be stored on one fiche or film, thereby creating an archive and saving space.

The Supreme Court rejected a claim by the publishers that the LEXIS/NEXIS databases were similar in nature to microfiche or microfilm. Those media, the Court argued, reproduced the articles and the pages of the publications as they originally appeared in print. For example, if an article was in the second column on the third page of the newspaper, it would still be found in that position on microfilm. It was true that an article could be enlarged and isolated away from the rest of its context (ads and other articles) but the context was there nonetheless.

The LEXIS/NEXIS database, on the other hand, was a huge collection of material separate from its original context, or place, in the newspaper among the other articles from that day. Justice Ruth Bader Ginsburg wrote for the majority: "Such a storage and retrieval system effectively overrides the Authors' exclusive right to control the individual reproduction and distribution of each article."

Copyright Law

Article I, Section 8, Clause 8 of the Constitution says that Congress shall have the power: "To promote the Progress of Science and the useful Arts, by securing for limited Times to Authors and Inventors the exclusive Right to their respective Writings and Discoveries."

The first copyright law in the United States was enacted soon after the Constitution was ratified in 1790. It provided a federal copyright term (meaning the copyright was protected by the federal government, not the state government) of 14 years from the date of publication, renewable for an additional 14 years if the author was still alive after the first 14 years were over. That meant an author or creator would have the exclusive rights to his or her creation, and all profits from it would go to him or her. After the term expired, anyone could copy, publish, and distribute those works without the permission of the creator. At that point, the works were considered part of what is called the "public domain," and available for use.

Congress expanded the federal copyright term to 42 years in 1831 (28 years from publication, renewable for an additional 14 years), and to 56 years in 1909 (28 years from publication, renewable for an additional 28 years).

A case called *Stevens v. Gladding* (1855) placed copyright law before the Supreme Court. A man named Isaac Cady bought a copper plate of a map of Rhode Island at an auction in Bristol County, Massachusetts. He was excited because he knew he could take the engraved copper sheet and run it through a printing press. The engraved plate would be inked and paper pressed onto it, creating a print. So Cady had copies of the map printed and sold them. The owner of the map's copyright filed suit in District Court, claiming his copyright had been infringed. The District Court ruled in favor of Cady, saying it was within his right to do as he wished with the plate.

The case reached the Supreme Court on appeal. James Stevens, arguing for himself, said: "It is immaterial how, or where, or from whom these respondents obtained these maps for sale; it is the publishing, the exposing to sale, the selling of these maps without the author's consent, which constitutes the violation of the copyright."

Justice Benjamin Robbins Curtis, speaking for the Court, explained that the only question in the case was whether or not the sale of the plate carried with it the sale of the copyright. Curtis said that just as it was necessary for the owner of the plate to purchase paper, ink, and a press, it was also necessary to purchase the rights to the print the map. If he did not have those rights, he could do whatever else he wanted with the plate—he could keep it, sell it, or use it as a decoration, but he could not print and sell maps from it. The Court reversed the decision of the District Court and ruled for the copyright holder.

Infringement Damages

In cases where copyright infringement occurred, the Supreme Court has had to decide what the limits of compensation should be. A case called *Sheldon v. Metro–Goldwyn Pictures Corp.* (1940) dealt with a play that was made into a movie. A scandalous Scottish murder trial that took place in 1857 was the basis for a play called *Dishonored Lady.* The play was copyrighted in 1930, and negotiations were started with MGM Pictures to sell the rights to the play for $30,000.

The negotiations with the playwright, Edward Sheldon, fell through, and MGM instead bought the rights to an English novel called *Letty Lynton.* This novel was based on the same Scottish trial and was published in 1930. MGM filmed the movie, and it was released in 1932. It starred Joan Crawford and Robert Montgomery, two of the biggest stars of the era. The movie was so popular that Joan Crawford's ruffled dress inspired 500,000 women to buy look-alike dresses that were on sale in Macy's department stores.

The author of the play was angry. He found that though the story was in public domain, there were actually distinct details of his play that MGM used in the film, so he filed a lawsuit claiming infringement.

The District Court originally found in favor of MGM, but the Court of Appeals reversed and ordered the District Court to figure out how much money was owed to the playwright for the infringement. The District Court then awarded Sheldon $587,604, the total net profit that MGM made from the movie. MGM felt this was very unfair. On appeal by MGM, the Court of Appeals thought $587,604 was too much money. They decided that the amount of money should be set at one-fifth of the net profit.

Now the playwright was unhappy, because his award had been reduced to $117,000. Yet this number was still higher than what the "expert witnesses" in the case said the original play had contributed to the finished product (between 0 percent and 12 percent).

The Supreme Court, in a decision written by Chief Justice Charles Evans Hughes, said that Sheldon should be satisfied with the amount he received. He returned to the question examined by the Court of Appeals—where did the profits come from? Were all the profits due to the play that was "stolen"? Hughes noted that a great deal of effort and talent goes into making a movie, including the production and props,

ACCIDENTAL INFRINGEMENT

THE CASE *Sheldon v. Metro-Goldwyn Pictures Corp.* (1940) dealt with a story that was in the public domain, but was infringed based on a play made of the story. In this activity, you will create a one-page dialogue based on a true story from Scottish history. The goal is to understand the difficult nature of infringement cases. The true story is as follows:

"Sir James Stewart, a Scotsman, and George Wharton, an Englishman, were friends. One day Wharton said something unkind to Stewart, and Stewart hit him. They resolved to fight the next day at an appointed spot. Once they made the date, they sat together in friendship and drank some wine. When they rose to part ways, Wharton said, 'Our next meeting will not part so easily.' The next day, the men met and fought each other courageously. Each one fell to the ground with many wounds, and each one died."

YOU'LL NEED

✔ Computers (or pen and paper)
✔ Printer
✔ At least 5 friends or classmates

Split your friends into three or four two-person teams. Each team should write a play script with between 25 and 50 lines of dialogue about the story shown here. The only thing each script must feature is the line said by Wharton: "Our next meeting will not part so easily." Print out a copy of each version of the story for each of the teams so that everyone has all the stories. Each team should review the other stories against its own, and team members should see if they find places where they feel their story line or dialogue was copied.

the actors, and the director. Many thousands of people are drawn to see a movie only by the names of the stars. Hughes also noted that movie rights are often sold for relatively small sums. The Supreme Court kept the award at $117,000.

Another case that dealt with damages from copyright infringement was *Woolworth v. Contemporary Arts* (1952). This case revolved around a small statue of a dog in a cute pose. A company named Contemporary Arts made the small dog figures and sold them to gift shops. Then, one day, they noticed that a nearly identical cocker spaniel statue was being sold in the "five-and-dime" chain store Woolworth.

It turned out that Woolworth had unknowingly bought 1,524 dog statues from a different source and sold them in 34 different Woolworth stores. Contemporary Arts filed a lawsuit against Woolworth. The District Court found that Woolworth should pay damages of $5,000. The retailer argued that their entire profit from the 1,524 dogs was only $899.16, and that was all they should have to pay.

The Supreme Court struck down this argument. Justice Robert Houghwout Jackson wrote that the Court had to be flexible when dealing with copyright issues. If profits were the measure of damages, then Woolworth could add in various expenses, employees' salaries, heating and lighting bills, display expenses, taxes, etc., and accountants could wither away the profit to virtually nothing. After all the deductions, they could claim they made a profit of just 25 cents. This would only encourage infringement by others. The copyright rules were "designed to discourage wrongful conduct." The $5,000 award stood.

Infinite Copyright?

In 1976, Congress again updated the copyright laws. For works created by individuals, the 1976 Act provided that copyright protection would run from the work's creation, not publication. Protection would last until 50 years after the author's death. For anonymous works, and works copyrighted by corporations, the 1976 Act provided a term of 75 years from publication or 100 years from creation, whichever expired first. For published works with existing copyrights, the 1976 Act granted a total copyright term of 75 years from publication (19 years more than what was granted under the 1909 Act).

The Copyright Term Extension Act (CTEA) was passed by Congress and signed by President Bill Clinton in 1998. It toughened the rules of the 1976 Act by extending protection to 70 years after the author's death and 95 years from publication or 120 years from creation for anonymous or corporate-created work. For published works with existing copyrights already in effect, the term went from 75 years to 95 years.

Some publishers and businesspeople were upset by the copyright extensions. In particular, they knew that some important creations were scheduled to be released into the public domain before the CTEA. Mickey Mouse, who first appeared in the late 1920s, was the most notable of these creations. Once Mickey Mouse went into the public domain, it would mean that anyone could use Mickey anywhere without getting permission from Disney.

A man named Eric Eldred ran a Web site that allowed users to access electronic versions of classic books that were in the public domain. One book he had planned to scan and post to the Web site was *Horses and Men,* a short-story collection by Sherwood Anderson. The book was published in 1923 and its copyright was scheduled to run out in 1998 (after 75 years). Then Congress passed the CTEA. Eldred was angry. He felt that copyrights were never intended to last so long.

Eldred decided to sue the government, and others joined him. The original suit was filed in early 1999. The District Court and the Court of Appeals both ruled in favor of the government. The case reached the Supreme Court on appeal by Eldred's lawyer a few years later in 2002.

In *Eldred v. Ashcroft* (2003), the petitioners argued that the CTEA violated the Copyright Clause and the First Amendment. They argued that allowing Congress to extend existing copyrights violated the "limited Times" mentioned in the Copyright Clause by making the copyright perpetual through repeated extensions. Once the copyright on existing works had been fixed at 75 years, that was the limit. Eldred and his supporters did not have a problem with Congress creating new guidelines for future works. They simply felt that once a limit had been set for existing copyrights, that limit could not be changed. They also felt that extending copyrights for so long failed to "promote the progress of science" as specified in the Copyright Clause.

The Court disagreed with these arguments. The Supreme Court upheld the CTEA as constitutional by a vote of 7–2. They felt Congress was correct in modifying the copyright laws, saying, "It is generally for Congress, not the courts, to decide how best to pursue the Copyright Clause's objectives."

The Court also stated that copyright was not so restrictive, and that "fair use" of copyrighted works was allowable: "[C]opyright gives the holder no monopoly on any knowledge. A reader of an author's writing may make full use of any fact or idea she acquires from her reading."

Lawrence Lessig

Lawrence Lessig served as a law clerk for Justice Antonin Scalia from 1990 to 1991. He is considered one of the foremost experts on intellectual property law. He represented Eric Eldred in the landmark case *Eldred v. Ashcroft* (2003), arguing against the Copyright Extension Act.

Q: *Isn't it up to Congress to interpret the Copyright Clause and make a determination about how long copyrights should extend?*

Lessig: Since Chief Justice John Marshall's famous opinion in *Marbury v. Madison,* it has been understood that the job of "interpreting" Congress's power is not Congress's alone. The Constitution was written, Marshall wrote, so that the limits intended by the framers "would not be forgotten." So no, it is not Congress's job to determine the limits on its own power. Within those limits, of course, Congress should have a great deal of discretion. But the question we asked the Court to interpret was the limits on Congress's power.

Q: *Did the big corporations that own some of these films and characters put too much pressure on Congress?*

Lessig: Special interests did what they do best: lobby to get laws passed which favor them. In this case, Congress did not adequately consider the harm these extensions would produce, even if it was quite aware of the benefit to these special interests. But Congress's mistake in balancing these interests was not the question we asked the Supreme Court to address: we wanted the Court to interpret the limits on Congress's power, not second-guess its view about that balance.

Q: *How does the Internet play into the whole copyright issue? Doesn't the Internet create an atmosphere with no apparent boundaries?*

Lessig: In one sense, yes. In another sense, the Internet enables an extraordinary range of creative and archival capacity. One important concern that we raised was whether the regime of copyright regulation—designed for a very different technical environment—continues to make sense, constitutionally, in light of these new capacities.

Though the Supreme Court often makes news with its decisions, it is the people and politics of the day that determine the cases it hears. The cases that go before the Supreme Court are very much a mirror of society. They reflect the concerns of the American people about the freedoms granted and restrictions placed on them by their government. The cases may also reflect changing technology and changing moral values.

It is the Court's duty to hear these complex issues and then set standards through rulings. Americans look to the Supreme Court to light a path into sometimes dark and unexplored areas of law. As the years pass, the Supreme Court is certain to make many more landmark decisions that change our country.

Though many battles will be waged and protests will be marched, Americans will always regard the Supreme Court as the nation's most important keeper of the constitutional flame. Along with the Constitution written by the founding fathers, the Justices will continue to look to the wisdom and intent of some of the Court's great Justices of the past—John Jay, John Marshall, Oliver Wendell Holmes, Thurgood Marshall, and others. Though the cases of the future are unknown, we can be sure that the nation's rich past will help guide the Court. Its ability to inject the challenges of tomorrow with both fresh new thought as well as legal and historical precedent of centuries past are what make the Supreme Court such a unique and important institution.

AFTERWORD

by James A. Baker III, former U.S. Secretary of State

What does the future hold for the Supreme Court? I do not foresee any structural changes in the Supreme Court during the coming decades, since there is little reason to alter the size of the Court or the manner in which the Justices are appointed. However, the Court can be expected to address many new and challenging legal issues that will arise as the world changes. In the future, the Court likely will be asked to settle a variety of complex copyright and intellectual property questions that are evolving as new technologies arise.

Another set of legal issues likely to take up much of the Court's time as the years pass will come from growing globalism, which will put pressure on America's court system to conform with international law and laws in other countries. Additionally, the war on international terrorism can be expected to continue to spark an array of legal questions about law enforcement and the rights of individuals—inside and outside of the country.

I feel certain that, as always, the Supreme Court will be able to rise to these new challenges.

Resources

Justices of the Supreme Court of the United States

Chief Justices

DATES OF SERVICE

1789–1795	John Jay
1795–1795	John Rutledge
1796–1800	Oliver Ellsworth
1801–1835	John Marshall
1836–1864	Roger B. Taney
1864–1873	Salmon P. Chase
1874–1888	Morrison Remick Waite
1888–1910	Melville Weston Fuller
1910–1921	Edward Douglass White
1921–1930	William Howard Taft
1930–1941	Charles Evans Hughes
1941–1946	Harlan Fiske Stone
1946–1953	Fred Moore Vinson
1953–1969	Earl Warren
1969–1986	Warren Earl Burger
1986–2005	William H. Rehnquist
2005–	John G. Roberts Jr.

Associate Justices

DATES OF SERVICE

1790–1791	John Rutledge
1790–1810	William Cushing
1789–1798	James Wilson
1790–1795	John Blair
1790–1799	James Iredell
1792–1793	Thomas Johnson
1793–1806	William Paterson
1796–1811	Samuel Chase
1799–1829	Bushrod Washington
1800–1804	Alfred Moore
1804–1834	William Johnson
1807–1823	Henry Brockholst Livingston
1807–1826	Thomas Todd
1811–1835	Gabriel Duvall
1812–1845	Joseph Story
1823–1843	Smith Thompson
1826–1828	Robert Trimble

Associate Justices (continued)

1830–1861	John McLean
1830–1844	Henry Baldwin
1835–1867	James Moore Wayne
1836–1841	Philip Pendleton Barbour
1837–1865	John Catron
1838–1852	John McKinley
1842–1860	Peter Vivian Daniel
1845–1872	Samuel Nelson
1845–1851	Levi Woodbury
1846–1870	Robert Cooper Grier
1851–1857	Benjamin Robbins Curtis
1853–1861	John Archibald Campbell
1858–1881	Nathan Clifford
1862–1881	Noah Haynes Swayne
1862–1890	Samuel Freeman Miller
1862–1877	David Davis
1863–1897	Stephen Johnson Field
1870–1880	William Strong
1870–1892	Joseph P. Bradley
1873–1882	Ward Hunt
1877–1911	John Marshall Harlan
1881–1887	William Burnham Woods
1881–1889	Stanley Matthews
1882–1902	Horace Gray
1882–1893	Samuel Blatchford
1888–1893	Lucius Quintus C. Lamar
1890–1910	David Josiah Brewer
1891–1906	Henry Billings Brown
1892–1903	George Shiras Jr.
1893–1895	Howell Edmunds Jackson
1894–1910	Edward Douglass White
1896–1909	Rufus Wheeler Peckham
1898–1925	Joseph McKenna
1902–1932	Oliver Wendell Holmes
1903–1922	William Rufus Day
1906–1910	William Henry Moody
1910–1914	Horace Harmon Lurton
1910–1916	Charles Evans Hughes
1911–1937	Willis Van Devanter
1911–1916	Joseph Rucker Lamar
1912–1922	Mahlon Pitney
1914–1941	James Clark McReynolds
1916–1939	Louis Dembitz Brandeis
1916–1922	John Hessin Clarke
1922–1938	George Sutherland
1923–1939	Pierce Butler
1923–1930	Edward Terry Sanford
1925–1941	Harlan Fiske Stone
1930–1945	Owen Josephus Roberts
1932–1938	Benjamin Nathan Cardozo
1937–1971	Hugo Lafayette Black
1938–1957	Stanley Forman Reed
1939–1962	Felix Frankfurter
1939–1975	William Orville Douglas
1940–1949	Frank Murphy
1941–1942	James Francis Byrnes
1941–1954	Robert Houghwout Jackson
1943–1949	Wiley Blount Rutledge
1945–1958	Harold Hitz Burton
1949–1967	Tom Campbell Clark
1949–1956	Sherman Minton
1955–1971	John Marshall Harlan
1956–1990	William J. Brennan Jr.

Associate Justices *(continued)*

1957–1962	Charles Evans Whittaker
1958–1981	Potter Stewart
1962–1993	Byron Raymond White
1962–1965	Arthur Joseph Goldberg
1965–1969	Abe Fortas
1967–1991	Thurgood Marshall
1970–1994	Harry A. Blackmun
1972–1987	Lewis F. Powell Jr.
1972–1986	William H. Rehnquist
1975–	John Paul Stevens
1981–2006	Sandra Day O'Connor
1986–	Antonin Scalia
1988–	Anthony M. Kennedy
1990–	David H. Souter
1991–	Clarence Thomas
1993–	Ruth Bader Ginsburg
1994–	Stephen G. Breyer
2006–	Samuel A. Alito Jr.

First Through Fifteenth Amendments to the United States Constitution

The first ten Amendments are commonly known as the Bill of Rights. They were ratified in 1791.

First Amendment

Congress shall make no law respecting an establishment of religion, or prohibiting the free exercise thereof; or abridging the freedom of speech, or of the press; or the right of the people peaceably to assemble, and to petition the Government for a redress of grievances.

Second Amendment

A well regulated Militia, being necessary to the security of a free State, the right of the people to keep and bear Arms, shall not be infringed.

Third Amendment

No Soldier shall, in time of peace, be quartered in any house, without the consent of the Owner, nor in time of war, but in a manner to be prescribed by law.

Fourth Amendment

The right of the people to be secure in their persons, houses, papers, and effects, against unreasonable searches and seizures, shall not be violated, and no Warrants shall issue, but upon probable cause, supported by Oath or affirmation, and particularly describing the place to be searched, and the persons or things to be seized.

Fifth Amendment

No person shall be held to answer for a capital, or otherwise infamous crime, unless on a presentment or indictment of a Grand Jury, except in cases arising in the land or naval forces, or in the Militia, when in actual service in time of War or public danger; nor shall any person be subject for the same offence to be twice put in jeopardy of life or limb; nor shall be compelled in any criminal case to be a witness against himself, nor be deprived of life, liberty, or property, without due process of law; nor shall private property be taken for public use, without just compensation.

Sixth Amendment

In all criminal prosecutions, the accused shall enjoy the right to a speedy and public trial, by an impartial jury of the State and district wherein the crime shall have been committed, which district shall have been previously ascertained by law, and to be informed of the nature and cause of the accusation; to be confronted with the witnesses against him; to have com-pulsory process for obtaining witnesses in his favor, and to have the Assistance of Counsel for his defence.

Seventh Amendment

In Suits at common law, where the value in controversy shall exceed twenty dollars, the right of trial by jury shall be preserved, and no fact tried by a jury, shall be otherwise re-examined in any Court of the United States, than according to the rules of the common law.

Eighth Amendment

Excessive bail shall not be required, nor excessive fines imposed, nor cruel and unusual punishments inflicted.

Ninth Amendment

The enumeration in the Constitution, of certain rights, shall not be construed to deny or disparage others retained by the people.

Tenth Amendment

The powers not delegated to the United States by the Constitution, nor prohibited by it to the States, are reserved to the States respectively, or to the people.

* * * * * * * *

Eleventh Amendment

Passed by Congress March 4, 1794. Ratified February 7, 1795.

Note: Article III, Section 2, of the Constitution was modified by Amendment Eleven.

The Judicial power of the United States shall not be construed to extend to any suit in law or equity, commenced or prosecuted against one of the United States by Citizens of another State, or by Citizens or Subjects of any Foreign State.

Twelfth Amendment

Passed by Congress December 9, 1803. Ratified June 15, 1804.

Note: A portion of Article II, Section 1 of the Constitution was superseded by the Twelfth Amendment.

The Electors shall meet in their respective states and vote by ballot for President and Vice-President, one of whom, at least, shall not be an inhabitant of the same state with themselves; they shall name in their ballots the person voted for as President, and in distinct ballots the person voted for as Vice-President, and they shall make distinct lists of all persons voted for as President, and of all persons voted for as Vice-President, and of the number of votes for each, which lists they shall sign and certify, and transmit sealed to the seat of the government of the United States, directed to the President of the Senate;—the President of the Senate shall, in the presence of the Senate and House of Representatives, open all the certificates and the votes shall then be counted;—The person having the greatest number of votes for President, shall be the President, if such number be a majority of the whole number of Electors appointed; and if no person have such majority, then from the persons having the highest numbers not exceeding three on the list of those voted for as President, the House of Representatives shall choose immediately, by ballot, the President. But in choosing the President, the votes shall be taken by states, the representation from each state having one vote; a quorum for this purpose shall consist of a member or members from two-thirds of the states, and a majority of all the states shall be necessary to a choice. [And if the House of Representatives shall not choose a President whenever the right of choice shall devolve upon them, before the fourth day of March next following, then the Vice-President shall act as President, as in case of the death or other constitutional disability of the President.—]* The person having the greatest number of votes as Vice-President, shall be the Vice-President, if such number be a majority of the whole number of Electors appointed, and if no person have a majority, then from the two highest numbers on the list, the Senate shall choose the Vice-President; a quorum for the purpose shall consist of two-thirds of the whole number of Senators, and a majority of the whole number shall be necessary to a choice. But no person constitutionally ineligible to the office of President shall be eligible to that of Vice-President of the United States.

———

Superseded by Section 3 of the Twentieth Amendment.

Thirteenth Amendment

Passed by Congress January 31, 1865. Ratified December 6, 1865.

Note: A portion of Article IV, Section 2, of the Constitution was superseded by the Thirteenth Amendment.

Section 1. Neither slavery nor involuntary servitude, except as a punishment for crime whereof the party shall have been duly convicted, shall exist within the United States, or any place subject to their jurisdiction.

Section 2. Congress shall have power to enforce this article by appropriate legislation.

Fourteenth Amendment

Passed by Congress June 13, 1866. Ratified July 9, 1868.

Note: Article I, Section 2, of the Constitution was modified by Section 2 of the Fourteenth Amendment.

Section 1. All persons born or naturalized in the United States, and subject to the jurisdiction thereof, are citizens of the United States and of the State wherein they reside. No State shall make or enforce any law which shall abridge the privileges or immunities of citizens of the United States; nor shall any State deprive any person of life, liberty, or property, without due process of law; nor deny to any person within its jurisdiction the equal protection of the laws.

Section 2. Representatives shall be apportioned among the several States according to their respective numbers, counting the whole number of persons in each State, excluding Indians not taxed. But when the right to vote at any election for the choice of electors for President and Vice-President of the United States, Representatives in Congress, the Executive and Judicial officers of a State, or the members of the Legislature thereof, is denied to any of the male inhabitants of such State, being twenty-one years of age,* and citizens of the United States, or in any way abridged, except for participation in rebellion, or other crime, the basis of representation therein shall be reduced in the proportion which the number of such male citizens shall bear to the whole number of male citizens twenty-one years of age in such State.

Section 3. No person shall be a Senator or Representative in Congress, or elector of President and Vice-President, or hold any office, civil or military, under the United States, or under any State, who, having previously taken an oath, as a member of Congress, or as an officer of the United States, or as a member of any State legislature, or as an executive or judicial officer of any State, to support the Constitution of the United States, shall have engaged in insurrection or rebellion against the same, or given aid or comfort to the enemies thereof. But Congress may by a vote of two-thirds of each House, remove such disability.

Section 4. The validity of the public debt of the United States, authorized by law, including debts incurred for payment of pensions and bounties for services in suppressing insurrection or rebellion, shall not be questioned. But neither the United States nor any State shall assume or pay any debt or obligation incurred in aid of insurrection or rebellion against the United States, or any claim for the loss or emancipation of any slave; but all such debts, obligations and claims shall be held illegal and void.

Section 5. The Congress shall have the power to enforce, by appropriate legislation, the provisions of this article.

———
Changed by Section 1 of the Twenty-Sixth Amendment.

Fifteenth Amendment

Passed by Congress February 26, 1869. Ratified February 3, 1870.

Section 1. The right of citizens of the United States to vote shall not be denied or abridged by the United States or by any State on account of race, color, or previous condition of servitude.

Section 2. The Congress shall have the power to enforce this article by appropriate legislation.

Glossary

affirm—uphold (a lower court ruling)

affirmative action—policy of setting goals for minority participation in business or college admissions, for example

amendment—an addition to the Constitution, which has to be ratified by the states

amicus **brief**—a brief filed by an outside party on behalf of one of the parties in a case

amicus curiae—Latin term for "friend of the court"

appeal—take a case to the next highest court when you lose

appellant—the party that is appealing a lower court's decision

appellate—having the power to review the judgment of another court

appellee—the party against whom a case is being appealed

apportionment—creating election districts based on population

Bill of Rights—the first Ten Amendments to the Constitution

brief—a legal document submitted to the Supreme Court, in which all pertinent legal issues are discussed and summarized

concur—agree; a concurring opinion agrees with the majority opinion, usually with some added insights or cautions

copyright—a creator's exclusive rights and protection for a written work or artwork, for example

defendant—the person who is being charged with a crime or sued in court

dissent—disagree; a dissenting opinion disagrees with the majority opinion and spells out the reasons why

due process—the principle of receiving the full rights granted in the Bill of Rights

ex parte—on behalf of

in forma pauperis—a filing with the Supreme Court as someone who cannot afford the normal fees

infringement—unlawfully usurping someone else's copyright

injunction—a court order that either requires a party to stop an activity or directs a party to do something

jurisdiction—the authority to interpret and apply the law

litigation—the act of bringing and pursuing a lawsuit

loophole—a legal "way out" to get around the provisions of a law

monopoly—a company's complete control of a product or service, with no competition

oral argument—the one-hour period when attorneys get to argue before the Supreme Court Justices

patent—a creator's exclusive rights and protection for an invention

per curiam—by the court

petitioner—someone who asks the Supreme Court to hear their case

plaintiff—the person who files a lawsuit

precedent—a judicial decision that creates a new legal rule that can be used as an example or guide in the future

remand—return; send back to a lower court for further action (such as sentencing or awarding monetary damages)

respondent—the opposing party named in a petitioner's request

reverse—overturn (a lower court ruling)

standing—the ability of a party to demonstrate the legal right to initiate a lawsuit, including proof that one is (or will be) harmed by a law and that there is a case or controversy that can be resolved by legal action

stare decisis—the principle of using a precedent rather than overturning it

stay—a court order to stop or suspend an activity

syllabus—a brief summary of the Court's decision that precedes the written opinion

term—the normal session of the Supreme Court, from fall to spring

trademark—a creator's exclusive rights and protection for a company name, logo, or slogan

writ of *certiorari*—a decision by the Supreme Court to hear an appeal from a lower court

writ of *habeas corpus*—a petition to a prison official ordering that an inmate be brought to court so it can be determined whether or not that person is being detained lawfully

writ of *mandamus*—a court order directing an official or a lower court to perform a duty or service

Web Sites

American Civil Liberties Union (ACLU)

www.aclu.org

The Web site of the American Civil Liberties Union contains much information on First Amendment and other decisions, as well as a summary of the rights championed by the ACLU. There are news stories on the main page. If you click into the "Supreme Court" tab, it takes you into a page that has more stories and historical information about the interaction of the ACLU and the nation's highest Court. You can also learn about the history of the ACLU.

Cornell Legal Information Institute

www.law.cornell.edu/supct/index.html

The Cornell Web site features the text of many Supreme Court and other lower court decisions. You can search chronologically or by case topic. The index includes cases from 1990 to the present, as well as historic decisions.

Findlaw for Legal Professionals

www.findlaw.com/casecode/supreme.html

This site has an archive of the full opinions of many hundreds of Supreme Court cases from the late 19th century to the present. You can search by year or by case name. The main page, www.findlaw.com (click on the "For Legal Professionals" tab), contains news coverage about legal issues in the news.

Landmark cases

www.landmarkcases.org

This site focuses on several landmark decisions and offers some key lessons about those decisions. Cases include *Marbury v. Madison* (1803), *Plessy v. Ferguson* (1896), *Mapp v. Ohio* (1961), *Miranda v. Arizona* (1966), *Tinker v. Des Moines* (1969), and *Texas v. Johnson* (1989).

Library of Congress

www.loc.gov

The Library of Congress online has images of many of the Court's Justices, as well as letters and other materials pertaining to some landmark cases (such as

Brown v. Board of Education, 1954). Click on "American Memory" and type a term in the search box.

National Archives

www.archives.gov/historical-docs

The National Archives offers access to images of key documents in American history. Many of these documents are available on the "America's Historical Documents" page, such as the Emancipation Proclamation, the *Brown v. Board of Education* (1954) decision, and the Bill of Rights.

Oyez

www.oyez.org

The Oyez site is very user-friendly. It has summaries of a vast number of Supreme Court cases that show which Justices were involved and which attorneys argued the cases. You can search cases by type (for example, "free speech"). There is also biographical information on all the Justices who ever served on the Court.

Supreme Court

www.supremecourtus.gov

The Supreme Court Web site has information about the traditions and procedures of the Court and has text of recent decisions. It also gives information about hours and procedures for visiting the Court in person and detailed rules for arguing before the Supreme Court.

Supreme Court Historical Society

www.supremecourthistory.org

The Historical Society Web site gives details about the Court's history, broken down by era of each Chief Justice. There is a discussion of how the Court works. The site also gives bibliographic information about other resources.

Bibliography

Aaseng, Nathan. *You Are the Supreme Court Justice.* Minneapolis: The Oliver Press, Inc., 1994.

Abbott, John S. C., and Russell H. Conwell. *Lives of the Presidents of the United States from Washington to the Present Time.* Portland: H. Hallett and Company, 1885.

Adams, James Truslow. *The March of Democracy.* New York: Charles Scribner's Sons, 1933.

Bloom, Sol. *The Story of the Constitution.* Washington, D.C.: United States Sesquicentennial Commission, 1937.

Bugliosi, Vincent. *The Betrayal of America: How the Supreme Court Undermined the Constitution and Chose Our President.* New York: Thunder's Mouth Press/Nation Books, 2001.

Carson, Hampton L. *The Supreme Court of the United States: Its History.* Philadelphia: John V. Huber Company, 1891.

Chafee Jr., Zechariah. *Free Speech in the United States.* Cambridge: Harvard University Press, 1942.

Croscup, George E. *United States History with Synchronic Charts Maps and Statistical Diagrams.* New York: Cambridge Book Corporation, 1913.

Evans, J. Edward. *Freedom of Speech.* Minneapolis: Lerner Publications Company, 1990.

Friedman, Leon. *The Supreme Court: Know Your Government.* New York: Chelsea House Publishers, 1987.

Fribourg, Marjorie G. *The Supreme Court in American History: Ten Great Decisions.* Philadelphia: Macrae Smith Company, 1965.

Harrison, Maureen and Steve Gilbert, eds. *Landmark Decisions of the United States Supreme Court.* Beverly Hills: Excellent Books, 1991.

Hickok, Eugene W. and Gary L. McDowell. *Justice vs. Law: Courts and Politics in American Society.* New York: The Free Press, 1993.

Lawson, Don. *Landmark Supreme Court Cases.* Hillside, NJ: Enslow Publishers, Inc., 1987.

Lindop, Edmund. *The Bill of Rights and Landmark Cases.* New York: Franklin Watts, 1989.

Irons, Peter. *The Courage of Their Convictions: Sixteen Americans Who Fought Their Way to the Supreme Court.* New York: The Free Press, 1988.

Irons, Peter, ed. *May It Please the Court: The First Amendment.* New York: The New Press, 1997.

Pascoe, Elaine. *Freedom of Expression: The Right to Speak out in America.* Brookfield, CT: The Millfield Press, 1992.

Rehnquist, William H. *The Supreme Court.* New York: Alfred A. Knopf, 2001.

Story, William W., ed. *Life and Letters of Joseph Story.* Boston: Charles C. Little and James Brown, 1851.

Wasby, Stephen L. *The Supreme Court in the Federal Judicial System.* Chicago: Nelson–Hall Publishers, 1993.

Williams, Stephen K., ed. *United States Supreme Court Reports, Vols. 58, 59, 60, 61: Cases Argued and Decided in the Supreme Court of the United States in the December Terms, 1854–1857.* Newark, NJ: The Lawyers' Co-operative Publishing Company, 1884.

Yalof, David Alistair. *Pursuit of Justices: Presidential Politics and the Selection of Supreme Court Nominees.* Chicago: The University of Chicago Press, 1999.

Interview Sources

James Baker III, e-mail interview, 2005

William Barr, telephone interview, 2005

Griffin B. Bell, e-mail interview, 2005

Victoria Jean Benson, telephone interview, 2005

David Boies, telephone interview, 2005

Benjamin Civiletti, telephone interview, 2005

Mario Cuomo, telephone interview, 2005

Walter Dellinger, telephone interview, 2005

Michael Dukakis, e-mail interview, 2005

Gathie Barnette Edmonds, telephone interview, 2005

Steven Engel, telephone interview, 2005

Cathy Kuhlmeier Frey, written interview, 2005

Rudolph Giuliani, telephone interview, 2005

Lillian Gobitis Klose, telephone interview, 2005

Alberto Gonzalez, e-mail interview, 2006

Lawrence Lessig, e-mail interview, 2005

Dollree Mapp, telephone interview, 2005

Jim McCollum, e-mail interview, 2005

Edwin Meese III, telephone interview, 2005

Tim Miller, e-mail interview, 2005

Walter Mondale, telephone interview, 2005

Robert Morgenthau, telephone interview, 2005

Ralph Nader, e-mail interview 2005.

Theodore Olson, e-mail interview, 2005

Robert Reich, e-mail interview, 2005

Jane Roe, e-mail interview, 2005

William Ruckelshaus, e-mail interview, 2005

Morley Safer, telephone interview, 2005

Donna and Ellery Schempp, telephone and e-mail interview, 2005

James Sensenbrenner, e-mail interview, 2005

Arlen Specter, e-mail interview, 2005

Kenneth Starr, telephone interview, 2005

Dick Thornburgh, telephone interview, 2005

John Tinker, e-mail interview, 2005

Kurt Vonnegut, personal interview, 1994

Seth Waxman, telephone interview, 2005

INDEX

Also available by Richard Panchyk

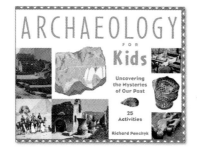

American Folk Art for Kids

With 21 Activities
Forewords by William C. Ketchum Jr.,
author of *American Folk Art*,
and *Mr. Imagination*

Ages 9 & up
Four-color interior, 100 color photos

"Will encourage a wide range of students to reconsider what makes an object art and perhaps to reconnect with their own cultural heritage."

—*Booklist*

"Great supplemental material for art teachers or homeschoolers on an often overlooked topic."

—*School Library Journal*

978-1-55652-499-8 $16.95 (CAN $22.95)

Archaeology for Kids

Uncovering the Mysteries of Our Past,
25 Activities

Ages 9 & up
Two-color interior, 60 b & w photos,
19 line drawings, 4 maps

"An enjoyable history lesson and science project all in one."

—*Today's Librarian*

"Much more than a run-of-the-mill activity guide."

—*Science News*

978-1-55652-395-3 $16.95 (CAN $18.95)

Galileo for Kids

His Life and Ideas, 25 Activities
Foreword by Buzz Aldrin

Ages 9 & up
Two-color interior, 50 b & w photos

"Fascinating . . . full of useful and insightful information. A good read."

—*Science Books & Films*

"A good choice for those interested in integrating history and science curriculums."

—*School Library Journal*

978-1-55652-566-7 $18.95 (CAN $20.95)

World War II for Kids

A History with 21 Activities
Foreword by Senator John McCain

Ages 9 & up
Two-color interior, 65 b & w photos,
10 line drawings, 2 maps

Selected by the Children's Book Council and the National Council for Social Studies as a Notable Social Studies Trade Book for Young People

"This well-written, well-researched book belongs on every reference bookshelf in American schools and libraries. It is a must-read book for kids and adults."

—*Children's Literature*

"Jam-packed with information that kids will find fascinating."

—*Today's Parent*

978-1-55652-455-4 $17.95 (CAN $21.95)

CHICAGO
REVIEW
PRESS

Distributed by IPG
www.ipgbook.com

www.chicagoreviewpress.com

Available at your favorite bookstore, by calling (800) 888-4741, or at www.chicagoreviewpress.com